Benson John Lossing

Mount Vernon

The Home of Washington

Benson John Lossing

Mount Vernon
The Home of Washington

ISBN/EAN: 9783337289706

Printed in Europe, USA, Canada, Australia, Japan

Cover: Foto ©ninafisch / pixelio.de

More available books at **www.hansebooks.com**

Mount Vernon, the Home of Washington.

DESCRIPTIVE.
HISTORICAL
AND PICTORIAL.
— BY —
BENSON J. LOSSING, LL.D.
With 160 Illustrations.

ENGRAVED ON STEEL AND WOOD,
CHIEFLY FROM ORIGINAL DRAWINGS BY THE AUTHOR.

CINCINNATI:
JOHN C. YORSTON & COMPANY.

TO THE

AMERICAN PEOPLE

THIS VOLUME

CONTAINING MEMORIALS OF THE HOME-LIFE OF THEIR

ILLUSTRIOUS EXEMPLAR AND FRIEND,

RESPECTFULLY INSCRIBED BY

THE AUTHOR.

PREFACE.

The title of this volume is so fully indicative of its character, that scarcely a word of "foretalk," as the Saxon expresses it, seems necessary; the following explanation, however, appears proper:

During frequent visits to Mount Vernon, the almost life-long home of Washington, and to Arlington House, the residence of his adopted son, George Washington Parke Custis, who inherited a large portion of the household furniture of the family of the Beloved Patriot, the author of this volume made careful drawings of the objects delineated in this book. Diligent search was also made elsewhere for memorials of the domestic life of Washington, for both pictorial illustrations and for correct descriptions. Careful transcriptions of documents; the study of accounts of the home-life at Mount Vernon, given by distinguished visitors, and the collection of isolated facts from various sources, with the drawings, have afforded the materials of which this volume is composed.

It was a fortunate circumstance that these materials, now presented in this collected form, were gathered and hoarded before the last of the honored name of Washington who inhabited the mansion on the Potomac, had departed, for he took away with him almost every relic of the venerated patriot which remained at his home. These, with the precious memorials of Washington at Arlington House, were scattered or swept out of existence by the fierce tempest of the late Civil

War, and may never be seen again. This volume, therefore, has the great merit of being the only rare and precious depository of the likenesses and descriptions of things once associated with the person and daily private life of Washington.

But for this work, all semblance of such objects would have been lost to the American people and the world, forever. It is a work that can never be rivalled, for obvious reasons, and it must, therefore, remain a rare and precious treasure in every American household into which it may be welcomed.

This book presents, in its contents and their arrangement in proper order, a more complete picture of the home-life at Mount Vernon, than any other work. The narrative begins with the period of Washington's earliest associations with Mount Vernon, while he was a mere lad, and delineates, with pen and pencil, the most prominent events and objects of his surroundings in private life until the last scenes of his death and burial, and the rendering of public honors to his memory by the nation. It also contains a complete catalogue of the books in Washington's library, and an inventory of his household furniture of every kind at the time of his death. This catalogue and inventory show, in minute detail, how the mansion at Mount Vernon was furnished, in all its parts, by its distinguished master. The book also contains some account of the early home of the Washington family in England; a copy of Washington's last Will and Testament; a copy of Mrs. Washington's Will, and the Act of Incorporation of the *Mount Vernon Ladies' Association of the Union*, the present possessors of the venerated mansion and the surrounding grounds on the Potomac River.

Benson J. Lossing.

PREFACE.

The following extracts, from a brilliant poem by Harvey Rice, entitled, "MOUNT VERNON," are here appended by the publishers as eminently appropriate to the subject of the book; to which are added the "Testimonies of Celebrated Men" to the life and character of the great hero, and some "Maxims" extracted from his deathless writings.

MOUNT VERNON.*

On yonder swelling height,
   With ivied oaks and cedars crowned,
Where Freedom's banner floats in light,
   And every whispering sound
Breathes of the past; 'tis consecrated ground.†

Pilgrim, ascend the steep,
   And there, with true and feeling heart,
On VERNON's brow deep silence keep;
   Ay, let the tear-drop start
While proud yet hallowed thoughts a balm impart.

Nature hath marked the spot
   Where sleeps the great, the good, the wise
Entombed, yet ne'er to be forgot;
   Ah! there the hero lies,
The man of weighty deeds and high emprise.

---

*The complete poem is published, *beautifully illustrated*, by Lee & Sheppard, Boston.

†Mount Vernon, consecrated as the home of Washington, is pleasantly situated in the County of Fairfax, Virginia, on the South Bend of the Potomac, and has an elevation of two hundred feet above the surface of the river, which at this point is two miles wide. The old family mansion, which crowns the hill, was originally built by Washington's uncle, who gave it the name of Mount Vernon, in honor Admiral Vernon, under whom he had served in the British Navy.

PREFACE.

'Twas there in counsels grave,
   That statesmen, noblest of the land,
Their solemn pledge to Freedom gave,
    And boldly took their stand
     In her defense, united heart and hand.

In all her wide domain,
   Say, where has Nature lavished more
To please the eye, the heart to gain,
    Or bid the fancy soar,
     Than here upon Potomac's peaceful shore?

'Twas here, retired, he sought
   A tranquil life, to love endeared—
He who the stern resolve had wrought—
    In days of gloom uncheered,
     To strike for human rights, though traitors sneered.

Musing, methinks I hear,
   The chieftain's voice, the foeman's tread,
And shouts of men who knew not fear,
    Onward to victory led,—
     Our brave old sires, with Freedom's banner spread.

'Mid subtle foes combined,
   How firm was he, that gallant one,
Ordained of Heaven to bless mankind—
    COLUMBIA's noblest son,
     The pride of earth, the noble WASHINGTON!

Sternly he led the van,
   The champion of his country's cause,
Sworn to defend the rights of man,
    His country's, and her laws,
     Against a sway that half the world o'erawes.

And well they earned their fame,
   Who fixed on Freedom's star their gaze,
And fought and bled in Freedom's name,
   And 'mid the battle's blaze
   Bore off the palm, in those heroic days.

On VERNON'S rugged side,
   Where eagles stoop to build the nest,
There let the hero, with his bride,
   In hallowed slumber rest—
   His fittest monument the mountain's crest.

Oh, may the land that's free
   Ne'er fall a prey to faction's blight,
But with her glorious history,
   Still blend a holier light,
   To cheer her sons, and guide them in the right!

* * * * * * * * *

TESTIMONIES

—TO THE—

LIFE AND CHARACTER OF WASHINGTON.

"He lives! ever lives, in the hearts of the free,
The wing of his fame spreads across the broad sea;
He lives where the banner of Freedom's unfurled;
The pride of his country, the wealth of the world."

      "His work is done;
But while the race of mankind endure,
Let his great example stand
Colossal seen of every land,
And keep the soldier firm, the statesman pure,
Till, in all lands, and thro' all human story,
The path of duty be the way to glory."—*Tennyson.*

"It matters very little what immediate spot may have been the birthplace of such a man as Washington. No people can claim, no country can appropriate him. The boon of Providence to the human race, his fame is eternity, and his dwelling-place creation."—*Charles Phillips.*

"Washington did the two greatest things which, in politics, man can have the privilege of attempting. He maintained, by peace, that independence of his country which he had acquired by war. He founded a free government, in the name of the principles of order, and by re-establishing their sway."—*Guizot.*

"Hail, patriot Chief, all hail! Historic Fame
In purest gold hath traced thy glorious name!
Earth has Niagara, the sky its sun,
And proud mankind its only Washington."
—*Albert B. Street.*

"It is the happy combination of rare talents and qualities, the harmonious union of the intellectual and moral powers, rather than the dazzling splendor of any one trait, which constitutes the grandeur of his character. If the title of *great man* ought to be reserved for him who can not be charged with an indiscretion or a vice; who spent his life in establishing the independence, the glory and durable prosperity of his country; who succeeded in all that he undertook, and whose successes were never won at the expense of honor, justice, integrity, or by the sacrifice of a single principle—this title will not be denied to Washington."—*Jared Sparks.*

"Vice shuddered at his presence, and virtue always felt his fostering hand."—*General Lee.*

"I love the patriot sages,
  Who, in the days of yore,
In combat met the foemen,
  And drove them from our shore;
Who flung our banner's starry field
  In triumph to the breeze,
And spread broad maps of cities where
  Once waved the forest trees.

"I love the lofty spirit
  Impell'd our sires to rise,
To found a mighty nation
  Beneath the Western skies.
No clime so bright and beautiful
  As that where sets the sun;
No land so fertile, free and fair,
  As that of Washington."—*George P. Morris.*

MAXIMS AND MOTTOES OF WASHINGTON.

"Without virtue, and without integrity, the finest talents, and the most brilliant accomplishments, can never gain the respect and conciliate the esteem of the truly valuable part of mankind."

"Labor to keep alive in your breast that little spark of celestial fire called conscience."

"A good character is the first essential in a man. It is therefore highly important to endeavor, not only to be learned, but virtuous."

"Speak not evil of the absent, it is unjust."

"Ingratitude, I hope, will never constitute a part of my character, nor find a place in my bosom."

"I never wish to promise more than I have a moral certainty of performing."

"I shall never attempt to palliate my own foibles by exposing the errors of another."

"I am resolved that no misrepresentations, falsehoods, or calumny, shall make me swerve from what I conceive to be the strict line of duty."

"Promote, as an object of primary importance, institutions for the general diffusion of knowledge. In proportion as the structure of a government gives force to public opinion, it is essential that public opinion should be enlightened."

"This Government, the offspring of our own choice, uninfluenced and unawed, adopted upon full investigation and mature deliberation, completely free in its principles, in the distribution of its powers, uniting security with energy, and containing within itself a provision for its own amendment, has a just claim to your confidence and your support. Respect for authority, compliance with its laws, acquiescence in its measures, are duties enjoined by the fundamental maxims of true liberty."

"It is of infinite moment that you should properly estimate the immense value of your National Union to your collective and individual happiness; that you should cherish a cordial, habitual, and immovable attachment to it, accustoming yourself to think and speak of it as the palladium of your political safety and prosperity."

"To preserve is one's duty, and to be silent is the best answer to calumny."

"Born in a land of liberty; having early learned its value; having engaged in the perilous conflict to defend it; having, in a word, devoted the best years of my life to secure its permanent establishment in my own country, my anxious recollections, my sympathetic feelings, and my best wishes are irresistibly attracted, whensoever in any country I see an oppressed nation unfurl the banner of freedom."

"Republicanism is not the phantom of a deluded imagination. On the contrary, laws, under no other form of government, are better supported, liberty and property better secured, or happiness more effectually dispensed to mankind."

"Commerce and industry are the best mines of a nation."

"Associate with men of good quality if you esteem your own reputation, for it is better to be alone than in bad company."

"Be courteous to all, but intimate with few; and let those few be well tried before you give them your confidence."

"Every action in company ought to be with some sign of respect to those present."

"It is a maxim with me, not to ask what, under similar circumstances, I would not grant."

"A difference of opinion on political points is not to be imputed to free men as a fault. It is to be presumed that they are all actuated by an equally laudable and sacred regard for the liberties of their country."

"Let your heart feel for the afflictions and distresses of everyone."

"The consideration that human happiness and moral duty are inseparably connected, will always continue to prompt me to promote the progress of the former by inculcating the practice of the latter."

"I hate deception, even where the imagination only is concerned."

"I never suffer reports, unsupported by proofs, to have weight in my mind."

"Nothing is more a stranger to my breast, or a sin that my soul more abhors, than that black and detestable one of ingratitude."

CONTENTS.

	PAGE
Description of the Arms of the Washington Family....	27
The Washington Family in England	28
A Baronial Residence of the Family	30
Washington's Seals, and Books in his Library	31
Reference to his Birth-Place	32
The Family of Washington's Mother. His Birth	33
His Birth-day and Change in the Calendar	34
Home of the Washington Family on the Rappahannock	34
Place of Washington's Birth described	36
Letters of Washington and Richard Henry Lee, in childhood	37
Death of Washington's Father	38
Lawrence Washington. Admiral Vernon	39
Lawrence with Admiral Vernon on a Naval Expedition	40
Siege of Carthagena; Lawrence Washington at Home	41
Lawrence Washington's Mansion. Mount Vernon Estate	42
The first Mansion at Mount Vernon	43
The Surroundings of George Washington's Boyhood	43
Account of Lord Fairfax's Life and Death	44
Society at Mount Vernon. Young Washington prepares for Sea	45
His Mother interferes, and he returns to School	46
Wahington's first Love. Temptation and Constancy	47
His Early Sports and regular Occupation	48
Experience as a Surveyor and in Wood-craft	48
Appointed a public Surveyor. Disposition of his implements	49
Washington's Military Genius awakened	50
Lawrence and George Washington in Barbadoes. Lawrence dies	51
George inherits Mount Vernon and Paternal Estate	51
Conflicting interests of the English and French in America	52
Washington, a Virginia Major, performs a Perilous Errand	53
Major Washington leads an Expedition against the French	54
Washington continued in the Public Service. Commissioned a Colonel	55
First meeting of Washington and Braddock	56
Washington with Braddock. Battle of the Monongahela	57
His Personal Losses. His Errand to Boston	58

CONTENTS.

Enamored of Mary Phillips on the Banks of the Hudson........... 59
His rival, and their different destinies........................... 60
Washington leads Troops toward Fort Du Quesne.................. 60
End of Campaign. Return of Washington to Mt. Vernon........... 61
Delegate in the Virginia Assembly. His Courtship................. 61
Story of his Courtship continued................................... 62
Marriage engagement with Martha Custis........................... 63
The Young Widow's First Husband. Her Fortune................... 64
The Marriage; its Place and Circumstances......................... 65
The Washington Family at Mount Vernon........................... 66
Character of Mrs. Washington. Mt. Vernon Estate................. 67
Articles used in the House during Washington's Bachelorhood...... 68
Orders preparatory to the reception of a Wife..................... 69
Articles ordered by Washington as a Husband...................... 70
Articles used by a Virginia Lady, in 1760......................... 71
Works of Art ordered for the Mt. Vernon Mansion.................. 72
Articles used by a Virginia Boy a Century ago..................... 73
Articles used by a Virginia Girl a Century ago.................... 74
Glimpses of Domestic Arrangements at Mt. Vernon.................. 75
Washington's daily Life revealed by his Diaries................... 75
Social Enjoyments, Sports and Amusements.......................... 76
Mrs. Washington's Equipage for the Road........................... 76
Washington's fine Horses. His appearance on Horseback............ 77
The Equestrian Outfit of a Virginia Gentleman..................... 77
Aquatic Sports. Social enjoyments abroad.......................... 78
Washington in the Civil Service. Life at the Capital............. 78
Washington's Home Habits. Industry, Economy and Method........... 79
He writes with a Gold Pen. Keeps a Diary through Life............ 80
His Accounts, Correspondence, and attention to his Farm........... 81
Washington as a Farmer. His Table Habits.......................... 82
The Product of his Farm. Character of his Flour.................. 82
The Mount Vernon Wharf.. 83
Shadows of coming Events.. 84
Washington's long training for the approaching Struggle........... 85
George Mason, his neighbor and Friend............................. 86
Washington's Connection with the Church of England................ 86
The establishment of Pohick Church................................ 87
Washington as an Architect and Draughtsman........................ 88
Ministers at Pohick Church. Mason L. Weems....................... 89
Character and occupation of Weems................................. 90
Washington a Vestryman in Alexandria.............................. 91
Pohick Church in decay.. 91

CONTENTS. 15

The Author's experience in Pohick Church	92
The interior of the Church	93
Charles Wilson Peale, the Painter	94
Peale paints the first Portrait of Washington	95
Rembrandt Peale's account of Field, the Painter	96
History of the Study of Washington's Portrait	97
Peale paints a miniature Likeness of Mrs. Washington	98
Death of Mrs. Washington's Daughter	99
Tokens of the Storm of the Revolution	100
Washington chosen a Delegate to the First Continental Congress	101
Assembling of the Delegates. Conference at Mt. Vernon	102
Washington and Friends on their journey to Philadelphia	103
Opening of the First Congress. Its Character	104
Local changes at Mt. Vernon	105
Social gathering of a Patriot Army	106
Distinguished Visitors at Mount Vernon	107
Charles Lee and Horatio Gates	108
Character and Conduct of Charles Lee	109
Character and Career of Horatio Gates	110
Washington in the Virginia Assembly. Patrick Henry	111
News at Mount Vernon of the Battle of Lexington	112
Washington departs for Philadelphia	113
Congress and a Continental Army	113
Washington Commander-in-chief of the Continental Army	114
Mrs. Washington in Camp. Washington's Letters to her	114
Siege of Boston. Honors conferred on Washington	115
His Achievements in New Jersey. Hessian Flag	116
Washington's last Victory and last Trophy	117
Domestic and Social Life at Mount Vernon	118
Mount Vernon during the War. Temporizing rebuked	119
Arrival of Washington at Mount Vernon in 1781	120
Greeting of the Family and Servants. Distinguished Guests	120
Public Duty regarded as paramount to Private Interest	121
Washington hastens to join Lafayette	121
The Count de Rochambeau and Marquis de Chastellux	122
Washington's playful Letter to de Chastellux	123
De Chastellux's Widow. The Family at Mt. Vernon in 1781	124
A cotemporary's description of the Person and Character of Washington	125
Washington Visits his Mother on his way to Yorktown	126
John Parke Custis and his Family	126
Surrender of Cornwallis. Illness of J. P. Custis	127
Death of Mr. Custis. Washington adopts his Children as his own	127

Eleanor Parke and George Washington Parke Custis, Foster Children..... 128
Washington again visits his Mother and his Home. Ball at Fredericksburg... 129
News of a Treaty of Peace. How Washington received it............ 130
Washington's Announcement of Peace. Army disbanded..................... 131
British Evacuate New York. Washington parts with his Officers........... 131
He publicly resigns his Commission at Annapolis................................ 132
His satisfaction in returning to Private Life... 132
His Military Garments then laid aside.. 133
History of Washington'. Battle Sword. Franklin wills him his Cane..... 134
Morris's Poem on the Sword and Cane... 135
Washington's Camp Chest and Contents described.............................. 136
His Accommodations for a Dinner Party at West Point....................... 137
Washington's Camp Goblet. History of his Marquee.......................... 138
His Writing-Desk and its Associations... 139
The Marquee and its Revolutionary Associations................................. 139
Its occasional Uses and Usefulness after the War................................. 140
History of the Cincinnati Society.. 141
The Objects of the Society stated.. 142
State Societies. The Order of the Cincinnati...................................... 143
Description of the jewelled Order presented to Washington................. 144
Description of the Member's Certificate of the Cincinnati................... 144
Washington chosen first President of the Society................................ 146
A Merry and Happy Christmas day at Mount Vernon......................... 147
Washington's experience of the Happiness of Retirement................... 147
He resumes the old Social Habits of Mount Vernon............................ 148
Lafayette expected there. Letter to Madam Lafayette....................... 148
Simplicity of Life at Mount Vernon. Open Hospitality....................... 149
Enlargement of the House at Mount Vernon....................................... 149
Description of the Mansion as Washington left it............................... 150
Surroundings of the Mansion. Washington his own Architect............ 151
He provides for importing Pavement Stone from England.................. 152
He makes arrangements for the employment of English Mechanics.... 153
He imports the Tools for their use.. 154
Preparations for Ornamental Planting at Mount Vernon...................... 154
Description of the Lawn at the West front of the Mansion................. 155
Description of the arrangement of the Tree-planting......................... 156
Account of the Seed and Tool Houses, and Conservatory.................... 157
Account of the Tropical and other Plants that survived Washington... 158
An ancient Sago Palm described and delineated.................................. 159
Destruction of Washington's Conservatory by fire. Its Ruins............ 160
Account of the Ice-house and Dry-well at Mt. Vernon....................... 161

CONTENTS.

Description of the Summer House and its Surroundings	162
Washington's Minute Memorandum of Direction and Distances	163
Lafayette visits Mount Vernon	163
History of Lafayette's connection with the Continental Army	164
Portrait of Lafayette, by Charles Wilson Peale	164
Lafayette's arrival at New York. His Letter to Washington	165
His arrival at Mount Vernon. Crowd of Visitors there	165
Washington and Lafayette Free and Accepted Masons	166
Madam Lafayette presents Washington with a Masonic Apron	167
Subsequent History of that Apron	168
Other Masonic Regalia presented to Washington	169
Washington's Correspondence on the Subject	170
How the Regalia was made. Its History	170
Public honors given to Washington. Bronze Statue proposed	171
Washington's Portrait Painted by Dunlap	172
Plaster-cast taken of his Face by Wright	172
Wright's Work accidentally destroyed	173
Legislature of Virginia order a Statue of Washington	173
Account of the Statue. The Inscription	174
Public Proceedings concerning the Statue. Washington's Letter	174
Methods used for procuring a good Likeness	175
Houdon employed to make it. Jefferson's Letter	176
Arrival of Houdon at Mt. Vernon. His Work	176
Houdon's Method of obtaining a Likeness	177
Description and Delineation of the Statue	177
Gouverneur Morris the Model for the Figure	179
Pine, the Painter. His Professional Visit at Mount Vernon	180
Washington dislikes Sitting to Painters. Other Portraits by Pine	181
Elizabeth Parke and G. W. Parke Custis. History of Pine's Portrait	182
French Hounds sent to Mount Vernon	183
Washington's Pack before the Revolution. The French Hounds	184
A Magnificent Chimney-piece presented to Washington	185
Description of the Chimney-piece	186
Description of the Fire-place. Ornaments on the Shelf	188
Exchange of Presents. Asses from the Royal Stud at Madrid	189
Description of the Jack Asses. Completion of the Mansion	190
Washington employs Tobias Lear as Secretary	191
Condition of the Country. Necessity for Political changes	192
Washington Apprehensive concerning the Future. A Movement	193
Convention for Remodelling the Government. National Constitution	194
Col. Humphries a Resident at Mount Vernon. His Character	195
He brings a Present to Washington from the King of France	196

CONTENTS.

His Literary Labors at Mount Vernon ... 197
Distinguished Guests at Mount Vernon ... 198
Marchioness de Brienne Paints a Miniature of Washington ... 199
Allegorical Picture by Madam Van Berckel ... 200
History of the Picture. Other Distinguished Visitors ... 201
Brisot de Warville and his Visit at Mt. Vernon ... 202
Washington chosen to be the First President of the Republic ... 203
A Glass Manufacturer Welcomed at Mt. Vernon ... 204
Meeting of the First Congress under the Constitution ... 205
Washington reluctantly returns to Public Life ... 206
Messengers, at Mount Vernon, announce his Election ... 207
He Visits His Mother for the last time. The Interview ... 208
Washington's journey to New York. A continual Ovation ... 209
Changes in the Aspect of Mount Vernon ... 210
Public Receptions on the way to New York ... 211
Pleasant incidents at Philadelphia ... 212
Reception of the President Elect, at Trenton ... 213
His Aquatic Escort, and his Reception at New York ... 214
Washington Caricatured. His Inauguration ... 215
The Ceremony of Administering the Oath of Office ... 216
Bible used at the Inauguration. Mrs. Washington at Home ... 217
Her Domestic Habits ... 218
Etiquette at the Republican Court ... 219
Watches purchased by Washington and his Wife ... 220
Account of Washington's Watch and Seals. Mrs. W's Frugality ... 221
Mrs. Washington's Journey to New York ... 222
Her Reception. Family Dinner. Names of Guests ... 223
Description of the Dinner. Mrs. Washington's Receptions ... 224
The President's Receptions. His Appearance on such occasions ... 225
Disposition of his Dress Swords used on those occasions ... 226
How Visitors were received. The President's Residence in New York ... 227
The Presidential Mansion and Furniture ... 228
Seat of Government changed. Washington's Voyage to Rhode Island ... 229
He and his family set out for Mount Vernon ... 230
His State Barge. His Letter. Again at Mount Vernon ... 231
Labors of Congress. Key of the Bastile. France disturbed ... 232
Opening of the French Revolution ... 233
Perfidy in the Bastile. The People Exasperated ... 234
Destruction of the Bastile. Lafayette at the head of the Troops ... 235
Key of the Bastile and Drawing of the Prison sent to Washington ... 236
Thomas Paine's Letter on the Subject. Correspondence ... 236
Washington's Spy-glass. Anecdote connected with it ... 238

CONTENTS.

Washington's Pocket Spy-glass Presented to Andrew Jackson............. 239
Pistols Presented to Washington... 240
Bust of M. Necker Presented by Count D'Estaing. Notice of Necker... 241
Inscription on the Bust of Necker. Account of D'Estaing................... 242
Houdon's Bust of Lafayette at Mount Vernon.................................. 243
Virginia Presents a Copy to the City of Paris................................... 244
Ceremony of Presentation. Lafayette Highly Honored...................... 245
President Washington's English Coach.. 246
External Decorations of the Coach. Family Journey in it................... 247
Incompetency of the Coachman. Accidents..................................... 248
History of the Coach. Its Earnings when in ruins.............................. 249
Selection of a Residence for the President considered...................... 250
Question as to the Permanent Seat of the National Government......... 251
Washington Negotiates for a Residence. His Prudence and Caution... 252
He makes Suggestions about Interior Arrangements.......................... 253
Description of Sevres China Presented to Washington....................... 254
Description of Sevres China Presented to Mrs. Washington................. 255
How Sevres China is made. Seat of the National Government............ 256
Strife for the Possession of the National Capital. Decision................. 257
New Yorkers Dissatisfied. Caricatures and Satires............................ 258
Philadelphians no better Satisfied. Washington's Caution.................. 259
A House Hired. Washington's Journey to Philadelphia...................... 260
A Patriotic Tavern-Keeper. President and Family at Philadelphia...... 261
A gay Season in Philadelphia. Luxuries.. 262
Washington Suggests Wine Castors, called "Coasters"...................... 263
They are made. Wine Coolers from France. Their History................ 264
Washington's Family Plate Re-made.. 265
Description of the Plate. Washington again at Mt. Vernon................ 266
Use of some of the Plate at Arlington Spring.................................... 267
Washington makes a Tour through the Southern States..................... 268
His calculations as to Time. Incidents of the Tour............................ 269
His return Journey. Site of the National Capital............................... 270
District of Columbia. City laid out and named................................. 271
Opening of the Second Congress... 272
Earl of Buchan Presents a Relic of Sir William Wallace..................... 272
A Scotch Painter dines with Washington. The Dinner...................... 273
Miniature Made by the Painter. Correspondence with Earl of Buchan... 274
By Will, Washington recommits the Wallace Relic to Buchan............. 275
Washington again at Mt. Vernon. Paine's *Rights of Man*.................. 276
Effects of *Rights of Man*, in England. Washington's Industry........... 277
Sickness and Death in the Mount Vernon Family............................... 278
Washington's Generosity to his Nephew's Widow.............................. 279

His Love for Children and Young Company. His Foster Children........ 280
Training of the Foster Children... 281
A Harpsichord at Mount Vernon... 282
Washington's Second Inauguration as President of the Republic............. 283
Simplicity of the Ceremonies on the occasion..................................... 284
An Account of the Ceremonies, and Washington's Appearance................. 285
Washington Sacrifices Private Interest for the Public Good..................... 286
Yellow Fever in Philadelphia. Washington at Home........................... 287
Unskillful Farm Management at Mount Vernon.................................. 288
The President's Family avoid the Fever at Germantown........................ 289
Marriage of Philadelphia Belles to Foreign Ministers............................ 290
Washington's Farewell Address composed.. 290
Effect of the Publication of the Farewell Address................................. 291
Violence of Party Spirit felt by Washington....................................... 292
A Specimen of the Newspaper utterances.. 293
Washington retires to Private Life, at Mount Vernon............................ 294
Inauguration of John Adams as Second President................................ 295
Farewell Entertainment for Washington by Philadelphians..................... 296
An Eye-Witness's Account of the President's Table Customs.................... 297
Account of Washington's Table Traits continued.................................. 298
Washington and his Family return to Mt. Vernon. Lafayette's Son......... 299
Lafayette's Misfortunes.. 300
Washington's Sensibility when Speaking of them................................. 301
Bradford's *Lament of Washington*, a Poem...................................... 302
Lafayette's Suffering. His Devoted Wife and Children......................... 303
His Son seeks an Asylum in America. Cautious proceedings................. 304
Congress takes Action concerning Young Lafayette.............................. 305
Washington takes him to Mt. Vernon under his Protection..................... 306
Release of Lafayette. The Son returns to France................................. 306
Washington's Letter to Lafayette. Young Lafayette's Profile................. 307
Sharpless, the Artist... 308
His Portrait of the Washington Family. Lafayette and Custis............... 309
Sharpless's Profiles at Arlington House.. 310
Washington's Exquisite Enjoyment of Private Life............................... 311
His own description of his Daily Employments................................... 312
Washington's Inkstand. Repairs at Mount Vernon............................. 313
Mount Vernon Refurnished and Beautified.. 314
Description of Illuminators at Mount Vernon..................................... 315
Account of Furniture once at Mount Vernon...................................... 316
Washington Relics at Arlington House... 317
Elkanah Watson's Account of a Night at Mount Vernon....................... 318
Pictures by Winstanley, at Mount Vernon... 319

Presages of War with France. The French Directory........................ 320
Relations of the United States with France. Preparations for War......... 321
Washington appointed Commander-in-chief of the Army...................... 322
Hamilton to be Acting General-in-chief. Guests at Mount Vernon........... 323
The French Directory Humbled. Bonaparte in Power. War averted..... 324
Washington's Nephew, Lawrence Lewis, a resident at Mt. Vernon........... 324
Nelly Custis and her Suitors... 325
Correspondence on the Subject. Nelly's Confessions...................... 326
Marriage of Lawrence Lewis and Nelly Custis.............................. 327
Incidents of the Marriage. Mrs. Macauley Graham......................... 328
Washington's allusion to his own Death. Makes his Will.................. 329
His exposure to Wet and Cold... 330
Sudden and Severe Inflammation of the Throat and Chest................... 331
Home Remedies Applied without Effect..................................... 332
Physicians sent for. Critical Situation. His Wills...................... 333
Washington's Directions about his Papers. Death near.................... 334
His Consideration for every one. His Last Words......................... 335
His Death. Mrs. Washington at his Bedside............................... 336
The Room in which Washington Died, and its Furniture..................... 337
The Spectators of Washington's Death 338
Notice of Dr. Craik, his Friend and Physician............................ 339
Preparations for Washington's Burial. The Coffin........................ 340
The Funeral at Mt. Vernon.. 341
The Funeral Procession... 342
The Bier and Vault... 343
The old Family Vault at Mt. Vernon. A Villanous Act..................... 344
Washington's Death Announced to Congress. Proceedings................... 345
Funeral Oration by General Henry Lee, at the Request of Congress........ 346
Lee at Mt. Vernon. His Oration. Guard of Honor......................... 347
Mrs. Washington's Letter about the Removal of the Remains................ 348
Mrs. Washington in Affliction. Public Honors to Washington abroad..... 349
Death of Mrs. Washington. Bushrod Washington Heirs Mt. Vernon..... 350
A Survivor of Washington's Slaves. Bushrod Washington................... 351
Account and Portrait of that Survivor.................................... 352
Billy. Lafayette at the Tomb of Washington.............................. 353
A Ring containing Washington's Hair Presented to Lafayette............... 354
Re-entombment of Washington and his Wife 354
Account of that Re-entombment by an Eye-witness.......................... 355
The Bodies put in Marble Coffins... 356
The new Tomb and Vault... 357
Disposition of Washington's Personal Property............................ 358
Account of a Relic of Washington in a Boston Family...................... 359

CONTENTS.

A few Mementoes of Washington, at Mt. Vernon 360, 361
Washington's Address and Dinner Cards 362
Works of Art that long remained at Mount Vernon 363
The Pitcher Portrait and Eulogy of Washington 364
History of the Pitcher Portrait 365
Copy of the Eulogy on the back of the Pitcher Portrait ... 366, 367, 368
A Retrospect. Late Condition of Mt. Vernon 369
Mount Vernon Purchased by American Women 370
Mount Vernon Ladies' Association control it 371
Reflections 372
The English Home of the Washington Family 373
Washington's Library 375
The Grounds about Mount Vernon 394
Washington as a Free Mason 396
Houdon's Likeness of Washington 397
Shadow Portrait of Washington 399
How the Mansion at Mount Vernon was Furnished 400
Washington's Great Barn 410
Posthumous Honors 411
Washington's Will 420
Present Condition of Mount Vernon 425

LIST OF ILLUSTRATIONS.

	PAGE
Washington's Book-plate	27
Cave Castle	29
Washington Mortar	30
Washington's Seal	31
Washington's Seal-ring	31
Washington's Watch-seals	31
Fac-simile of Signatures of Jane and Mary Washington	32
Dutch Tile—half the size of the original	34
Residence of the Washington Family	35
Washington's Birth-place	36
Lawrence Washington	39
Admiral Vernon	40
The Vernon Medal	42
Washington's Telescope	50
Pack-saddle	53
Leathern Camp-chest	53
Washington's first Head-quarters	55
The Carey House in 1859	56

ILLUSTRATIONS.

	PAGE
Mary Phillips	59
Morris's House	60
Daniel Parke Custis	64
Mrs. Custis's Iron Chest	64
Mrs. Washington's Children	66
Mrs. Washington at the time of her Marriage	67
Chairs once at Mount Vernon	69
Custis Arms	74
Washington's Gold Pen with Silver Case	80
Fac-simile of Page-headings in Washington's Diary	80
Fac-simile of Entry in Washington's Diary	81
Mount Vernon Landing	83
Ground-plan and Elevation of Pohick Church	88
Mason L. Weems	90
Christ Church, Alexandria	91
Pohick Church in 1859	92
Pulpit in Pohick Church	93
Charles Willson Peale	95
Washington's Military Button	95
Washington as a Virginia Colonel, at the age of forty	96
Fac-simile of Peale's Receipt	97
John Parke Custis	98
Patrick Henry	103
General Charles Lee	108
General Horatio Gates	110
Gold Medal awarded to Washington for the Deliverance of Boston	116
Hessian Flag taken at Trenton	117
British Flag taken at Yorktown	118
Count de Rochambeau	121
Marquis de Chastellux	123
Eleanor Parke Custis	128
Washington's Military Clothes	133
The Sword and Staff	135
Washington's Camp-chest	136
Silver Camp-goblet	138
Washington's Travelling Writing-case	139
Washington's Tents in their Portmanteaux	140
Order of the Cincinnati	143
Order presented by French Officers	144
Cincinnati Society—Member's Certificate	145
Western Front of Mount Vernon in 1858	151
Section of shaded Carriage-way	154
General Plan of the Mansion and Grounds at Mount Vernon	155

ILLUSTRATIONS.

	PAGE.
Garden-house	157
Century-plant and Lemon-tree	158
View in the Flower-garden at Mount Vernon—the Sago Palm	159
Ruins of the Conservatory at Mount Vernon	160
Ice-house at Mount Vernon	161
Summer-house at Mount Vernon	162
Lafayette.—Painted by C. W. Peale, in 1778	166
Masonic Apron wrought by the Marchioness Lafayette	167
Houdon's Bust of Washington	177
Houdon's Statue of Washington	178
Elizabeth Parke Custis	182
G. W. P. Custis when a Child	183
Italian Chimney-piece	186
Tablet on the left of Chimney-piece	187
Centre Tablet	187
Tablet on the right of Chimney-piece	187
Porcelain Vases	188
Colonel David Humphreys	195
Engraving of Louis XVI	196
Washington and Lafayette	199
Washington's Destiny	200
Charles Thomson	207
Travelling Boot-jack	209
Ancient Entrance to Mount Vernon in 1858	210
Bible used at the Inauguration of Washington	216
Washington's Lepine Watch, Seal and Key	221
Washington's last Watch-seal	221
Washington's Dress Sword	225
Secretary and Circular Chair	229
Destruction of the Bastile	235
Key of the Bastile	237
Washington's Spy-Glass	238
Washington's Pistol	240
Bust of M. Necker	243
Bust of Lafayette	244
Washington's English Coach	246
Emblazoning on Washington's Coach	247
Picture of a Panel on Washington's Coach	248
Cincinnati China	254
Mrs. Washington's China	255
China Butter-bowl and Dish	256
Wine-coolers and Coaster	265
Specimens of Washington's Plate	266

ILLUSTRATIONS.

	PAGE
The Presidential Mansion	267
Martha Washington	275
Nelly Custis's Harpsichord	282
George Washington Lafayette	300
G. W. P. Custis at the age of seventeen years	308
Crayon Profile of Washington	310
Crayon Profile of Mrs. Washington	311
Washington's Inkstand	314
Mural Candelabra	315
Ancient Lantern	315
Sideboard, Tea-table and Punch-bowl	317
Washington's Silver Candlestick	317
Morning—a Landscape by Winstanley	319
Evening—a Landscape by Winstanley	319
Dr. James Craik	332
Bed and Bedstead on which Washington died	337
Room in which Washington died	338
Silver Shield on Washington's Coffin	341
Washington's Bier	343
The old Vault in 1858	344
General Henry Lee	346
McPherson's Blue	348
Bushrod Washington	351
Westford	352
Washington's Marble Coffin	356
Lid of Washington's Coffin	356
Washington's Tomb	357
Washington's Liquor-chest	361
Washington's Mirror	361
Water-mark	362
Washington's Address Card	362
Pitcher Portrait	364
Postscript	373
The Washington House, Brington	373
Inscription in the Washington House	374
Fac-simile of Washington's Memorandum	395
Masonic Portrait of Washington	397
Houdon's Mold from Washington's Face	398
Shadow Portraits	399
Washington's Circular Barn	411
Lutheran Church in Philadelphia	4.2
Washington Medal	412
Mrs. Washington's Signature	425

MOUNT VERNON, THE HOME OF WASHINGTON, AND ITS ASSOCIATIONS.

WASHINGTON'S BOOK-PLATE.

N many an ancient volume in the library at Mount Vernon, while the mansion remained in the possession of the Washington family, was the engraved book-plate of the illustrious proprietor, which displayed, as usual, the name and armorial bearings of the owner. The language of heraldry learnedly describes the family arms of Washington as "*argent*, two bars *gules* in chief, three *mullets* of the second. Crest, a raven, with wings, *indorsed proper*, issuing out of a ducal coronet, *or*." All this may be interpreted, a white or silver shield, with two red bars across it, and above them three spur rowels, the combination appearing very much like the stripes and stars on our national ensign. The crest, a raven of natural color issuing out of a golden ducal coronet. The three mullets or star-figures indicated the filial distinction of the third son.

Back into the shadowy past six hundred years and more we may look, and find the name of Washington presented with "honorable mention" in several counties in England, on the records of the field, the church, and the state. They were generally first-class agriculturists, and eminently loyal men when their sovereigns were in trouble. In that trying time for England's monarch, a little more than two hundred years ago, when a republican army, under the authority of a revolutionary parliament, was hunting King Charles the First, Sir Henry Washington, a nephew of the Duke of Buckingham, is observed as governor of Worcester, and its able defender during a siege of three months by the parliamentary troops under General Fairfax. And earlier than this, when Charles, as Prince Royal, was a suitor for the hand of the Infanta of Spain, we find a Washington attached to his person. The loyal James Howell, who suffered long imprisonment in Fleet-street Jail because of his attachment to Charles, was in the train of the Prince while at Madrid; and from that city he wrote to his "noble friend, Sir John North," in the summer of 1623, saying:

"Mr. *Washington*, the Prince his page is lately dead of a Calenture, and I was at his buriall under a Figtree behind my Lord of *Bristol's* house. A little before his death one *Ballard*, an *English* Priest, went to tamper with him, and Sir

Edmund Varney meeting him coming down the stairs out of *Washington's* chamber, they fell from words to blows: but they were parted. The business was like to gather very ill blood, and com to a great hight, had not Count *Gondamar* quasht it, which I beleeve he could not have done, unless the times had bin favorable; for such is the reverence they bear to the Church here, and so holy a conceit they have of all Ecclesiastics, that the greatest Don in Spain will tremble to offer the meanest of them any outrage or affront."

CAVE CASTLE.

From this loyal family came emigrants to America nine years after King Charles lost his head. These were two brothers, true Cavaliers, who could not brook the rule of Cromwell, the self-styled Lord Protector of England. They left their beautiful residence of Cave Castle, north of the Humber, in Yorkshire, and sought more freedom of life in the virgin soil of the New World. And in later years the representatives of the Washingtons and Fairfaxes, who were neighbors and friends in Virginia, found themselves, in political positions, opposed to those of their ancestors; that of the former being the great leader of a republican army, and of the latter a most loyal adherent of the crown.

The Washingtons who first came to America seem not to have been possessed of much wealth. They brought with them no family plate as evidences of it; for the heiress of the family had given her hand and fortune to an English baronet, the master of the fine estate of Studley Royal, where now the

WASHINGTON MORTAR.

eldest son of the late Earl of Ripon resides. It is believed that there is only one relic of the old Washington family in this country, and that is a small bronze mortar, having the letters "C. W." (the initials of CIMON WASHINGTON) and the date, "1664," cast upon it. That mortar is in Independence Hall, in Philadelphia.

The Northamptonshire family, from whom George Washington was descended, wore the motto seen upon his book plate — EXITUS ACTA PROBAT: "The end justifies the means;" and it was borne and heeded by the line from generation to generation, until the most illustrious of them all had achieved the greatest ends by the most justifiable means.

The annexed engraving is from an impression of General Washington's seal, bearing his family arms, attached to the death-warrant of a soldier executed at Morristown, in 1780. Below it is an engraving of the face of his seal-ring, which also bears his arms and motto; and also of two watch-seals which he wore together in early life. Upon each of the last two is engraved his monogram, one of them being a fac-simile of his written initials. One of these was lost by Washington himself on the bloody field of Monongahela, where Braddock was defeated in 1755; and the other by his nephew, in Virginia, more than twenty-five years ago. Both were found in the year 1854, and restored to the Washington family.*

WASHINGTON'S SEAL.

SEAL-RING.

WASHINGTON'S WATCH-SEALS.

Of all the volumes in the Mount Vernon library which contain Washington's book-plate none appears more interesting than Sir Matthew Hale's *Contemplations, Moral and Divine*, printed at the beginning of the last century. It is well worn by frequent use; for it was from that volume that Washington's mother drew many of those great maxims which she instilled into the mind of her son, and which had a powerful influence in

---

* This statement is made on the authority of Charles J. Bushnell, Esq., of New York, whose investigations in numismatic science and kindred subjects have been careful and extensive. The engravings of the seals are copied, by his permission, from a work of his now in preparation for the press.

moulding his moral character. Upon a fly-leaf of the volume are written, in bold characters, the names of the two wives of Augustine Washington, the father of our beloved Friend. These were JANE BUTLER and MARY BALL. Their names were written by themselves, the first with ink that retains its original blackness, and the second with a color that has faded to the tint of warm sepia.

FAC-SIMILE OF SIGNATURES.

These signatures send the thoughts on busy retrospective errands to the pleasant mansions and broad and fertile plantations of Virginia, when the Old Dominion was as loyal to the second King George of England as to the second King Charles in the days of Berkeley, almost a hundred years before; or when royal governors held vice-regal courts at Williamsburg, the capital of the Commonwealth twenty years after republican Bacon's torch had laid old Jamestown in ashes. Especially do they send the thoughts to the beautiful spot near the Potomac, half way between Pope's and Bridge's Creek, in Westmoreland, where stood a modest mansion, surrounded by the holly and more stately trees of the forest, in which lived Mary, the mother of the great Washington.

In the possession of an old Virginian family may be seen a picture, in which is represented a rampant lion holding a globe in his paw, a helmet and shield, a vizor strong, and coat of mail and other emblems of strength and courage; and for a motto the words, from Ovid, *Cœlumque tueri*. On the back of the picture is written:

"The coat of arms of Colonel William Ball, who came from England with his family about the year 1650, and settled at the mouth of Corotoman River, in Lancaster county, Virginia, and died in 1669, leaving two sons, William and Joseph, and one daughter, Hannah, who married Daniel Fox. William left eight sons (and one daughter), five of whom have now (Anno Domini 1779) male issue. Joseph's male issue is extinct. General George Washington is his grandson, by his youngest daughter, Mary." Here we have the American pedigree of the mother of Washington.

In that modest mansion near the Potomac, of which we have just spoken, a great patriot was born of a mother eight-and-twenty years of age, when the popular William Gooch was royal governor of Virginia; and in an old family Bible, in Hanover county, of quarto form, dilapidated by use and age, and covered with striped Virginia cloth, might have been seen, a few years ago, the following record, in the handwriting of the father of that Patriot:

"George Washington, son to Augustine and Mary his wife, was born y⁰ 11th day of February, 1731–2, about ten in the morning, and was baptized the 3d of April following; Mr. Beverly Whiting and Captain Christopher Brooks, godfathers, and Mrs. Mildred Gregory godmother."

Almost three hundred years ago Pope Gregory the Thirteenth ordained that ten days should be added to the tally of all past time since the birth of Jesus, to make up some fractional deficiencies in the calendar; and twenty years after the above record was made, the British government ordered the Gregorian calendar, or new style, as it was called, to be adopted. The deficiency was then eleven days, and these were added. So we date the birth of Washington, and celebrate its anniversary, on the twenty-second instead of the eleventh of February.

Washington's birth-place was a "four-roomed house, with a chimney at each end," perfectly plain outside and in. The

DUTCH TILE.—HALF THE SIZE OF THE ORIGINAL.

only approach to ornament was a Dutch-tiled chimney-piece in the best room, covered with rude pictures of Scriptural scenes; but around the mansion there were thrift and abundance. George was the eldest of his mother's six children, and only his infant years were passed under the roof where he first saw the light; for fire destroyed the house, and his father removed to an estate in Stafford county, near Fredericksburg, and dwelt in an equally plain mansion, pleasantly seated near the north bank of the Rappahannock River.

RESIDENCE OF THE WASHINGTON FAMILY.

Of the birth-place of Washington nothing now remains but a chimney and a few scattered bricks and stones; and around it, where the smiles of highest culture were once seen, there is an aspect of desolation that makes the heart feel sad. Some decayed fig-trees and tangled shrubs and vines, with here and there a pine and cedar sapling, tell, with silent eloquence, of neglect and ruin, and that decay has laid its blighting fingers upon every work of man there. The vault of the Washington family, wherein many were buried, is so neglected that some of the remains exposed to view have been carried away by plunderers. All around it are stunted trees, shrubs, and briers; and near it may be seen fragments of slabs once set up in commemoration of some of that honored family.

WASHINGTON'S BIRTH-PLACE.

On the spot where Washington was born, the late George Washington Parke Custis, a grandson of Mrs. Washington, placed a piece of freestone in 1815, with the simple inscription:

HERE,

ON THE 11TH OF FEBRUARY, 1732,

GEORGE WASHINGTON WAS BORN

"We gathered together," says Mr. Custis, in a published account, "the bricks of the ancient chimney that once formed the hearth around which Washington, in his infancy, had played, and constructed a rude kind of pedestal, on which we reverently placed the FIRST STONE, commending it to the respect and protection of the American people in general, and the citizens of Westmoreland in particular." But such respect and protection have been withheld, and that stone is now in fragments and overgrown with brambles.

In this vicinity lived some of the Lees, always a distinguished family in Virginia; and one of the most intimate of Washington's friends, in his earliest childhood, was Richard Henry Lee, afterward the eminent statesman and patriot. They were very nearly of the same age, Lee being one month the oldest. I have before me a copy of a letter written by each when they were nine years old, and which are supposed to be among the earliest, perhaps the very first, epistles penned by these illustrious men. They were sent to me a few years ago, by a son of Richard Henry Lee (who then possessed the originals), and are as follows:

RICHARD HENRY LEE TO GEORGE WASHINGTON.

"Pa brought me two pretty books full of pictures he got them in Alexandria they have pictures of dogs and cats and tigers and elefants and ever so many pretty things cousin bids me send you one of them it has a picture of an elefant and a little indian boy on his back like uncle jo's sam pa says if I learn my tasks good he will let uncle jo bring me to see you will you ask your ma to let you come to see me.

"Richard henry Lee."

GEORGE WASHINGTON'S REPLY.

"Dear Dickey I thank you very much for the pretty picture book you gave me. Sam asked me to show him the pictures and I showed him all the pictures in it; and I read to him how the tame Elephant took care of the master's little boy, and put him on his back and would not let any body touch his master's little son. I can read three or four pages sometimes without missing a word. Ma says I may go to see you and stay all day with you next week if it be not rainy. She says I may ride my pony Hero if Uncle Ben will go with me and lead Hero. I have a little piece of poetry about the picture book you gave me, but I mustnt tell you who wrote the poetry.*

<blockquote>
"G. W.'s compliments to R. H. L.,
And likes his book full well,
Henceforth will count him his friend,
And hopes many happy days he may spend.
</blockquote>

"Your good friend,
"George Washington.

"I am going to get a whip top soon, and you may see it and whip it."

Augustine Washington died in the spring of 1743, when his son George was eleven years of age, and by his last will and testament bequeathed his estate of Hunting Creek, upon a bay and stream of that name, near Alexandria, to Lawrence Washington, a son by his first wife, Jane Butler. It was a

---

* In a letter to me, accompanying the two juvenile epistles, Mr. Lee writes: "The letter of Richard Henry Lee was written by himself, and, uncorrected, was sent by him to his boy-friend, George Washington. The poetical effusion was, I have heard, written by a Mr. Howard, a gentleman who used to visit at the house of Mr. Washington."

noble domain of many hundred acres, stretching for miles along the Potomac, and bordering the estates of the Fairfaxes, Masons, and other distinguished families.

LAWRENCE WASHINGTON.

Lawrence, who seems to have inherited the military spirit of his family, had lately been to the wars. Admiral Vernon, commander-in-chief of England's navy in the West Indies, had lately chastised the Spaniards for their depredations upon British commerce, by capturing Porto Bello, on the isthmus of Darien. The Spaniards prepared to strike an avenging blow, and the French determined to help them. England and her colonies were aroused. Four regiments, for service in the West Indies, were to be raised in the American colonies; and from Massachusetts to the Carolinas, the fife and drum of the recruiting sergeant were heard. Lawrence, then a spirited young man of twenty-two, was among the thousands who caught the infection, and obtaining a captain's

ADMIRAL VERNON.

commission, he embarked for the West Indies in 1741, with between three and four thousand men under General Wentworth. That officer and Admiral Vernon commanded a joint expedition against Carthagena, in South America, which resulted in disaster. According to the best authorities not less than twenty thousand British soldiers and seamen perished, chiefly from a fatal sickness that prevailed, especially among the troops who were commanded by General Wentworth. To that scourge Thompson, in his "Summer," thus touchingly alludes:

> "You, gallant Vernon, saw
> The miserable scene; you, pitying, saw
> To infant weakness sunk the warrior's arm;
> Saw the deep-racking pang, the ghastly form,
> The lip pale-quivering, and the beamless eye
> No more with ardor bright; you heard the groans
> Of agonizing ships, from shore to shore;
> Heard, nightly plung'd amid the sullen waves,
> The frequent corse—while on each other fixed,
> In sad presage, the blank assistants seemed,
> Silent, to ask, whom fate would next demand."

In the midst of that terrible pestilence the system of Lawrence Washington received those seeds of fatal disease against whose growth it struggled manfully for ten years, and then yielded.

Lawrence returned home in the autumn of 1742, the provincial army in which he had served having been disbanded, and Admiral Vernon and General Wentworth recalled to England. He had acquired the friendship and confidence of both those officers. For several years he kept up a correspondence with the former, and received from him a copy of a medal struck in commemoration of the capture of Porto Bello by Admiral Vernon. This was preserved at Mount Vernon until Washington's death, and is probably in possession of some member of the family. The only specimen of the medal I have ever seen is in my own possession, from which the engraving was made.

THE VERNON MEDAL.

Lawrence intended to go to England, join the regular army, and seek preferment therein; but love changed his resolution and the current of his life, for

"Love rules the court, the camp, the grove,
And man below, and saints above."

Beautiful Anne, the eldest daughter of the Honorable William Fairfax, of Fairfax county, became the object of his warm attachment, and they were betrothed. Their nuptials were about to be celebrated in the spring of 1743, when a sudden attack of gout in the stomach deprived Lawrence of his father. But the marriage took place in July. All thoughts of military life as a profession passed from the mind of Lawrence, and, taking possession of his Hunting Creek estate, he erected a plain, substantial mansion upon the highest eminence along the Potomac front of his domain, and named the spot MOUNT VERNON, in honor of the gallant admiral.

In that mansion Lawrence resided until his death, and but little change was made in its appearance from the time when it came into the possession of his brother George by inheritance, until the close of the Old War for Independence. It has been described as a house of the first class then occupied by thrifty Virginia planters; two stories in height, with a porch in front, and a chimney built inside, at each end, contrary to the prevailing style. It stood upon a most lovely spot, on the brow of a gentle slope which ended at a thickly-wooded precipitous river bank, its summit nearly one hundred feet above the water. Before it swept the Potomac with a magnificent curve, its broad bosom swarming with the graceful swan, the gull, the wild duck, and smaller water-fowl; and beyond lay the green fields and shadowy forests of Maryland.

When Lawrence was fairly settled, with his bride, in this new and pleasant home, little George was a frequent and much-petted visitor at Mount Vernon. His half-brother loved him tenderly, and after their father's death he took a paternal interest in all his concerns. The social influences to which he was subjected were of the highest order. The Fairfaxes held the first rank in wealth and social position, both in England and in Virginia; and the father-in-law of Lawrence, who occupied a beautiful country seat not far from Mount Vernon, called Belvoir, was a man of distinction, having served as an officer of the British army in the East and West Indies, and officiated as governor of New Providence, one of the Bermudas. He now managed an immense landed estate belonging to his cousin, Lord Fairfax, a tall, gaunt, rawboned, near-sighted man, upon whom had fallen the snows of sixty winters, and who, made shy and eccentric by disappointed love in early life, was now in Virginia, and living at Belvoir, but secretly resolving to go over the Blue Mountains of the West, and make his home in the deep wilderness, away from the haunts of men. Thither he went a few years later, and in the great valley of Virginia took up his abode in a lodge at a spot where he resolved to build a manor-house, in the midst of ten thousand acres of arable and grazing land, call it Greenway Court, and live, a solitary lord over a vast domain. But the mansion was never built, and in that lodge (which remained until a few years ago) the lord of the manor lived during all the stormy days of the French and Indian war, and as a stanch loyalist throughout the struggles of the Americans for independence, until the news came one day that his young friend Washington had captured Cornwallis and all his army. Then, says tradition, he called to his servant and said, "Come, Joe, carry me to my bed, for I'm sure it's high time for me to die!"

> "Then up rose Joe, all at the word,
>   And took his master's arm,
> And to his bed he softly led
>   The lord of Greenway farm.
> Then thrice he called on Britain's name,
>   And thrice he wept full sore.
> Then sighed—'O Lord, thy will be done!'
>   And word spake never more.'

It was early in 1782, at the age of ninety-two years, that Lord Fairfax died at Greenway Court, loved by many for his generosity and benevolence.

Lawrence Washington was also distinguished for his wealth

and intelligence. He was adjutant-general of his district, with the rank and pay of major, and at this time was a popular member of the Virginia House of Burgesses. At Mount Vernon and at Belvoir the sprightly boy George, who was a favorite everywhere, became accustomed to the refinements and amenities of English social life, in its best phases, and this had a marked influence upon his future character.

There were other influences there which made a deep impression upon the mind of the thoughtful boy. Sometimes the companions-in-arms of his brother, or officers from some naval vessel that came into the Potomac, would be guests at Mount Vernon, and perils by field and flood would be related. In these narratives Sir William Fairfax often joined, and related his experience in the far-off Indies, in marches, battles, sieges, and retreats. These fired the soul of young Washington with longings for adventure, and accordingly, we find him, at the age of fourteen years, preparing to enter the English navy as a midshipman, a warrant having been procured. His brother and Mr. Fairfax encouraged his inclination, and his mother's reluctant consent was obtained. A vessel-of-war was lying in the Potomac, and the lad's luggage was on board, when his mother received the following letter from her brother, in England, dated Stratford-by-Bow, 19th May, 1747:

"I understand that you are advised and have some thoughts of putting your son George to sea. I think he had better be put apprentice to a tinker, for a common sailor before the mast has by no means the common liberty of the subject; for they will press him from a ship where he has fifty shillings a month and make him take twenty-three, and cut, and slash, and use him like a negro, or rather like a dog. And, as to any considerable preferment in the navy, it is not to be expected, as there are always so many gaping for it here who have interest, and he has none. And if he should get to be master of a Virginia ship (which it is very difficult to do), a planter that has three or four hundred acres of land and three or four slaves, if he be industrious, may live more comfortably, and leave his family in better bread, than such a master of a ship can. * * * * He must not be too hasty to be rich, but go on gently and with patience, as things will naturally go. This method, without aiming at being a fine gentleman before his time, will carry a man more comfortably and surely through the world than going to sea, unless it be a great chance indeed. I pray God keep you and yours.

"Your loving brother,
"Joseph Ball."

This letter, without doubt, made the mother decide to act according to the desire of her heart, for already a friend had written to Lawrence, "I am afraid Mrs. Washington will not keep up to her first resolution. * * * * I find that one word against his going has more weight than ten for it." She could not expose her son to the hardships and perils of the British navy, so vividly portrayed by his uncle. Her consent was withdrawn, and George Washington, with disappointed ambition, returned to school, fell desperately in love with a "lowland beauty" (who reciprocated not his passion, but became the mother of General Henry Lee), indited sentimental verses, as young lovers are apt to do, sighed for a time in great unhappiness, and then went to live with his brother at Mount Vernon, in partial forgetfulness that he had once dreamed that

> "She was his life,
> The ocean to the river of his thoughts,
> Which terminated all."

Now it was that young Washington's real intimacy with the Fairfax family commenced, and an attachment was formed between himself and George William Fairfax, his senior by six or seven years, who had just brought his bride and her sister to Belvoir.

Young Washington's heart was tender and susceptible, and that bride's beautiful sister tried its constancy to his first love very sorely. To his young friend "Robin," he wrote: "My residence is at present at his lordship's, where I might, was my heart disengaged, pass my time very pleasantly, as there is a very agreeable young lady lives in the same house (Colonel George Fairfax's wife's sister); but as that is only adding fuel to fire, it makes me the more uneasy, for by often and unavoidably being in company with her, revives my former passion for your Lowland Beauty; whereas, was I to live more retired from young women, I might in some measure alleviate my sorrows, by burying that chaste and troublesome passion in the grave of oblivion." Thus wrote George Washington before he was sixteen years of age.

He was soon taken from these temptations. He was a tall, finely-formed, athletic youth, and Lord Fairfax, who was a passionate fox-hunter, though old in years, invited him one day to join him in the chase. His lordship was so charmed with his young friend's boldness in the saddle and enthusiastic pursuit of the hounds and game, that he took him to his bosom as a companion; and many a hard day's ride this young and old man had together after that, in the forests of Virginia.

But a more noble, because a more useful pursuit than the mere pleasures of the chase, now offered its attractions to the lad. Master Williams had taught him the mysteries of surveying, and the old Lord Fairfax, having observed his practice of the art at Mount Vernon, and his extreme care and accuracy, proposed to him to go to his broad possessions beyond the Blue Ridge, where lawless intruders were seated, and prepare his domain for settlement, by running boundary lines between large sections. The lad gladly acceded to the proposition, and just a month from the time he was sixteen years of age, he set off upon the arduous and responsible enterprise. And to this day a little log-house, near Battle Town, in Clarke county, is pointed out to the traveller, wherein the young surveyor lodged; and in the same county, not far from Winchester, stood, a few years ago, the lodge of Greenway Court.

In the wilderness, around the south branch of the Potomac, the future Leader received those lessons in wood-craft — that personal knowledge of the country and its dusky inhabitants, and, above all, that spirit of self-reliance which was ever a most marked and important trait in his character — which fitted him for the great duties of a commander.

So satisfactory were young Washington's services on that occasion, that he received, soon after his return, the appointment of public surveyor, and upon the records of Culpepper county may be read, under date of July 20th, 1749 (O. S.), that "GEORGE WASHINGTON, Gent., produced a commission from the President and Master of William and Mary College, appointing him to be surveyor of this county, which was read, and thereupon he took the usual oaths to his Majesty's person and government, and took and subscribed the abjuration oath and test, and then took the oath of a surveyor, according to law." Part of each year he was beyond the Alleghanies, with no other instruments than compass and chain, acquiring strength of limb and purpose for future great achievements, and putting money in his purse at the rate of a doubloon and sometimes six pistoles a day. These expeditions he always remembered as the greatest pleasures of his youth.

After Washington's death, more than fifty years later, the simple compass and chain and other mathematical instruments of his earlier and later years, were distributed among his family connections, but only one of them, a small library instrument, was mentioned in his will, as follows:

"To David Stuart I give my large shaving and dressing table, *and my telescope.*"

Dr. Stuart married the widow of John Parke Custis, the son of Mrs. Washington. The telescope was some years ago in possession of his granddaughter, wife of the Reverend A. B. Atkins, of Germantown, Pennsylvania.

And now another and more extended field of action opened before the young resident at Mount Vernon. Beneath the roof of that pleasant mansion, toward the spring of 1751, he received from acting Governor Burwell the commission of adjutant of his military district, with the rank and pay of major. It was an acceptable honor. His military spirit was kindling; for it had been fanned by old Major Muse, a fellow-soldier with Lawrence at Carthagena, who was a fre-

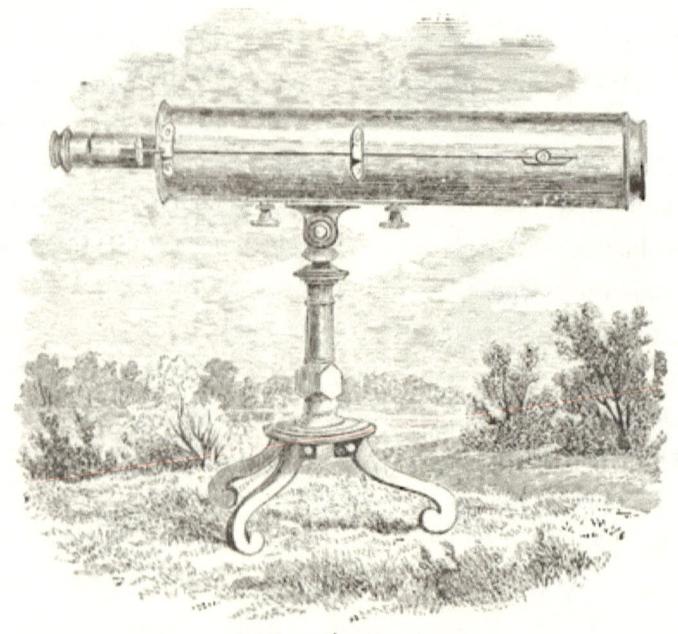

WASHINGTON'S TELESCOPE.

quent and welcome guest at Mount Vernon, and by the stout Dutchman, Van Braam (who afterward figured ingloriously in history), who had taught him the art of fencing.

Young Washington had scarcely taken his initial steps in the performance of his new duties when he was drawn from public life. Dark and ominous shadows were alternating with the sweet domestic sunlight that smiled so pleasantly around Mount Vernon. They were cast by the raven wing of the angel of disease. A hectic glow was upon the cheeks of Lawrence Washington, and his physicians advised him to go to the more genial climate of Barbadoes in search of health. George went with him. It was in bright September, 1751, when they sailed, and in dark and stormy January he returned to tell the anxious wife of his brother that her loved one must go to Bermuda in the spring; for the hectic glow was growing brighter and his manly strength less. She was preparing to join him there, when word came that hope's promises had faded forever, and that her husband was coming home to die. He came when the bloom of May was upon the land, and before the close of July he was laid in the grave, at the early age of thirty-four years, leaving a wife and infant child.

And now George Washington, a noble youth of twenty, his fine manly face a little scarred by the smallpox, that seized him while he was in Barbadoes, was at Mount Vernon as the faithful executor of the last will and testament of his brother. He was also prospective heir of that whole beautiful domain, Lawrence having left it to his daughter, with the proviso that in the event of her death that and other lands should become the property of George. That contingency soon occurred. Little Jenny died, and George Washington became the owner of Mount Vernon. Already, by the will of his father, he was the proprietor of the paternal estate on the Rappahannock. Now he ranked among the wealthier of the planters of the Old Dominion.

The development of great and stirring events soon called Washington to the forests, not with compass and chain, and field-book, but with sword and pistol, and diplomatic commission. Then his hero-life began.

For a thousand years a national feud had existed between Gauls and Britons—French and English; and their colonists, seated a little way apart in the New World, cherished this sentiment of utter dislike. It was intensified by jealousy; for they were competitors for a prize no less than that of supreme dominion in America.

The English were planters—the French were traders; and while the stations of the latter were several hundred miles in the interior, away from the settlements of the former, on the seaboard, the equanimity of both parties was quite undisturbed. But when, after the capture of Louisburg by the English, in 1745, the French adopted vigorous measures for opposing the extension of British power in America; when they built strong vessels at the foot of Lake Ontario; made treaties of friendship and alliance with the Delaware and Shawnee tribes of Indians; strengthened their fortress at the mouth of the Niagara River, and commenced the erection of a cordon of fortifications, more than sixty in number, between Montreal and New Orleans, the English were aroused to immediate and effective action, in defence of the territorial rights conceded to them in their ancient charters. By virtue of these, they claimed absolute dominion westward to the Pacific Ocean, south of the latitude of the north shore of Lake Erie; while the French claimed a title to all the territory watered by the Mississippi and its tributaries, because they had made the first explorations and settlements in that region. The claims of the real owner—the Indian—were not considered. It was a significant question, asked by a messenger sent by sachems to Mr. Gist, agent of the English Ohio Company—"Where is the Indian's land? The English claim it all on one side of the river, the French on the other. Where does the Indian's land lie?"

At length English traders who went to the Ohio region were driven away or imprisoned by the French, and the latter commenced building forts south of Lake Erie. Governor Dinwiddie, of Virginia, thought these proceedings rather insolent, and he sent Major Washington, then less than twenty-two years of age, to carry a letter of remonstrance to the French commander in that region.

Seven persons besides Major Washington composed the expedition, and among them was Van Braam, Washington's Dutch fencing-master, who could speak French fluently, and went as interpreter. They assembled at Williamsburg, and made every preparation for a journey of several hundred miles on horseback, through an unbroken wilderness. They were furnished by the governor with horses, pack-saddles, tent, arms, ammunition, a leathern camp-chest, provisions,

PACK-SADDLE.

LEATHERN CAMP-CHEST.

and every other necessary, and on the 31st of October, 1753, departed for the head-waters of the Ohio. They made a most perilous journey, and, after an absence of seven weeks, Major Washington again stood in the presence of Governor Dinwiddie, his mission fulfilled to the satisfaction of all. Two days afterward he returned, first to his mother's home, near Fredericksburg, then to Belvoir, and finally to Mount Vernon, where he spent a greater portion of the winter and spring of 1754.

But Major Washington was not allowed to remain long in seclusion. In the late expedition he had exhibited qualities too great and useful to be suffered to repose. War with the French appeared inevitable. The latter continued their hostile preparations in the Ohio region, and a colonial military force, to be sent thither, was organized in the spring of 1754. Colonel Joshua Fry was appointed its commander, and Major Washington his lieutenant.

For a while Mount Vernon appeared like a recruiting station. At length all preparations were completed, and on the 2d of April, Major Washington, with the advanced corps, marched from Alexandria toward the Ohio. After a toilsome journey of eighteen days, over the Blue Ridge, they reached the mouth of Wills' Creek (now Cumberland), where Washington, for the first time, occupied a house for his headquarters as a military commander. It was the dwelling of a pioneer. It has long since passed away, but the pencil has preserved its features, and now, at the distance of time of more than a hundred years, we may look upon the portrait of Washington's first Head-Quarters.

It is not our purpose to trace the events of Washington's life in their consecutive order. We propose to give delineations of only such as held intimate relations with his beautiful

WASHINGTON'S FIRST HEAD-QUARTERS.

home on the Potomac, which, for more than forty years, was to him the dearest spot on the earth.

During the war between the French and English, that commenced in earnest in 1755, when Braddock came to America as commander-in-chief of the British forces, until the close of the campaign of 1758, when the French and their dusky allies were driven from the forks of the Ohio, Washington was almost continually in the public service, and spent but little time at Mount Vernon. He had been promoted to Colonel in 1754, but, on account of new military arrangements by the blundering, wrong-headed, narrow-minded Governor Dinwiddie, he had left the service with disgust, and retired to the quiet of private life at Mount Vernon, with a determination to spend his life there in the pursuits of agriculture—pursuits which he always passionately loved, and longed for most earnestly when away from them.

General Braddock, an Irish officer of forty years' experience in the army, came to America with two regiments early in 1755, and called a council of royal governors at Alexandria, to arrange a regular campaign against the French. Braddock soon heard, from every lip, encomiums of the character of Colonel Washington, and he invited him to Alexandria. Mount Vernon was only a little more than an hour's ride distant, and Washington, whose military ardor was again aroused by preparations for conflict, was swift to obey the summons. From Mount Vernon he had looked upon the ships-of-war and transports upon the bosom of the Potomac that bore Braddock and his troops, and the thought that only a few miles from his dwelling, preparations were in progress for a brilliant campaign, under the command of one of the most experienced generals of the British army, stirred the very depths of his soul, and made him yearn to go again to the field.

THE CAREY HOUSE IN 1859

At the residence of Jonathan Carey, where Braddock made his head-quarters, the young provincial colonel and the veteran general first met, at the close of March. Carey's was then the finest house in Alexandria, surrounded by a noble lawn that was shaded by lofty forest trees, and its gardens extending down a gentle slope to the shore of the Potomac. Now it stands within the city, hemmed in by buildings and paved streets, and forms a part of Newton's Hotel. The convention of governors met in it in April, and there the ensuing campaign was planned.

Braddock invited Washington to join his military family, as aid, with the rank he had lately borne. The mother of the young colonel hastened to Mount Vernon to persuade him not to accept it. She urged the claims of his and her own affairs upon his attention, as strong reasons for him not to enter the army again, and for two days she held his decision in abeyance, for filial obedience was one of the strongest sentiments of Washington's nature. But it was not strong enough to restrain him on this occasion—or, rather, God's will must be obeyed—and he left Mount Vernon for Alexandria, after her departure for the Rappahannock, and was welcomed into Braddock's family with joy by Captains Orme and Morris.

On the 9th of July following we behold him upon the bloody field of the Monongahela, shielded by God's providence, untouched by ball or bayonet, arrow or javelin, while carnage was laying its scores of victims around him, and his commander was borne mortally wounded from the field—we behold him riding from point to point, bringing order out of confusion, and leading away from that *aceldama* the shattered battalions of the proud army of the morning to a place of safety and repose. Then he returned to Mount Vernon, weak from recent sickness and exposure in the field. In his little library there he wrote to his brother, then a member of the House of Burgesses at Williamsburg, and thus summed up his military career:

"I was employed to go a journey in the winter, when I

believe few or none would have undertaken it, and what did I get by it? My expenses borne! I was then appointed, with trifling pay, to conduct a handful of men to the Ohio. What did I get by that? Why, after putting myself to a considerable expense in equipping and providing necessaries for the campaign, I went out, was soundly beaten, and lost all! Came in, and had my commission taken from me; or, in other words, my command reduced, under pretence of an order from home. I then went out a volunteer with General Braddock, and lost all my horses, and many other things. But this being a voluntary act, I ought not to have mentioned it; nor should I have done it, were it not to show that I have been on the losing order ever since I entered the service, which is now nearly two years."

But what wonderful and necessary lessons for the future had Washington learned during that time!

Mount Vernon saw but little of its master during the next four years; for the flame of war lighted up the land from Acadia, and along the St. Lawrence, away down to the beautiful Cherokee country, in Western Georgia and Carolina, and Washington was most of the time in camp, except from December, 1757, until March, 1758, when he was an invalid at home.

In February, 1756, we find him, accompanied by two aides, journeying to Boston, to confer with General Shirley concerning military rank in Virginia. Little did he then think that twenty years later he would again be there directing a siege against the New England capital, in command of rebels against the crown he was then serving!

We find him lingering in New York, on his return. The

young soldier, apparently invincible to the mortal weapons of war, was sorely smitten there by the "sly archer" concealed in the bright eyes, blooming cheeks, and winning ways of Mary Phillipse, the heiress of a broad domain, stretching many a mile along the Hudson. The young soldier lingered

MARY PHILLIPSE.

in her presence as long as duty would permit, and he would fain have carried her with him to Virginia as a bride, but his natural diffidence kept the momentous question unspoken in his heart, and his fellow aide-de-camp in Braddock's family, Roger Morris, bore away the prize. Mary Phillipse did not become the mistress of Mount Vernon, but reigned, as beauteous queen, in a more stately mansion on the bank of the

Harlem River, where, twenty years later, Washington, as leader of a host of Americans, in arms against the king, held his head-quarters, the master and mistress of the mansion being proscribed as " enemies to their country!"

MORRIS'S HOUSE.

But, three years later, there was a presiding angel over the mansion on Mount Vernon. Meanwhile the tramp of steeds, the clangor of arms, and every sound betokening warlike preparations, were heard there, and the decisive campaign of 1758 was opened.

Washington went to the camp as soon as his health would permit; and toward Fort du Quesne, at the confluence of the forks of the Ohio, quite a large army made its way. Wasting delays and weary marches consumed the summer time: and late in autumn, having traversed deep forests and rugged mountains, the invading army found rest, beyond the Alleghanies. Colonel Washington, with an advanced guard, took possession of all that was left of Fort du Quesne, where Pittsburg now stands. It had been the prize for which Braddock contended—the nest from which came the vultures that preyed upon the frontier settlements. Over its smoking ruins the red cross of St. George was unfurled, where for four years had waved the lilies of France. Then French dominion ceased southward of Lake Erie; and the young hero, whose wisdom, skill, and valor had contributed so largely toward the accomplishment of that result, returned to Mount Vernon sick and wearied, fully resolved to leave the army forever, and seek repose and happiness, usefulness and fair fame, in domestic and civil life.

For these Washington was now prepared. During the previous spring, while on his way to Williamsburg, from his camp at Winchester, he had been taught to love one of the best of Virginia's daughters; and in the autumn, while he was making his toilsome march toward Fort du Quesne, he had been elected a delegate to the Virginia House of Burgesses.

The story of Washington's love and courtship is simple, yet full of the elements of romance. No words can better tell that story than those used for the purpose, in after years, by a grandson of the lady.* "It was in 1758," he says, "that Washington, attired in military undress, and attended by a body servant, tall and *militaire* as his chief, was crossing William's Ferry over the Pamunkey River, a branch of the York River. On the boat touching the southern or New Kent side, the soldier's progress was arrested by one of those personages who give the beau ideal of the Virginia gentleman of the old *régime* — the very soul of kindliness and hospitality.

---

* The late George Washington Parke Custis, the adopted son of Washington. See Custis's *Recollections of Washington*. New York. 1859.

It was in vain the soldier urged his business at Williamsburg, important communications to the governor, etc. Mr. Chamberlayne, on whose domain the *militaire* had just landed, would hear of no excuse. Colonel Washington's was a name and character so dear to all the Virginians that his passing by one of the old castles of the Dominion without calling and partaking of the hospitalities of the host was entirely out of the question.

"The colonel, however, did not surrender at discretion, but stoutly maintained his ground, till Chamberlayne bringing up his reserve, in the intimation that he would introduce his friend to a young and charming widow, then beneath his roof, the soldier capitulated, on condition that he should dine — only dine — and then, by pressing his charger and borrowing of the night, he would reach Williamsburg before his Excellency could shake off his morning slumbers. Orders were accordingly issued to Bishop, the Colonel's body-servant and faithful follower, who, together with the fine English charger, had been bequeathed by the dying Braddock to Major Washington, on the famed and fatal field of the Monongahela. Bishop, bred in the school of European discipline, raised his hand to his cap, as much as to say, ' Your honor's orders shall be obeyed.'

"The colonel now proceeded to the mansion, and was introduced to various guests (for when was a Virginian domicile of the olden time without guests?) and, above all, to the charming widow. Tradition relates that they were mutually pleased on this their first interview. Nor is it remarkable. They were of an age when impressions are strongest. The lady was fair to behold, of fascinating manners and splendidly endowed with worldly benefits. The hero, fresh from his early fields, redolent of fame, and with a form on which

> "'Every god did seem to set his seal,
> To give the world assurance of a man.'

"The morning passed pleasantly away; evening came, with Bishop, true to his orders and firm at his post, holding the favorite charger with one hand, while the other was waiting to offer the ready stirrup.

"The sun sank in the horizon, and yet the colonel appeared not. And then the old soldier marvelled at his chief's delay. ''Twas strange, 'twas passing strange—surely he was not wont to be a single moment behind his appointments, for he was the most punctual of all punctual men.' Meantime, the host enjoyed the scene of the veteran on duty at the gate, while the colonel was so agreeably employed in the parlor, and proclaiming that no guest ever left his house after sunset, his military visitor was, without much difficulty, persuaded to order Bishop to put up the horses for the night.

"The sun rode high in the heavens the ensuing day, when the enamored soldier pressed with his spur his charger's side, and speeded on his way to the seat of government, where, having dispatched his public business, he retraced his steps, and, at the White House, a marriage engagement took place."

That "charming widow" was Martha Custis, daughter of John Dandridge, whose husband, Daniel Parke Custis, had been dead between two and three years. He had left her with two young children and a very large fortune in lands and money, the legal evidence of which, in the form of deeds, mortgages, bonds, and certificates of deposit in the Bank of

DANIEL PARKE CUSTIS.

England, were contained in a strong iron box, which is carefully preserved by her descendants, at their beautiful seat at Arlington, on the Potomac, opposite Washington City.

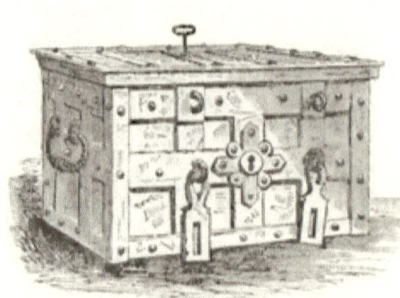

MRS. CUSTIS'S IRON CHEST.

"And much," continues the writer we have quoted, "hath the biographer heard of that marriage of Washington, from the grayhaired domestics who waited at the board where love made the feast and the Virginia colonel was the guest.

"'And so you remember,' I said to old Cully, my grandmother's servant, when in his hundredth year—'and so you remember when Colonel Washington came a-courting your young mistress?'

"'Ay, master, that I do,' said Cully. 'Great times, sir, great times—shall never see the like again.'

"'And Washington looked something like a man—a proper man, hey, Cully?'

"'Never seed the like, sir—never the like of him, though I have seen many in my day—so tall, so straight, and then he sat on a horse and rode with such an air! Ah, sir, he was like no one else! Many of the grandest gentlemen, in the gold lace, were at the wedding; but none looked like the man himself.'"

The marriage of Washington occurred on the 17th of January, (6th Old Style), 1759, at the "White House," the residence of his bride, in New Kent county, not far from Williamsburg. The officiating clergyman was the Reverend David Mossom, who, for forty years was rector of the neighboring parish of St. Peter's. Washington was then an attendant member of the House of Burgesses, and for three months, while official duties detained him at Williamsburg, he resided at the "White House." When the session had ended, he returned to Mount Vernon, taking with him the future mistress of the mansion, and her two children, John Parke and Martha Parke Custis.

Then commenced that sweet domestic life at Mount Vernon, which always possessed a powerful charm for its illustrious owner. He early wrote to his friend, Richard Washington, in London:

MRS. WASHINGTON'S CHILDREN.

"I am now, I believe, fixed in this seat with an agreeable partner for life, and I hope to find more happiness in retirement than I ever experienced in the wide and bustling world." He was then seven-and-twenty years of age, and over six feet two inches in height, and admirably proportioned. His hair was a rich dark-brown; his eyes grayish-blue and expressive of deep thought; his complexion florid, and his features regular and rather heavy.

Washington's wife was three months younger than himself. She was a small, plump, elegantly formed woman. Her eyes were dark and expressive of the most kindly good nature; her complexion fair; her features beautiful; and her whole face beamed with intelligence. Her temper, though quick, was sweet and placable, and her manners were extremely winning. She was full of life, loved the society of her friends, always

MRS. WASHINGTON AT THE TIME OF HER MARRIAGE.

dressed with a scrupulous regard to the requirements of the best fashions of the day, and was, in every respect, a brilliant member of the social circles which, before the revolution, composed the vice-regal court at the old Virginia capital.

Washington, at this time, possessed an ample fortune, independent of that of his wife. His estate of Mount Vernon he described as most pleasantly situated in "a high, healthy country; in a latitude between the extremes of heat and cold, on one of the finest rivers in the world—a river well stocked with various kinds of fish at all seasons of the year, and in the spring with shad, herrings, bass, carp, sturgeon, etc., in abundance. The borders of the estate," he continued, " are washed by more than ten miles of tide-water; several valuable fisheries appertain to it; the whole shore, in fact, is one entire fishery." Such was the delightful home to which Washington took his bride in the spring of 1759.

At that time, almost every manufactured article for domestic use, was imported from England. It is amusing and interesting to observe the difference in the items of orders sent out to London from Mount Vernon within the space of two years. First, as a bachelor, Washington orders:

" Five pieces of Irish Linnen.
1 piece finest Cambric.
2 pr. fine worked ruffles, at 20s. a pr.
2 setts compleat shoe brushes.
½ doz. pr. thread hose, at 5s.
1 compleat Saddle and Bridle, and 1 sett Holster caps, and Housing of fine Blue Cloth with a small edging of Embroidering round them.
As much of the best superfine blue Cotton Velvet as will make a Coat, Waistcoat, and Breeches for a Tall Man, with a fine silk button to suit it, and all other necessary trimmings and linings, together with garters for the Breeches.
6 prs. of the very neatest shoes, viz: 2 pr. double channelled pumps; two pr. turned ditto, and two pair stitched shoes, to be made by one Didsbury over Colonel Beiler's last, but to be a little wider over the instep.
6 prs. gloves, 3 pairs of which to be proper for riding, and

to have slit tops; the whole larger than the middle size."

A little later, in apparent expectation of a wife at some future day, the careful bachelor prepares the mansion for her reception. In September, 1757, he wrote to Richard Washington, saying:

"Be pleased, over and above what I have wrote for in a letter of the 13th of April, to send me 1 doz. Strong Chairs, of

CHAIRS ONCE AT MOUNT VERNON.

about 15 shillings a piece, the bottoms to be exactly made by the enclosed dimensions, and of three different colors to suit the paper of three of the bed-chambers, also wrote for in my last. I must acquaint you, sir, with the reason of this request. I have one dozen chairs that were made in the country; neat, but too weak for common sitting. I therefore propose to take the bottoms out of those and put them into these now ordered, while the bottoms which you send will do for the former, and furnish the chambers. For this reason the workmen must be very exact, neither making the bottoms larger nor smaller than the dimensions, otherwise the change can't be made. Be kind enough to give directions that these chairs, equally with the others and the tables, be carefully packed and stowed. Without this caution, they are liable to infinite damage."

In 1759 (the year of Washington's marriage), we have the order of a husband instead of that of a bachelor. The items are quite different, and were evidently dictated by the sweet little wife, leaning lovingly, perhaps, upon the broad shoulder of her noble lord. He directs his friend in London to send him:

"1 Salmon-colored Tabby [velvet] of the enclosed pattern, with Sattin flowers; to be made in a sack and coat.

1 Cap, Handkerchief, and Tucker [a piece of lace or linen pinned to the top of women's stays] and Ruffles, to be made of Brussells lace or Point, proper to be worn with the above negligée; to cost £20.

1 piece Bag Holland, at 6s. a yard.

2 fine flowered Lawn Aprons.

2 double handkerchiefs.

2 prs. women's white silk hose.

6 pr. fine cotton do.

4 pr Thread do. four threaded.

1 p. black and 1 pr. white Sattin Shoes of the smallest fives

4 pr Callimanco do

1 fashionable Hat or Bonnet.
6 p. Women's best Kid Gloves.
6 pr. ditto mitts.
½ doz. Knots and Breast Knots.
1 doz. round Silk stay laces.
1 black Mask.
1 doz most fashionable Cambrick Pocket Handkerchiefs.
2 pr. neat Small Scissors.
1 lb Sewing Silk, shaded.
Real Miniken pins and hair pins, and 4 pieces Binding Tape.
Six lbs perfumed powder.
3 lbs best Scotch Snuff.
3 lbs best Violette Strasbourg Snuff.
1 pr narrow white Sattin ribbon, pearl edge.
A puckered petticoat of a fashionable color.
A silver Tabby velvet petticoat.
2 handsome breast flowers.
Hair pins—sugar candy.
2 pr. small silver Ear-rings for servants
8 lbs Starch.
2 lbs Powdered Blue.
2 oz. Coventry Thread, one of which to be very fine.
1 case of Pickles to consist of Anchovies, Capers, Olives, Salad Oil, and one bottle Indian Mangoes.
1 Large Cheshire Cheese.
4 lbs Green Tea.
10 gross best Corks.
25 lbs best jar Raisins.
25 lbs Almonds, in the Shell

1 hhd best Porter.
10 loaves double and 10 single refined Sugar.
12 lbs best mustard.
2 doz. Jack's best playing cards.
3 gallons of Rhenish in bottles.
100 lbs white Biscuit.
1½ doz. Bell glasses for Garden.
1 more Window Curtain and Cornice.
2 more Chair bottoms, such as were written for in a former invoice."

Such were Washington's orders for his house at that time. These items were followed by others pertaining to his farming operations and the servants upon his estate; and also medicines for family use.

And now, the mansion at Mount Vernon having an accomplished mistress to preside over its hospitalities, and to receive and entertain some of the best society of Virginia, articles of taste were introduced to embellish it. In the handwriting of the master we find the duplicate of an order, as follows:

"DIRECTIONS FOR THE BUSTS.—One of Alexander the Great; another of Julius Cæsar; another of Charles XII. of Sweden; and a fourth of the King of Prussia.

"N. B. These are not to exceed fifteen inches in height, nor ten in width.

"2 other Busts of Prince Eugene and the Duke of Marlborough, somewhat smaller.

"2 Wild Beasts, not to exceed twelve inches in height, nor eighteen in length.

"Sundry ornaments for Chimney-piece."

These items indicate the military taste of Washington at that time, and show his reverence for the great military leaders of whom history had made her enduring records. Many years later, when Washington had become as renowned as they, the Great Frederick sent him a portrait of himself, accompanied by the remarkable words—" From the Oldest General in Europe to the Greatest General in the World!"

Two years after his marriage, Washington sent the following order to Robert Carey, Esq., in London:

"FOR MASTER CUSTIS, 8 YEARS OLD.

" 1 handsome suit of Winter Cloathes.

A suit of Summer ditto, very light.

2 pieces Nankeens with trimmings.

1 silver laced hat.

6 pair fine Cotton Stockings.

1 pr fine worsted ditto.

4 pr. Strong Shoes.

1 pr. neat Pumps.

1 p. gloves.

2 hair bags.

1 piece ribbon for ditto.

1 p. silver Shoe and Knee buckles.

1 p. Sleeve buttons.

A Small Bible neatly bound in Turkey, and John Parke Custis wrote in gilt letters on the inside of the cover.

A neat Small Prayer Book bound as above, with John Parke Custis, as above.

1 piece Irish linen, at 1s.

3 pr shoes for a boy 14 y'rs old.

CUSTIS'S ARMS.

3 p. Coarse Stockings for do.
2 pr Women's Strong Shoes, size 8.
2 p'r Stockings for do.
50 ells Osnaburgs.
A suit of livery Cloathes for the above boy of 14. A hat for do.
"NOTE.—Let the livery be suited to the arms of the Custis family."

"FOR MISS CUSTIS, 6 YEARS OLD.

"A coat made of fashionable Silk.
A fashionable Cap or Fillet with bib apron.
Ruffles and Tucker—to be laced.
4 fashionable dresses to be made of Long lawn.
2 fine Cambric frocks.
A Sattin Capuchin hat and neckatees.
A Persian quilted coat.
1 pr. pack thread Stays.
4 p. Calamanco Shoes, 6 pr leather ditto and
2 p'r Sattin do. with flat ties.
6 pr fine Cotton Stockings, 4 pr White Wors'd Do.
12 p'r Mitts. 6 p'r Gloves, white Kids.
1 p'r Silver Shoe buckles.
1 pr. neat sleeve buttons,
6 handsome Egrets* different sorts.
6 yds Ribbon Do.

---

* An *Egrette* or *Aigrette* was an ornament for the head then much used by people of fashion. They were sometimes made of tufts of feathers, diamonds, etc., but more frequently of ribbons. In the above invoice both kinds were ordered.

1 pr. little Scissors.

3 M (thousand) large pins.   3 M short whites.

3 M Minikens.

1 Fashionable dressed Doll to cost a guinea.   1 Do. at 5s.

A box Gingerbread, Toys & Sugar Images and Comfits.

A neat Small Bible, bound in Turkey, and Martha Parke Custis wrote on the inside in gilt letters.

A Small Prayer Book, neat and in the same manner.

12 yards coarse green Callimanco.

The above things to be put into a Strong Trunk—separate from J. P. Custis's, whose will likewise be put into a Trunk, each having their names.

1 very good Spinet [a small harpsichord], to be made by Mr. Plinius, Harpsichord Maker, in South Audley Street, Grosvenor Square.

"It is begged as a favor that Mr. Carey would bespeak this instrument as for himself or a friend, and not let it be known y' is intended for exportation.

"Send a good assortment of spare strings to it.

"Books according to the enclosed List—to be charged equally to both John Parke Custis and Martha Parke Custis—likewise one Ream of Writing paper."

These specimens of orders which were sent out annually to England, are given as glimpses of the domestic arrangements at Mount Vernon, and the style in which the wealthier Virginia families, of cultivated tastes, lived before the Revolution It is evident that Washington and his family indulged in all the fashionable luxuries (not extravagances) of the day, pertaining to the table and the wardrobe; and in the absence of positive proof, these invoices would afford the strongest infer entia, evidences that they spent much of their earlier years in the enjoyment of social pleasures.

Washington's Diaries bear still stronger, because positive testimony to the fact. During some months, two or three times a week he records the result of a day's sport thus: "Went a hunting with Jacky Custis, and catched a fox, after three hours chase. Found it in the creek:" or, "Mr. Bryan Fairfax, Mr. Grayson and Phil. Alexander came home by sunrise. Hunted and catched a fox with these, Lord Fairfax, his brother, and Colonel Fairfax—all of whom with Mr. Fairfax and Mr. Wilson of England, dined here." Afterward, two days in succession: "Hunted again with the same company."

Still more frequently he noted the arrival and departure of guests. One day the Fairfaxes, or Masons, or Thurstons, or Lees would be there; and the next day he and "Mrs. Washington, Mr. and Miss Custis" would "dine at Belvoir." And so the round of visiting went on. Mount Vernon was seldom without a guest. The hunting day, which occurred so frequently, generally ended in a dinner there or at Belvoir, a little lower on the Potomac—more frequently at the former; and the hospitalities of the house were kept up in a style which none but a wealthy planter could afford. "Would any one believe," Washington says in his diary of 1768, "that with a *hundred and one cows*, actually reported at a late enumeration of the cattle, I should still be obliged to buy butter for my family?"

For Mrs. Washington and her lady visitors he kept a chariot and four horses, with black postillions in livery; and these were frequently seen and admired upon the road between

Mount Vernon and Alexandria, or the neighboring estates. He took great delight in horses. Those of his own stable were of the best blood, and their names, as well as those of his dogs, were registered in his household books. When abroad, he always appeared on horseback; and as he was one of the most superb men and skilful horsemen in Virginia, he must have made an imposing appearance, especially when fully equipped for the road, with the following articles, which were ordered by him from London, in one of his annual invoices:

"1 Man's Riding-Saddle, hogskin seat, large plated stirrups, and everything complete. Double-reined bridle and Pelham Bit, plated.

A very neat and fashionable Newmarket Saddle-Cloth.

A large and best Portmanteau, Saddle, Bridle and Pillion Cloak-Bag Surcingle; checked Saddle-cloth, holsters, &c.

A Riding Frock of handsome drab-colored Broadcloth, with plain double-gilt Buttons.

A Riding Waistcoat of superfine scarlet cloth and gold Lace with Buttons like those of the Coat.

A blue Surtout Coat.

A neat Switch Whip, silver cap.

Black Velvet Cap for Servant."

Thus attired, and accompanied by Bishop, his favorite body servant, in scarlet livery, Washington was frequently seen upon the road, except on Sunday morning, when he always rode in the chaise, with his family, to the church at Pohick or at Alexandria.

Like other gentlemen living near the Potomac, Washington was fond of aquatic sports. He kept a handsome barge, which, on special occasions, was manned by black oarsmen in livery. Pleasant sailing-boats were frequently seen sweeping along the surface of the river, freighted with ladies and gentlemen going from mansion to mansion on its banks—Mount Vernon, Gunston Hall, Belvoir, and other places—on social visits.

Washington and his wife frequently visited Annapolis and Williamsburg, the respective capitals of Maryland and Virginia. For fifteen consecutive years he was a member of the Virginia House of Burgesses, and Mrs. Washington spent much of her time with him at Williamsburg during the sessions. Both fond of amusements, they frequently attended the theatrical representations there and at Annapolis, that entertainment being then a recent importation from England, the first company of actors, under the direction of Lewis Hallam, having first performed in the Maryland capital in 1752. They also attended balls and parties given by the fashionable people of Williamsburg and Annapolis, and frequently joined in the dance. But after the Revolution Washington was never known to dance, his last performance being in a minuet, of which he was very fond, on the occasion of a ball given at Fredericksburg in honor of the French and American officers then there, on their way north, after the capture of Cornwallis, toward the close of 1781.

But it must not be supposed, that during these years of his earlier married life, Washington's time was wholly, or even chiefly, occupied in the pleasures of the chase and of social intercourse. Far from it. He was a man of great industry and method, and managed his large estates with signal industry and ability. He did not leave his farms to the entire care of his overseers. He was very active, and continually, even when absent on public business, exercised a general supervision of his affairs, requiring a carefully prepared report of all operations to be transmitted to him weekly, for his inspection and suggestions.

He was very abstemious, and while his table always furnished his guests with ample and varied supplies for their appetites, he never indulged in the least excess, either in eating or drinking. He was an early riser, and might be found in his library from one to two hours before daylight in winter, and at dawn in summer. His toilet, plain and simple, was soon made. A single servant prepared his clothes, and laid them in a proper place at night for use in the morning. He also combed and tied his master's hair.

Washington always dressed and shaved himself. The implements he then used have been preserved, as interesting relics, in the family of Doctor Stuart, who, as we have observed, married the widow of John Parke Custis, the son of Mrs. Washington. Though neat in his dress and appearance, he never wasted precious moments upon his toilet, for he always regarded time, not as a gift but as a loan, for which he must account to the great Master.

Washington kept his own accounts most carefully and methodically, in handwriting remarkable for its extreme neatness and uniformity of stroke. This was produced by the constant use of a *gold pen*. One of these, with a silver case, used by Washington during a part of the old war for independence, he presented to his warm personal friend, General Anthony Walton White, of New Jersey, one of the most distinguished and patriotic of the cavalry officers of that war in the southern campaigns. It was in the possession of Mrs. Eliza M.

Evans, near Brunswick, New Jersey, the only surviving child of General White. In one end of the silver pen-case was a sliding tube for a common black-lead pencil, the convenient "ever-pointed" pencil being unknown in Washington's time. That was invented by Isaac Hawkins, and patented by him, in London, in 1802.

WASHINGTON'S GOLD PEN WITH SILVER CASE.

From his youth Washington kept a diary. For many years these records of his daily experience were made on the blank leaves of the *Virginia Almanac*, "Printed and sold by Purdie

Where & how — my time is spent
Remarks & Occs. — in April. —
Acct of the Weather — in April

FAC-SIMILE OF PAGE-HEADINGS IN WASHINGTON'S DIARY.

and Dixon, Williamsburg." They are headed respectively, as seen in the engraving, which is a fac-simile from one of his early diaries after his marriage. Under similar headings in these almanacs, and in small blank pocket-books, this man of mighty labors kept such records, from day to day, for more than forty years; and he frequently noted therein minute particulars concerning his agricultural operations, in the style of the sentence on the next page, which was copied from his diary for March, 1771.

Thus minutely journalizing his agricultural proceedings, keeping his own accounts, making all his own surveys, and, even before the Revolution, having an extensive correspond-

> 20th Began to Manufacture my wheat with the water of Piney Branch, which being insufficient to keep the Mill constantly at work, & Country Custom coming in, no great progress could be made.—

FAC-SIMILE OF ENTRY IN WASHINGTON'S DIARY.

ence, Washington found much daily employment for his pen. The labors in his library, and a visit to his stables, usually occupied the hours before breakfast. After making a frugal meal of Indian cakes, honey, and tea or coffee, he would mount his horse and visit every part of his estate where the current operations seemed to require his presence, leaving his guests to enjoy themselves with books and papers, or otherwise, according to their choice. He rode upon his farms entirely unattended, opening the gates, pulling down and putting up the fences, and inspecting, with a careful eye, every agricultural operation, and personally directing the manner in which many should be performed. Sometimes the tour of his farms, in the course of the morning might average, in distance, twelve or fifteen miles; and on these occasions his appearance was exceedingly plain. The late Mr. Custis, his adopted son, has left on record a description of him on one of these occasions, in the latter years of his life, which he gave to a gentleman who was out in search of Washington:

"You will meet, sir," said young Custis to the inquirer, "with an old gentleman riding alone, in plain drab clothes, a broad-brimmed white hat, a hickory switch in his hand, and carrying an umbrella with a long staff which is attached to his saddle-bow—that, person, sir, is General Washington."* The umbrella was used to shelter him from the sun, for his skin was tender and easily affected by its rays.

His breakfast hour was seven o'clock in summer and eight in winter, and he dined at three. He always ate heartily, but was no epicure. His usual beverage was small beer or cider, and Madeira wine. Of the latter he often drank several small glasses at a sitting. He took tea and toast, or a little well-baked bread, early in the evening, conversed with or read to his family, when there were no guests, and usually, whether there was company or not, retired for the night at about nine o'clock.

So carefully did Washington manage his farms, that they became very productive. His chief crops were wheat and tobacco, and these were very large—so large that vessels that came up the Potomac, took the tobacco and flour directly from his own wharf, a little below his deer-park in front of his mansion, and carried them to England or the West Indies. So noted were these products for their quality, and so faithfully were they put up, that any barrel of flour bearing the brand of "GEORGE WASHINGTON, MOUNT VERNON," was exempted from the customary inspection in the British West India ports.

---

* "Recollections and Private Memoirs of Washington, by his Adopted Son," page 168.

MOUNT VERNON LANDING.

Upon the spot where that old wharf once stood, at the foot of a shaded ravine scooped from the high bank of the Potomac, through which flows a clear stream from a spring, is a rickety modern structure, placed there for the accommodation of visitors to Mount Vernon, who are conveyed thither by a steamboat twice a week. There may be seen the same ravine, the same broad river, the same pleasant shores of Maryland beyond; but, instead of the barrels of flour, the quintals of fish, and the hogsheads of tobacco which appeared there in Washington's time, well-dressed men and women—true pilgrims to a hallowed shrine, or mere idle gazers upon the burial place of a great man—throng that wharf as they arrive and depart on their errands of patriotism or of curiosity.

And now the dawn of great events, in which Washington was to be a conspicuous actor, glowed in the eastern sky. From the Atlantic seaboard, where marts of commerce had begun to spread their meshes (then small and feeble) for the world's traffic, came a sound of tumult; and the red presages of a tempest appeared in that glowing orient. At first, that sound was like a low whisper upon the morning air, and, finally, it boomed like a thunder-peal over the hills and valleys of the interior, arousing the inhabitants to the defence of the immunities of freemen and the inalienable rights of man.

Time after time, for the space of a hundred years, the decree had gone forth from British councils, that the Anglo-American colonists should be the *commercial* as well as *political* vassals of the crown; and chains of restrictions upon trade had been forged by an unwise and unrighteous policy, and fastened upon the lusty arms of the young giant of the West. And from time to time the giant, not all unconscious of his strength, yet docile because loyal, had spoken out mild remonstrances with deferential words. These had been heard with scorn, and answered by renewed offences.

An extravagant administration had exhausted the national exchequer, and the desperate spendthrift, too proud to borrow of itself by curtailing its expenditures, seemed to think nothing more honorable than a plea of bankruptcy, and sought to replenish its coffers by taking the money of the Americans without their consent, in the form of indirect taxation. This was in violation of the great republican postulate, that

TAXATION AND REPRESENTATION ARE INSEPARABLE.

And when the well-known stamp act was signed by the king and its requirements and its penalties were proclaimed in America, the tempest of which we have spoken was aroused. It swept from the sea to the mountains, and from the mountains to the sea, until those who had sown the wind, were alarmed at the harvest they were reaping.

At Mount Vernon there was a spirit that looked calmly, but not unconcernedly, upon the storm, and, with prophetic vision, seemed to perceive upon the shadowy political sky the horoscope of his own destiny. Washington was a member of the Virginia House of Burgesses, and had listened from his seat to the burning words of Patrick Henry, when he enunciated those living truths, for the maintenance of which the husbandman of Mount Vernon drew his sword a few years later. His soul was fired with the sense of oppression and the thoughts of freedom, yet his sober judgment and calculating prudence repressed demonstrative enthusiasm, and made him a firm, yet conservative patriot.

Among those who came to Mount Vernon at this time, and for years afterward, to consult with Washington respecting public affairs, was his neighbor and friend of Gunston Hall, George Mason. He was six years older than Washington, of large, sinewy frame, an active step and gait, locks of raven blackness, a dark complexion, and a grave countenance, which was lighted up by a black eye, whose glance was felt with power by those upon whom it chanced to fall. He was one of the most methodical of men, and most extensive of the Virginia planters at that time; and like Washington from Mount Vernon, shipped his crops from his own wharf, near his elegant mansion of Gunston Hall. He was proud, yet extremely courteous; and while no man could be a warmer and more faithful friend than he, his bearing was such as to excite admiration rather than love. His strong mind was thoroughly cultivated, and he was conversant with the minute particulars of English general history, and especially with the political history of the English empire. His mind was quick to perceive; his judgment equally quick to analyze and arrange; and these qualities made him a most skilful statesman. In council he was eminently wise; in debate he was distinguished for extraordinary ability; and as a political writer, he was without a peer in his country, when the rising dispute with Great Britain was occupying the thoughts of men in both hemispheres. Such was the man with whom, at Mount Vernon and at Gunston Hall, Washington held close conference for many years, while the flame of the Revolution was slowly kindling.

The storm of the stamp act season passed by, but it was succeeded by many others. In the intervals Washington was engaged in agricultural pursuits at Mount Vernon, and the pleasures of social life. In all the public affairs of his neighborhood, he was an active participant; and as early as 1765, the year when the stamp act became a law, he was a vestryman of both Truro and Fairfax parishes, in which Pohick in the country, and Christ Church in Alexandria, were the respective places of worship. In that year his name is appended to a declaration, with others, that he would "be conformable to the Doctrines and Discipline of the Church of England, as by law established." With his name appear those of George Mason, George William Fairfax, Edward Payne, Captain Charles Broadwater, and more than twenty others.

During the earlier years of his married life, Washington attended Pohick church, seven miles from Mount Vernon, more frequently than any other. The first church of that name was a frame building, and stood on the south side of Pohick creek, about two miles from the present edifice. About the year 1764, it became so dilapidated as to be no longer fit for use. The parishioners were called together to consult upon the erection of a new one. Among those assembled was Washington, and the father of George Mason, then advanced in years and greatly respected. When the question of the location of the new church came up for consideration, there was a difference of opinion. Mr. Mason was in favor of the old site, and Washington was opposed to it. Mr. Mason made a pathetic appeal in favor of the old site, pleading that there was the spot where their fathers had worshipped, and it was consecrated by their graves which surrounded it. Washington and others took the ground that the spot was far less convenient for the parish than a more central one. The subject took a shape that required more reflection, and a second meeting was called. Meanwhile, Washington made a careful survey of the whole neighborhood, marking the place of every house, and the relative distances, on a distinct map. When the second meeting was held, Mason again appealed to the sympathies of the people, when Washington appealed to their common sense, by simply presenting his map and explaining it in a few words. His almost mute argument prevailed, and the site of the present church was selected.

Preparations were now made for the erection of the new church, but it was not completed until the year 1773. Washington drew the ground-plan and elevation of the building for the use of the architect, and these (the originals) are before me while I write. They are very neatly sketched with China ink, upon good drawing paper, and occupy a space thirteen by fifteen inches square. The engraving is from a carefully

GROUND PLAN AND ELEVATION OF POHICK CHURCH.

drawn copy on a small scale, but shows every line as seen in Washington's drawing.

Of the ministers who officiated at Pohick, there were none

more beloved than the Reverend Lee Massey. He was the companion of Washington from his youth, and at his solicitation, and that of Mason, Fairfax, M'Carty, Chichester and others of that parish, he was induced to relinquish the profession of the law, study divinity, and become their pastor. His speech becoming impaired by the loss of his front teeth, he left the pulpit, and studied medicine as a means of affording relief to the poor.

Another clergyman, who officiated occasionally at Pohick church, after the regular stated services of the Church of England had ceased there, was the eccentric Mason L. Weems, the earliest biographer of Washington. The style of that biography was so attractive to the uncultivated readers of his day, that it passed through some forty editions, and even now it finds a sale. His character appears to have been a curious compound of seriousness and levity, truthfulness and exaggeration, reverence and profanity. He was an itinerant in every sense of the word. He was a man of considerable attainments as a scholar, physician and divine; and his benevolence was unbounded. When a boy of fourteen years, he was found at night teaching half-clad, half-fed children, who gathered eagerly around him; and all through life he was ready to share a crust with the unfortunate. He used wit and humor freely on all occasions. "Whether in private or public, in prayers or preaching," says Bishop Meade, "it was impossible that either the young or old, the grave or the gay, could keep their risible faculties from violent agitation." He would pray with the negro servants at night, and fiddle for them by the road-side by day. For many years he was a travelling bookseller, preaching when invited, haranguing the people at courts, fairs, and other public gatherings, and selling the Bible out of one hand and Paine's *Age of Reason* out of the other, alleging as an excuse for the latter performance, that he always carried the antidote with the poison. His fund of

MASON L. WEEMS.

anecdote was inexhaustible; and after giving a promiscuous audience the highest entertainment of fun, he found them in good mood to purchase his books. At Mount Vernon he was always a welcome guest, for Washington loved his goodness of heart and overlooked his foibles. Mr. Weems died at Beaufort, South Carolina, in May, 1825, at an advanced age.

After the Revolution, for reasons not clearly seen, Washington attended Christ Church, at Alexandria (of which he was a vestryman), instead of Pohick. Others of the latter parish followed, and after a while regular services ceased in that part of

the country. Washington owned a pew in Christ Church from
the establishment of the parish, in 1764, and occupied it constantly
after 1783, until his death. Some of his name have
held possession of it ever since. Judge Bushrod Washington

CHRIST CHURCH, ALEXANDRIA.

succeeded the General in its occupancy, then his nephew, John
A. Washington, the father of the late proprietor of Mount
Vernon, and lastly, that proprietor himself. Christ Church, at
Alexandria, was finished in 1773, and Washington paid the
highest price for a pew in it.

I visited Pohick Church many years ago, and found it falling
rapidly into decay. It stood upon an eminence north of
Pohick Creek, on the border of a forest that extended almost
uninterruptedly to Mount Vernon. Around it were the ancient
oaks of the primeval wood, interspersed with chestnuts and
pines. It was just at twilight when I reached the old fane, and
after making a sketch of it, I passed on to seek lodgings for the

night. The next day was the Sabbath, and being informed that a Methodist meeting was to be held in the church, I repaired thither at the usual hour, and took a seat in Washington's pew, near the pulpit. There I awaited the slow gathering of the little auditory. When all had assembled, men and

POHICK CHURCH IN 1858.

women and children, white and black, the whole congregation numbered only twenty-one persons. I could not refrain from drawing a parallel with the scenes of other days under that venerated roof, when some of the noblest of Virginia's aristocracy worshipped there, while clergymen, in surplice and gown, performed the solemn and impressive ritual of the Church of England. Now, a young man, with nothing to distinguish him from other men but a white cravat, stood as teacher within the old chancel by the side of the ancient communion-table. He talked sweetly of Christian charity:

> "Oh, the rarity
> Of Christian charity!"

and asked the little company to join with him in singing the hymn—

> "Come, Holy Spirit! Heavenly Dove!"

When the service was over, I made note, with pen and pencil, of all within. It was a melancholy task, for decay with its busy fingers was at work all around me, making sure prophecies of the speedy desolation of a building hallowed by associations with the beloved Washington. Upon the wall, back of the chancel, were still inscribed, the *Law*, the *Creed*, and the *Lord's Prayer*, upon which the eyes of Washington and his friends had rested a thousand times. A large proportion of the panes of glass were broken from the windows, admitting freely the wind and the rain, the bats and the birds. The elaborately wrought pulpit, placed by itself on one side of the church, was sadly marred by desecrating hands. Under its sounding-board, a swallow had built her nest; and upon the book ledge the fowls of the air had evidently perched. These things brought to memory the words of the "sweet singer of Israel"— "Yea, the sparrow has found a home, and the swallow a nest for herself, where she may lay her young, even thine altar, O Lord of Hosts!"

PULPIT IN POHICK CHURCH.

In the spring of 1772 there was a stranger at Mount Vernon, in errand and person. He was one-and-thirty years of age, slender in form, with a sweet and thoughtful face. He was a native of Maryland, and had been a saddler's apprentice at Annapolis, the capital of the province. In boyhood he had been as beautiful as a girl, and at twenty he was a handsome young man. At that age he felt spiritual aspirations for the life of an artist; and when, two or three years later, he said to a retired painter who resided a few miles from Annapolis, "Show me, Mr. Hesselius, how you mix such beautiful tints for your canvas, and I will give you the best saddle that I can make," a new world was opening to his enraptured vision. At that moment his true artist life began, for the generous painter revealed to him the coveted secret. Then the occupations of watchmaker, silversmith, carver, and saddler, in which he had severally engaged, were abandoned for the pursuit of art, except when stern necessity compelled him to employ them in earning his daily food. Thus he worked on until a way was opened for him to go to England and place himself under the instruction of Benjamin West, the great American painter, then the loved companion of the king. Two years he remained with West, and in 1769, Charles Willson Peale, the young artist referred to, returned to his native country and set up his easel as a portrait painter at Annapolis and Baltimore with wonderful success.

The fame of the young painter soon reached Mount Vernon, and he was invited there to delineate, for the first time, the form and features of the noble "lord of the manor." He executed the commission admirably, and produced a fine portrait of Washington at the age of forty years, life size, a little more than half-length, and in the costume of a colonel of the twenty-second regiment of the Virginia Militia. The coat is blue, with red facings, and bright metal buttons, having the

CHARLES WILLSON PEALE.

number of the regiment ("22") cast upon them. The waistcoat and breeches are also red, and the sash, a faded purple.

When, in 1797 or '98, Field, an English miniature painter and engraver of some eminence, visited Mount Vernon, he slept in a room in which hung Washington's old military coat. The painter cut off one of the buttons, and brought it away with him, regarding the transaction as a pious theft, no doubt, because prompted by veneration for the owner.

WASHINGTON'S MILITARY BUTTON.

That button was in the possession of John F. Watson, Esq.,

the venerable annalist of Philadelphia and New York, and at his house in Germantown the annexed sketch of it was made.

WASHINGTON AS A VIRGINIA COLONEL AT THE AGE OF FORTY.

Field had a pleasant countenance and fine portly figure. He was, on the whole, rather fat, and loved his ease. "When at Centreville, on the eastern shore of Maryland, in 1798," says Rembrandt Peale, in a recent letter to a friend, "Field and I took a walk into the country, after a rain. A wide puddle of water covered the road beyond the fence on both sides. I climbed the fence and walked round, but Field, fat and lazy, in good humor paid an old negro to carry him on his shoulders over the water. In the middle of it, Field became so convulsed with laughter, that he nearly shook himself off the old man's back."

Field went to Canada, studied theology a little, was ordained a priest of the Established Church, and became a bishop.

The portrait painted by young Peale, at that time, was the first that was ever made of Washington. From the study he then made, he painted the fine picture which hung at Mount Vernon until the owner's death, and since that time has graced the walls of Arlington House, the home of the late George Washington Parke Custis. The study —the really first portrait, was afterward dressed in the continental costume. This remained in possession of the artist and his family until the Peale gallery, in Philadelphia, was sold a few years ago, when it was purchased by Charles S. Ogden, Esq., in whose possession it now rests.

FAC-SIMILE OF PEALE'S RECEIPT

While at Mount Vernon at that time, Peale painted a miniature of Mrs. Washington, for her son, John Parke Custis, then a youth of eighteen, for which Washington, as his guardian, paid ten guineas, according to a receipt in the hand-writing of Washington, and signed by the artist, a fac-simile of which is on the preceding page.

JOHN PARKE CUSTIS.

Peale's miniatures were exquisitely painted, and very much sought after. A few years later he painted a portrait, in miniature, of young Custis, who was then General Washington's aide; also of his wife, the second daughter of Benedict Calvert, of Maryland, a descendant of Lord Baltimore. He also painted a portrait of that lady, life size, before her marriage, in which she is represented as a beautiful young girl in equestrian costume, the riding-jacket being open in front, and on her head a riding-hat with a feather. The miniature of John Parke Custis, from which our engraving was copied, was in the possession of Mrs. Washington until her death, and was afterwards the property of his granddaughter, the wife of the late Colonel Robert E. Lee, of Arlington House, Virginia.*

A shadow fell upon Mount Vernon in the spring of 1773. No child had blessed the union of Washington and his wife, and her two children received the most tender parental care and solicitude from their step-father. He appeared to love them as his own. Martha was a sweet girl, of gentle temper, graceful form, winning ways, and so much a brunette, that she was called "the dark lady." Just as she was blooming into womanhood, pulmonary consumption laid its withering hand upon her. For several months her strength had been failing, and letters filled with expressions of anxiety went frequently from her mother to Washington, who was engaged in his duties in the House of Burgesses at Williamsburg. At length a most alarming letter reached him. He had just made arrangements to accompany Lord Dunmore, the governor, on a long tour of observation west of the mountains, but he hastened to Mount Vernon. He found the dear child in the last moments of earthly life. His manly spirit was bowed with grief, and with deep feeling he knelt at the side of her bed and prayed most earnestly for her recovery. Upon the wings of that holy prayer her spirit ascended, and when he arose and looked upon her pale and placid face, Death had set its seal there. She expired on the nineteenth of June,

---

* Mr. Peale painted many other portraits of Washington, life size and in miniature. For an account of these, see note to the chapter on *Washington's Portraits,* in Custis's *Recollections and Private Memoirs of Washington.*

when in the seventeenth year of her age. Her departure left a great void in the heart of the mother, and Washington remained for some time at Mount Vernon, in seclusion, to console his afflicted wife, instead of taking the contemplated journey with the governor.

And now the flames of the Revolution were rapidly kindling all over the land. The representatives of royal authority had been buffeted in Boston, and acts of parliament had been set at naught, in such manner, that an indignant decree went forth from the throne, that the port of the New England capital should be shut, and the entire machinery of the colonial government be clogged, until the people there should show practical signs of penitence for their political sins. The people defied the ministerial power, and laughed at ministerial anathemas. Then a new governor, with armed soldiers, took possession of Boston, and, with iron heel, crushed its commerce and its prosperity.

Hot was the indignation of the colonists over the length and breadth of the land, and to every stroke of resistance given by the people of Massachusetts, those of Virginia abetted and gave loud acclamations of applause. For ten long years the people, in separate communities, had petitioned and remonstrated in vain. Now there was a universal desire for unity of action, and a GENERAL CONGRESS was proposed, in accordance with a suggestion made by Doctor Franklin. It received a hearty response in every colony, and the 5th of September, 1774, was the time agreed upon for such congress to assemble, and Philadelphia the place.

For a long time Washington had been much engaged in the discussion of the momentous political questions of the day. He was firm in his opinion, but no enthusiast; and with cautious but unwavering step, he had walked in the path of opposition to ministerial measures. He heartily approved of a General Congress; and when, after the Virginia Assembly, of which he was a member, had been dissolved by the governor, and met in informal convention, to consult upon the expedient of holding another council to elect representatives to a general congress, he was warmly in favor of the measure. And when that congress met, he was among the delegates chosen for the important business of conferring, in solemn earnestness, upon the destinies of a nation.

Washington was now fairly embarked upon the stormy ocean of political life in troublous times—"times," as Paine afterward said, "that tried men's souls." Vast were the stakes that he pledged. Life, fortune, honor, and every social enjoyment were all imperilled; and while his friend and neighbor of Gunston Hall as warmly espoused the same cause, those of Belvoir adhered to the crown.

The sports of the chase, social visiting, and almost every amusement of life now ceased at Mount Vernon. Grave men assembled there, and questions of mighty import were considered thoughtfully and prayerfully, for Washington was a man of prayer from earliest manhood.

At length the time arrived for the assembling of the national congress, and from all the colonies, except Georgia, the delegates began to make their way toward Philadelphia, some on horseback, others in coaches or chaises, but none by public conveyances, for there were few of these even in the most populous provinces. Some travelled alone, others in pairs; and as they approached the Delaware or the Schuylkill, they found themselves in companies. What a glorious spectacle! From twelve strong viceroyalties, containing an aggregate population of almost three millions of people, the best and the wisest among them, obedient to the public will, were on their way, through vast forests, and over rugged mountains, across broad rivers, and broader morasses, and through richly cultivated districts, cheerful villages, and expanding cities, to a common goal, there to meet, deliberate, and confederate, for the welfare, not only of a continent, but of the world! It was a moral spectacle such as had been hitherto unrecorded by the pen of history.

On Wednesday morning, the 31st of August, 1774, two men approached Mount Vernon on horseback. One of them was a slender man, very plainly dressed in a suit of ministers' gray, and about forty years of age. The other was his senior in years, likewise of slender form, and a face remarkable for its expression of unclouded intelligence. He was more carefully dressed, more polished in manners, and much more fluent in conversation than his companion. They reached Mount Vernon at seven o'clock, and after an exchange of salutations with Washington and his family, and partaking of breakfast, the three retired to the library and were soon deeply absorbed in the discussion of the great questions then agitating the people of the colonies. The two travellers were Patrick Henry and Edmund Pendleton. A third, the silver-tongued Cicero of Virginia, Richard Henry Lee, was expected with them, but he had been detained at Chantilly, his seat in Westmoreland.

All day long these three eminent Virginians were in council; and early the next morning they set out on horseback for Philadelphia, to meet the patriots from other colonies there. Will Lee, Washington's huntsman, and favorite body servant, now that

PATRICK HENRY.

Bishop had become too old and infirm to be active, was the only attendant upon his master. They crossed the Potomac at the Falls (now Georgetown), and rode far on toward Baltimore, before the twilight. On the 4th of September, the day before the opening of the Congress, they breakfasted at Christina Ferry (now Wilmington), and dined at Chester; and that night Washington, according to his diary, "lodged at Doctor Shippen's, in Philadelphia, after supping at the New Tavern." At that house of public entertainment he had lodged nearly two years before, while on his way to New York to place young Custis in King's (now Columbia) College.

At ten o'clock on Monday morning, the 5th of September, 1774, the First Continental Congress commenced its sessions in Carpenter's Hall, in Philadelphia. The members first assembled at the City Tavern, and marched in procession to the Hall. They organized the congress by choosing Peyton Randolph—a large, fleshy, good-looking Virginian, five-and-forty years of age—as president; and for secretary they appointed Charles Thomson, a lean man, with hollow, sparkling eyes, hair quite thin and gray, and a year younger than the president, though bearing marks of premature old age. Thomson was an accomplished Pennsylvanian; and, notwithstanding he appeared so old at the age of forty-four, he lived fifty years longer, while the florid, healthful-looking Randolph died the very next year, within an hour after eating a hearty dinner at Richard Hill's country seat, near Philadelphia.

The business of the congress was opened by Patrick Henry, and the session continued until the 26th of October, when they had laid the foundations of a new Republic, deep in the principles of Truth and Justice. They debated great questions with the dignity and wisdom of sages, and, by a large majority adopted the following resolution—a resolution which reaffirmed all previous resolves of the Americans to fight for freedom rather than submit to inglorious political servitude:

"*Resolved*,—THAT THIS CONGRESS APPROVE THE OPPOSITION OF THE INHABITANTS OF MASSACHUSETTS BAY TO THE EXECUTION OF THE LATE ACTS OF PARLIAMENT; AND IF THE SAME SHALL BE ATTEMPTED TO BE CARRIED INTO EXECUTION BY FORCE, IN SUCH CASE, ALL AMERICA OUGHT TO SUPPORT THEM IN THEIR OPPOSITION.

The Congress closed their important labors by putting forth some of the most remarkable state papers that ever appeared in the annals of the nations. The perusal of them drew from the Earl of Chatham the most enthusiastic encomiums, in a speech in the House of Lords. "When your lordships," he said, "look at the papers transmitted to us from America; when you consider their decency, firmness, and wisdom, you cannot but respect their cause, and wish to make it your own. For myself, I must declare and avow, that in all my reading and study of history (and it has been my favorite study—I have read Thucydides, and have studied and admired the master states of the world), that for solidity of reasoning, force of sagacity, and wisdom of conclusions, under such a complication of circumstances, no nation or body of men can stand in preference to the Congress at Philadelphia."

It was in a congress composed of such men that Washington distinguished himself. Although he did not engage in the public debates (for he had no talent for extempore speaking), and his name does not appear in the published proceedings of the Congress as a member of any committee during the session, his diary shows that he was assiduous in his attendance at Carpenter's Hall; and there is ample evidence that his mind had much to do in the general conduct of the business, and especially in the preparation of the state papers alluded to. When Patrick Henry was asked, on his return from Philadelphia, whom he considered the greatest man in the congress, he replied: "If you speak of eloquence, Mr. Rutledge of South Carolina is by far the greatest orator; but if you speak of solid information and sound judgment, Colonel Washington is unquestionably the greatest man on that floor."

When the Congress adjourned, Washington returned to Mount Vernon, full of desires for a reconciliation with the parent government, and for peacefulness in the bosom of his family; yet without any well-grounded hope. The hand of inexorable circumstances was then making many and great changes in and around his beautiful home. The sunshine upon the fields, the forests and the river were as bright as ever; and the flowers bloomed as beautifully, and the birds sang as sweetly as ever, when another spring came, like the angel of the resurrection, to call forth the sleepers in the bosom of mother earth. But in the mansion death had left the memorial footsteps of its recent visit; and the discord of clashing opinions had almost hushed into silence the sweet voices of the social circle in which he had been accustomed to move. His friend of Belvoir was a loyalist and beyond the ocean; and that fine mansion, wherein the Washingtons and Fairfaxes had held generous intercommunication for a quarter of a century, was soon afterward consumed by fire. Its owner never returned to America, and the social intercourse of two long-tried friends was closed forever. George Washington and George William Fairfax never met again on the earth.

The Congress of 1774, doubtful concerning reconciliation with Great Britain upon terms to which the colonists could accede, adjourned, to meet again at the same place on the tenth of May following, unless the desired redress of grievances should speedily take place, and render another national council unnecessary. But the people, taught by long and bitter experience, expected no justice from a blinded ministry, and prepared for inevitable war. They aroused themselves, and organized into military companies for the purpose of discipline.

Suddenly, as if by magic, a vast army was formed. It was, as we have elsewhere observed, "strong, determined, generous, and panting for action, yet invisible to the superficial observer. It was not seen in the camp, the field, nor the garrison. No drum was heard calling it to action; no trumpet was sounded for battle. It was like electricity, harmless when latent, but terrible when aroused. It was all over the land. It was at the plough, in the workshop, and in the counting-room. Almost every household was its head-quarters, and every roof its tent. It bivouacked in every chamber; and mothers, wives, sisters, and sweethearts made cartridges for its muskets, and supplied its commissariat. It was the old story of Cadmus repeated in modern history. British oppression had sown dragon's teeth all over the land, and a crop of armed men were ready to spring up, but not to destroy each other." *

Washington, always covetous of rural pursuits and the quiet of domestic life, returned from Philadelphia with the intention of resuming them. But urgent calls to public duty drew him from them. The volunteer companies of his state sought his counsel, and offered him the general leadership; and he went from place to place, reviewing the assembled troops, and imparting wisdom which he had learned from his military experience. Meanwhile, his old companions in arms came frequently to Mount Vernon, for they snuffed the smoke of war from afar. Among these, Doctors Hugh Mercer, of Fredricksburgh, and James Craik, of Alexandria, were the most welcome, for these Washington loved much.

Other men more distinguished also made frequent visits to Mount Vernon. Among the most famous of these were General Charles Lee and Major Horatio Gates, both of whom had

* Lossing's *Life of Washington*, i. 470.

been officers of distinction in the British army, and were then residents in Virginia. These frequently accompanied Washington in his military excursions; and during the spring of 1775, they spent much time under his roof.

GENERAL CHARLES LEE.

Lee was a Welshman, and a year younger than Washington. He possessed fine manly physical proportions, and a fiery spirit which nothing, at times, could control. He had been engaged in the war with the French and Indians in America, in 1756 and a few succeeding years; and the Mohawks, who created him a chief among themselves, gave him the significant name of *Boiling Water*. Restless and ambitious, he engaged in the continental wars of Europe, wherever he could find employment. At one time we find him an aide to the king of Poland, and then a companion of that king's ambassador to Constantinople. Then we see him in England assailing the British ministry with his sarcastic pen, and by his ill nature and perverse judgment, shutting every door to his own advancement. Disappointed and still restless, he came to America in 1773, and travelled through most of the English provinces. In Virginia he met Major Gates, and was induced by that gentleman to purchase an estate near him, in Berkeley county. There he was residing when the war for independence was fairly kindling, and he espoused the cause of the patriots with a zeal that commanded their greatest admiration. He entered the army as the first major-general under Washington, became very popular with the great body of the people, and for awhile disputed a place in their attachment with Washington himself. His ambition soon conquered his prudence, and he became insolent and insubordinate toward his superiors. With apparent collusion with the enemy, he became a prisoner; endeavored, while a captive, to betray his adopted country; was restored to the army by exchange, but soon afterward was suspended from command because of bad conduct on the field of Monmouth; and died in Philadelphia in comparative poverty, in the autumn of 1782, at the age of fifty-one years. He was a brilliant man in many things, but his life exhibited few commendable traits of character. He was bad in morals and manners; profane and extravagant in language, and feared and loved neither God nor man. In his will he bequeathed his soul to the Almighty and his body to the earth, saying: "I desire most earnestly that I may not be buried in any church or churchyard, or within a mile of any Presbyterian or Anabaptist meeting-house; for, since I have resided in this country, I have kept so much bad company when living, that I do not choose to continue it when dead."

Major Gates was three years the senior of Washington, and is supposed to have been a natural son of Horace Walpole. He was an officer in the British army during the French and Indian war, and was with Braddock in the battle of the Monongahela, where he was severely wounded. He accom-

GENERAL HORATIO GATES.

panied General Mockton to the West Indies as his aide-de-camp, and expected great preferment after the campaign was over, as he was the bearer to the king of the tidings of the English victory at Martinico. He was disappointed, and, in 1772, he sold his commission of major, came to America, and purchased an estate in Berkeley county, Virginia, beyond the Blue Ridge.

Gates was the opposite of Lee in his social qualities, being a perfect gentleman in his deportment. He, also, espoused the republican cause at the kindling of the war, was appointed the first adjutant-general of the continental army, and arose to the rank of major-general. He was ambitious and vain; and, during the first half of the war, was seeking to take the place of Washington as supreme commander of the American armies.

His last active military command was in South Carolina, in the summer of 1780, where he lost his whole army. He returned to his estate in Virginia, where he lived until 1790, and then removed to a farm on Manhattan Island, near the city of New York. He was a member of the New York legislature one term, and died in the spring of 1806, at the age of seventy-eight years.

Washington was at Mount Vernon only a few weeks at a time, from the summer of 1774 until his retirement from the army in 1783. He was in the first continental Congress, as we have observed, during the autumn of 1774; was absent upon military services much of the time during the winter of 1775, and was a member of the Virginia Assembly in the spring, when Patrick Henry made his famous war speech, which was closed with the burning words: "What is it that gentlemen wish? What would they have? Is life so dear or peace so sweet, as to be purchased at the price of chains and slavery? Forbid it, Almighty God! I know not what course others may take, but as for me, GIVE ME LIBERTY OR GIVE ME DEATH!"

With these words of Henry ringing in his ears, Washington returned to Mount Vernon, and prepared for a journey to Philadelphia, there to take his seat as a member of the Second

Continental Congress. Just at the close of a mild April day, while he and his neighbor, Bryan Fairfax, with Major Gates, were discussing the stirring events at Williamsburg, connected with the seizure of powder belonging to the colony, by the royal governor, and the bold stand taken by Patrick Henry— events which were then arousing every republican heart in Virginia to action—a messenger came in haste from Alexandria, bearing intelligence of bloodshed at Lexington and Concord. That intelligence made a deep but widely different impression upon the minds of the three friends. The gentle Fairfax, even then inclined to enter the gospel ministry, which he afterward adorned, was drawn, by the ties of consanguinity and ancestral reverence, to the side of the parent country. He was much distressed by the tidings from the east, for he perceived the gathering of a cloud of miseries for his country, and the peril of all pleasant social relations.

Gates, ambitious of military glory, and eagerly looking for the honors and emoluments of office, for which he had long played the sycophant in London, was delighted by this opening of an avenue to a field of action wherein they might be won; while Washington, communing with the intuitions of his loftier spirit, became thoughtful and reserved, and talked little, but wisely, on the subject. But he resolved nobly and firmly to go zealously into whatever conflicts might arise for the defence of the liberties of his country. All regarded the event as the casting away of the scabbard, as the severing blow to colonial allegiance.

These friends parted company on the following day, and toward the evening of the 4th of May, Benjamin Harrison, one of the immortal fifty-six who afterward signed the Declaration of Independence, came to Mount Vernon, supped, lodged, and breakfasted, and departed with Washington, early in the morning of the 5th, for Philadelphia. They arrived at Chester on the 9th, and, while riding toward Philadelphia, with other southern delegates, were met, five or six miles from the city, by a cavalcade of five hundred gentlemen. Nearer the city, they were met by military companies, and by these, with bands of music, were escorted into and through the city " with great parade." On the following day, the new England delegates were received in a similar manner; and thus, in the midst of the homage and acclamations of the people, the representatives of thirteen viceroyalties assembled to confederate in the great work of constructing a new republic.

With the sword of defence in one hand, and the olive-branch of reconciliation in the other, the Congress went on in their solemn labors. The military genius and experience of Washington were continually acknowledged by his being placed as chairman of all the committees appointed for the conduct of military affairs; and to him was entrusted the important task of preparing rules and regulations for an army, and devising measures for the general defence.

Meanwhile, a large, but crude and ill-regulated army, had gathered around Boston, and was keeping the British regulars in close confinement upon that little peninsula. It possessed no other cohesion than that derived from a sense of mutual danger. The Congress perceived this, and resolved to consolidate and organize it by adopting it as a Continental army, with a commander-in-chief and assistant general officers. That adoption was formally made; and on Thursday, the 15th of June, two days before the battle of Bunker's Hill, George

Washington was chosen commander-in-chief of "all the continental forces raised or to be raised, for the defence of American liberty." The appointment was officially announced to him on the following day, and modestly accepted; and on the 18th he wrote a touching letter to his wife on the subject, telling her he must depart immediately for the camp; begging her to summon all her fortitude, and to pass her time as agreeably as possible; and expressing a firm reliance upon that Providence which had ever been bountiful to him, not doubting that he should return safe to her in the fall.

But he did not so return. Darker and darker grew the clouds of war; and, during more than seven years, Washington visited his pleasant home upon the Potomac but once, and then only for three days and nights. Mrs. Washington spent the winter in camp with her husband; and many are the traditions concerning her beauty, gentleness, simplicity, and industry, which yet linger around the winter-quarters of the venerated commander-in-chief of the armies of the Revolution. For many long years she was remembered with affection by the dwellers at Cambridge, Morristown, Valley Forge, Newburgh, and New Windsor. When, on each returning spring, she departed for her home on the Potomac, the blessings of thousands—soldiers and citizens—went with her, for she was truly loved by all.

Pleasant would it be to read the scores of letters written by Washington to his charming wife during all that campaigning period, and his subsequent services in civil life. That pleasure can never be enjoyed. Only one letter to her—the message informing her of his appointment to the command of the army—is known to be in existence, and that, with one to her son on the same subject, written on the following day, is carefully preserved at Arlington House, by her great-granddaughter, Mrs. Mary Custis Lee. Mrs. Washington destroyed all of her husband's other letters to herself, a short time before her death.

It is not our design to follow Washington in his career as a soldier, or even as a statesman, for in these his field of action was far away from Mount Vernon—the object of our illustrations. His career in each was noble; and even in his defeats in battle, he never lost a particle of the dignity of his character, nor the esteem of his countrymen. His caution and prudence were sometimes misunderstood, but they were always found to be the guaranties of success. For nearly nine months he cautiously watched the British army in Boston, and waited for strength sufficient to attack it with success, while the people, and even the Congress, became impatient and clamored for battle. At length the proper time came, and with skill and energy he prepared to strike an annihilating blow. The enemy saw their peril, fled to their ships, and escaped to Halifax, while the whole continent rang with the praises of Washington. The Congress decreed a gold medal to the victor. Duvivier, of Paris, cut the die; and to Mount Vernon the glittering testimonial of a nation's gratitude was afterward borne, upon which was inscribed: "THE AMERICAN CONGRESS TO GEORGE WASHINGTON, COMMANDER-IN-CHIEF OF ITS ARMIES, THE ASSERTORS OF FREEDOM: THE ENEMY FOR THE FIRST TIME PUT TO FLIGHT—BOSTON RECOVERED, 17TH MARCH, 1776."

Although excessively prudent, Washington was ever ready to strike a blow in the presence of greatest peril, when his judgment and inclination coalesced in recommending the per

GOLD MEDAL AWARDED TO WASHINGTON FOR THE DELIVERANCE OF BOSTON.

formance of the act. We see him with a handful of ill-disciplined, ill-fed, ill-clad soldiers, after a prudent flight of three weeks before a strong pursuing enemy, crossing a rapid river in the midst of floating ice, and darkness, and driving storm, and smiting a band of mercenary Germans at Trenton, who had been hired out by their avaricious princes to aid the British soldiery in butchering their fellow subjects. Victory followed the blow, and a few days afterward that victory was repeated at Princeton. Again the praises of Washington were upon every lip. The great Frederick of Prussia declared that the achievements of the American leader and his compatriots, between the twenty-fifth of December 1776, and the fourth of January, 1777—a space of ten days—were the most brilliant of any recorded in the annals of military action. A splendid flag, taken from the Hessians at Trenton, composed of two pieces of heavy white damask silk, bearing devices embroidered with gold thread, and the words FOR OUR PRINCE AND COUNTRY, in Latin, exquisitely wrought in needlework, was presented to Washington. It was afterward hung up in the great hall at Mount Vernon, but only on one occasion, for Washington was careful never to make even the most trivial display of mementos of his own valor. This flag was his first trophy of the kind in the war for independence.

And all through the war, prudence, sagacity, skill, energy, and great wisdom, marked the acts of Washington. His last battle was at Yorktown, where another trophy, similar to that at Trenton, was secured. It was the flag of the seventh British regiment, made of heavy twilled silk, six feet in length and five feet four inches in width.

HESSIAN FLAG TAKEN AT TRENTON.

The ground was blue; the central stripe of the cross red; the marginal ones white. In the centre was a crown, and beneath it a garter, with the usual inscription in Norman French—*Evil be to him who evil thinketh*—enclosing a full-blown rose, the floral emblem of England. This flag, with another, was presented to Washington by a resolution of the Congress, passed ten days after the victory, and was hung in the hall at Mount Vernon on the single occasion referred to. It had been sadly tattered during the conflict. Until a few years ago it occupied a place near the Hessian flag, in the Museum at Alexandria, where they were deposited by Mr. Custis, and labeled *Alpha* and *Omega*—the *first*

BRITISH FLAG TAKEN AT YORKTOWN.

and the *last* of the trophies won by Washington. The Museum and its contents were afterwards burned.

Lonely was the mansion at Mount Vernon without the master during the seven years and more that the war lasted. Yet it was by no means deserted. The only child of Mrs. Washington, John Parke Custis, with his wife and growing family, were there much of the time, for Washington had written to him a few days after his appointment to the command of the army: "At any time, I hope it is unnecessary for me to say, that I am always pleased with your and Nelly's abidance at Mount Vernon, much less upon this occasion, when I think it absolutely necessary for the peace and satisfaction of your mother; a consideration which I have no doubt will have due weight with you both, and require no arguments to enforce." Neighbors and friends also came frequently to cheer the temporary widowhood of the mistress. Lund Washington, the master's relative and friend, was the faithful manager of the estate, and he scrupulously obeyed the injunction of the owner, who said: " Let the hospitality of the house, with respect to the poor, be kept up. Let no one go away hungry. If any of this kind of people should be in want of corn, supply their necessities, provided it does not encourage them in idleness."

Nothing of importance, aside from the routine of plantation life, occurred at Mount Vernon after the summer of 1775, until 1781. At the former period, Lord Dunmore and his marauding followers, ascended the Potomac as far as Occoquan Falls, with the intention of making Mrs. Washington a prisoner, and desolating the estates of Gunston Hall and Mount Vernon. The Prince William militia gathered in large numbers to oppose him, and these, aided by a heavy storm, frustrated his lordship's designs, and he sailed down the river, after destroying some mills and other property.

Early in September, 1781, there was great commotion at Mount Vernon, greater than when, a few months before, small British armed vessels had come up the Potomac, plundering and destroying on every hand. One of these, on that occasion, had approached Mount Vernon with fire and sword, and Lund Washington had purchased the safety of the estate by giving the commander refreshments and supplies. For this the master of Mount Vernon rebuked him, saying, "It would have been a less painful circumstance to me to have heard that, in consequence of your non-compliance with their request, they had burned my house and laid my plantation in ruins."

On the 9th of September, 1781, there was an arrival more startling to the dwellers upon the Mount Vernon estate than that of an armed enemy upon the neighboring waters. It was the unexpected arrival of the master himself. . The allied French and American armies were then on their march toward

Virginia, to assist Lafayette and his compatriots in driving the invading Cornwallis from that state. Washington came from Baltimore late at night, attended only by Colonel Humphreys (one of his aides) and faithful Billy. They had left the Count de Rochambeau and the Marquis de Chastellux—one at Alexandria, and the other at Georgetown—to follow them in the morning. Very soon the whole household was astir, and the news flew quickly over the estate that the master had arrived. At early dawn the servants came from every cabin to greet him, and many looked sorrowfully upon a face so changed by the storms of successive campaigns, during more than six years that he had been absent.

None came earlier than Bishop, the venerable body-servant of the master in the old French war, who was now too old to go to the camp. He lived near the mansion, the Nestor of the plantations, and was overseer of one of the farms. No doubt he came, as was his custom on great occasions, fully equipped in his regimentals, made after the fashion of George the Second's time, to greet the man he so much loved. Bishop was then almost eighty years of age, with deep furrows upon his cheeks, a few gray locks upon his temples, and his once manly form bent gently by the weight of years, and shrunken by the suns of nearly fourscore summers.

On the morrow, the French noblemen, with their suites, arrived—Rochambeau first, and De Chastellux afterward—and all but the chief made it a day of rest. For him there was no repose. He was not permitted to pass even an hour alone with his wife. Public and private cares were pressing heavily upon him. He was on his way to measure strength with a powerful enemy, and his words of affection were few and hurried. All

COUNT DE ROCHAMBEAU.

the morning of the 10th he was closeted with his manager, and before dinner he wrote to Lafayette the first letter that he had dated at Mount Vernon since early in May, 1775, saying, " We are thus far on our way to you. The Count de Rochambeau has just arrived. General Chastellux will be here, and we propose, after resting to-morrow, to be at Fredericksburg on the night of the 12th. The 13th we shall reach New Castle ; and, the next day, we expect to have the pleasure of seeing you at your encampment." These calculations were correct ; they arrived at the camp of Lafayette, at Williamsburg, on the evening of the 14th.

Rochambeau and Chastellux were guests worthy of such a host. The former was of a noble Vendôme family. He was of medium height, slender in form, and then fifty-six years of age. He had been aide-de-camp to the Duke of Orleans, five-and-thirty years before, and had gained many laurels on the fields of battle, especially on that of Minden, which occurred a few months after Washington had taken his bride to Mount Vernon. A fine picture of that battle hung upon the walls at Mount Vernon for many years, and is now at Arlington House. Whether it was there to delight the eyes of Rochambeau on this occasion is a question that may not now be solved.

Rochambeau had come to America at the head of a large army, to assist the struggling colonists to cast off the British yoke. He came with the title of lieutenant-general, but, according to previous arrangement by the French court, he was to be second to Washington in command. He assisted nobly at the siege of Yorktown, where, little more than a month after this visit at Mount Vernon, Cornwallis and a large army surrendered to the allied forces. He returned to France, was made a field-marshal by the king, but was called to much suffering during the French Revolution. Bonaparte granted him a pension and the cross of grand officer of the legion of honor, in 1803. Four years afterward he died at the age of eighty-two.

De Chastellux was a much younger man than Rochambeau, heavier in person, very vivacious, fond of company, and exhibited all the elegances of manner of the older French nobility, to which class he belonged. He came to America with Rochambeau, but seems not to have been confined to the army, though bearing the title of major-general; for during the two years he was here, he travelled very extensively, and made notes and observations. These he printed on board the French fleet—only twenty-four copies—for distribution among his friends; but a few years afterward they were translated and published in two volumes, by an English traveller.

MARQUIS DE CHASTELLUX.

De Chastellux was the life of every company into which he was introduced, while in this country, and he left a very pleasant impression at Mount Vernon. In the library there, where he was entertained in the autumn of 1781, Washington wrote to him a playful letter in the spring of 1787, after receiving from the marquis an account of his marriage to an accomplished lady, a relative of the Duke of Orleans. "I saw," wrote Washington, "by the eulogium you often made on the happiness of domestic life in America, that you had swallowed the bait, and that you would as surely be taken, one day or another, as that you were a philosopher and soldier. So your day has at length come. I am glad of it, with all my heart and soul. It is quite good enough for you. Now you are well served for coming to fight in favor of the American rebels, all the way across the Atlantic ocean, by catching that terrible contagion—domestic felicity—which, like the smallpox or plague, a man can have only once in his life."

De Chastellux died in 1793, in the midst of the terrible storm of the French Revolution, and by it the fortunes of himself and wife seem to have been swept away, for his widow applied to Washington, two years afterward, for an allowance from our government, on account of the services of her husband, who was in active military duty near New York, and was in the siege at Yorktown. Her application was unsuccessful.

On the second day after Washington's arrival at Mount Vernon—the eleventh of September—the fourth anniversary of the battle of Brandywine—the mansion, then not nearly so large as now, was crowded with guests; and at dinner were met gentlemen and ladies from the country for miles around, who had not been at the festive board with the master of the feast since the war broke out. And there were children, too—tiny children, whom the master loved as his own, for they were the grandchildren of his wife. There were four of these. The eldest was a beautiful girl, five years old, who afterward married a nephew of Lord Ellenborough; and the youngest was a boy-baby, only six months old, who was afterward adopted as the child of Washington, became one of the executors of his will, and lived until 1857. These were the children of John Parke Custis and his fair young wife, Eleanor Calvert, and had all been born during the absence of the master from his home at Mount Vernon.

Here let us pause a moment and look with the eye of faith in the words of a fellow man, upon the person of the great patriot who sat at the head of the feast on that day. The year before, a writer in the *London Chronicle* (an anti-ministerial paper), who had seen Washington, thus vividly described him:

"General Washington is now in the forty-seventh year of his age. He is a tall, well-made man, rather large-boned, and has a genteel address. His features are manly and bold; his eyes of a bluish cast and very lively; his hair a deep brown; his face rather long, and marked with the smallpox; his complexion sunburnt, and without much color. His countenance sensible, composed, and thoughtful. There is a remarkable air of dignity about him, with a striking degree of gracefulness. He has an excellent understanding, without much quickness; is strictly just, vigilant, and generous; an affectionate husband, a faithful friend, a father to the deserving soldier; gentle in his manners, in temper reserved; a total stranger to religious prejudices; in morals irreproachable; and never known to exceed the bounds of the most rigid temperance. In a word, all his friends and acquaintances allow that no man ever united in his own person a more perfect alliance of the virtues of a philosopher with the talents of a general. Candor, sincerity, affability, and simplicity seem to be the striking features of his character; and, when occasion offers, the power of displaying the most determined bravery and independence of spirit."

Domestic felicity and social enjoyment were, at that time,

secondary considerations with Washington, and, on the morning of the 12th of September, he departed, with all his military guests, from his delightful dwelling-place, journeyed to Fredericksburg to embrace his aged mother and receive her blessing, and then hastened on toward Yorktown, where Cornwallis had intrenched himself with a view of overrunning Virginia.

There was great sorrow at Mount Vernon on the morning of the departure of the master. It was a grief to the devoted wife to part so soon from her husband, who was on his way to battle, perhaps to death; but more poignant was her grief as a mother, for John Parke Custis, her only surviving child, in whom her fondest earthly affections were centred, followed Washington to the field as his aide-de-camp. He was then in the flush of manhood, eight-and-twenty years of age, and full of promise. He was a member of the Virginia House of Burgesses, and very popular wherever known. He now went out to battle, for the first time, leaving his wife and children and his fond mother in the pleasant home at Mount Vernon, with every material comfort around them, but with hearts filled with sadness, and spirits agitated with anxiety and apprehension.

Oh, how eagerly did those wives and mothers at Mount Vernon watch for the courier who daily brought intelligence from the camp! At length there came a messenger with tidings which produced mingled joy and alarm. He came to tell of a triumph at Yorktown, and of mortal sickness at Eltham, thirty miles from the field where victory had been won. At Yorktown, the allied armies, after a siege of twelve days, had compelled Cornwallis to surrender, with all his army, seven thousand strong.

Joy was awakened all over the land as intelligence of this glorious event was spread, by swift couriers, from hamlet to hamlet, from village to village, from city to city. The name of Washington was upon every lip, as the Benefactor, the Liberator, the Saviour of his country. And there was peculiar joy and pride at Mount Vernon, when, at early dawn on a frosty morning, a messenger brought the intelligence that prophesied of peace and the speedy return of the loved ones to the safety and repose of domestic life.

But, as we have said, the same messenger brought intelligence that produced serious alarm, and preparations were immediately made at Mount Vernon, for a journey. Young Custis was very sick with camp fever at the house of Colonel Bassett, the husband of his mother's sister, at Eltham. His mother and wife were soon upon the road; and, in an agony of suspense, they urged the postillion to increase the speed of his horses. When they arrived at Eltham, all hope for the loved one's recovery had vanished.

Washington had sent his old and faithful friend, Doctor Craik, to attend the sufferer, and as soon as his arrangements at Yorktown could be completed, the chief followed. He arrived at Eltham " time enough" he wrote to Lafayette, " to see poor Mr. Custis breathe his last." In that hour the young wife was made a widow, and the mistress of Mount Vernon a childless woman. The great man bowed his head in deep sorrow, while his tears flowed freely. Then he spoke soothing words to the widowed mother, and said, "Your two younger children I adopt as my own." These were Eleanor Parke Custis and George Washington Parke Custis, the former two years and six months of age, and the latter only six months.

They both lived beyond the age of threescore and ten, and Eleanor was considered one of the most beautiful and brilliant women of her day. She married Lawrence Lewis, the favorite nephew of Washington. The nuptials were celebrated on the

ELEANOR PARKE CUSTIS.

chief's birthday, 1799. Three days before, Washington, as her foster-father, wrote from Mount Vernon to the clerk of Fairfax county court, saying:

"Sir: You will please to grant a license for the marriage of Eleanor Parke Custis with Lawrence Lewis, and this shall be your authority for so doing."

The portrait of this beautiful lady, from which our engraving is copied, was painted at Philadelphia by Gilbert Stuart. It adorned the mansion at Mount Vernon for several years, and was preserved with care among the Washington treasures of Arlington House.

Late in the autumn of 1781, Washington again visited Mount Vernon for a brief season. It was when he was on his journey to Philadelphia, in November, bearing the laurels of a victor. He was accompanied as far as Fredericksburg by a large retinue of American and French officers; and there, after an interview with his mother, he attended a ball given in honor of the occasion. The aged matron went with him to the assembly, and astonished the French officers by the plainness of her apparel and the quiet simplicity of her manners, for they expected to see the mother of the great chief distinguished by a personal display such as they had been accustomed to behold among the families of the great in their own country. They thought of the Dowager Queen of France, of the brilliant Marie Antoinette, and the high-born dames of the court of Louis the Sixteenth, and could not comprehend the vision.

Washington retired with his mother from the gay scene at an early hour, for there was grief in his heart because of the death of his beloved Custis; and, the next morning, attended by two aides and Billy, he rode to Mount Vernon. His stay there was brief. Public duties beckoned him forward. "I shall remain but a few days here," he wrote to General Greene, "and shall proceed to Philadelphia, when I shall attempt to stimulate Congress to the best improvement of our late success, by taking the most vigorous and effectual measures to be ready for an early and decisive campaign the next year."

Happily for the country, no other campaign of active military operations was needed; and, in the course of a few months, the war was virtually at an end. The desire for peace, which had long burned in the bosom of the British *people*, now found such potential expression, as to be heeded by the British *ministry*. The intelligence of the fate of Cornwallis and his army had fallen with all the destructive energy of a bombshell in the midst of the war party in parliament. When Lord North, the premier, heard of it, he paced the room violently, and, throwing his arms wildly about, exclaimed, "O God! it is all over! it is all over!" The stoutest declaimer in favor of bayonets and gunpowder, Indian and German mercenaries, as fit instruments for enslaving a free people, began to talk of the *expediency* of peace; and at length, by mutual consent, commissioners were appointed by the contending parties to treat for peace on the basis of the independence of the United States. They were successful; and, early in the spring of 1783, the joyful news, that a treaty had been signed at Paris, reached America, by the French ship *Triomphe*, sent for the purpose, by Count d'Estaing, at the request of Lafayette.

Washington was then, with his wife, at Newburgh, the headquarters of the continental army, happy in having just frustrated a scheme of some officers to produce a general mutiny among the discontented soldiers. The intelligence came to him in dispatches from Robert R. Livingston, the Secretary for Foreign Affairs, and also in a letter from Alexander Hamilton, and other New York delegates in Congress. It was hailed by the chief with joy, and he immediately wrote the following letter to Governor Clinton, which is copied from the original manuscript, now in the archives of the state of New York:

"HEAD-QUARTERS, *March* 27, 1783.

"DEAR SIR:—I take the first moment of forwarding to your Excellency the dispatches from the Secretary of Foreign Affairs, which accompany this. They contain, I presume, all the intelligence respecting Peace, on which great and glorious event permit me to congratulate you with the greatest sincerity."

Upon the envelope bearing the superscription, Washington wrote in large letters, with a broad dash under it—PEACE.

What a glorious word! What joy must have filled the heart of the commander-in-chief when he wrote that word! What dreams of repose upon the Potomac, in the quiet shades of his beautiful home must have been presented to his vision at that time! But many weary months were yet to intervene before he could see his beloved Mount Vernon.

It was not until the 1st of November following that all arrangements for the departure of the British army from our shores were completed.

The American army, by a general order of Congress, on the 3d of November, was disbanded, except a small force retained under a definite enlistment, until a peace establishment should be organized; and, on the 25th of that month, the British evacuated the city of New York—their last resting-place upon the soil of the United States—went on board their ships, and sailed for Nova Scotia and Europe, with a large number of loyalists.

On the 4th of December Washington parted with his officers at Fraunces' tavern in New York, and then proceeded toward Annapolis, where Congress was sitting, to resign into their hands his commission as commander-in-chief of the armies of the United States, which had been given him eight years and six months before. He stopped at Philadelphia, and presented his accounts to the proper fiscal officers, and arrived at Annapolis on Friday, the 19th, where he was joined by Mrs. Washington and many warm personal friends. On Monday he was present at a dinner ordered by the Congress, at which more than two hundred persons were seated; and that evening he opened a grand ball given in his honor, with Mrs. James Macubbin, one of the most beautiful women of her time.

At twelve o'clock, on the 23d, Washington entered the hall of Congress in the old State House at Annapolis, according to previous arrangement, and, in the presence of a great concourse of people, presented his resignation to General Thomas Mifflin, the president of that body, accompanying the act by a brief speech. This was responded to by Mifflin. The great Leader of the Continental Armies, now a private citizen, retired, followed by the audience; and the curtain fell upon the last solemn act in the great drama of the war for independence.

Washington now hastened to Mount Vernon, accompanied by many friends, as an escort of honor, among whom was Colonel Walker, one of the aides of the Baron Steuben, by whose hand he sent a letter to Governor Clinton, the first which he wrote at his home after his retirement. In it he said: "The scene is at last closed. I am now a private citizen on the banks of the Potomac. I feel myself eased of a load of public care. I hope to spend the remainder of my days in cultivating the affections of good men, and in the practice of the domestic virtues."

It was on Christmas eve, 1783, that Washington, a private citizen, arrived at Mount Vernon, and laid aside forever the

WASHINGTON'S MILITARY CLOTHES.

military clothes which he had worn perhaps through more than half the campaigns of the war just ended. Around them clustered many interesting associations, and they were preserved with care during the remaining sixteen years of his life. And they are still preserved, in a condition almost as perfect as when the illustrious owner hung them in his wardrobe for the last time. They are in a glass case, with other mementos of the FATHER OF HIS COUNTRY, in the Smithsonian Institution at Washington city. The coat is made of deep blue cloth, faced with a yellow called buff, with large plain gilt buttons. The waistcoat and breeches are made of the same kind of buff cloth as the facings of the coat.

On the same occasion, Washington laid aside his battle-sword which he had worn throughout all the later years of the war. It, too, hung at Mount Vernon for almost twenty years, and is carefully preserved in the same glass case in the Patent Office. It is a kind of hanger, incased in a black leather scabbard, with silver mountings. The handle is ivory, colored a pale green, and wound in spiral grooves with thin silver wire. It was manufactured by J. Bailey, in Fishkill, Duchess county, New York, and has the maker's name engraved upon the blade. The belt is of white leather, mounted with silver, and was doubtless used by Washington in the old French war, for upon a silver plate attached to it is engraved "1757."

With this sword is a long, knotty, black cane, with a golden head, which was bequeathed to Washington by Doctor Franklin, in the following clause in the codicil to his will:

"My fine crab-tree walking-stick, with a gold head curiously wrought in the form of a cap of liberty, I give to my friend, and the friend of mankind, *General Washington*. If it were a sceptre, he has merited it, and would become it. It was a present to me from that excellent woman, Madame de Forbach, the dowager Duchess of Deuxponts, connected with some verses which should go with it."

These "verses" have been lost, and for them we will substitute the beautiful ode, by Morris, alluding to these precious relics, entitled

"THE SWORD AND THE STAFF.

I.

"The sword of the Hero!
 The staff of the Sage!
Whose valor and wisdom
 Are stamp'd on the age!
Time-hallowed mementos
 Of those who have riven
The sceptre from tyrants,
 'The lightning from heaven.'

II.

"This weapon, O Freedom!
 Was drawn by thy son,
And it never was sheath'd
 Till the battle was won!
No stain of dishonor
 Upon it we see!
'Twas never surrender'd—
 Except to the free!

III.

"While Fame claims the hero
 And patriot sage,
Their names to emblazon
 On History's page,
No holier relics
 Will Liberty hoard,
Than FRANKLIN's staff, guarded
 By WASHINGTON's sword."

THE SWORD AND
THE STAFF.

In the same glass case are other interesting relics of Washington, the most conspicuous of which is his camp-chest, an old-fashioned hair trunk, twenty-one inches in length, fifteen in width, and ten in depth, filled with the table furniture used by the commander-in-chief during the war. The compartments are so ingeniously arranged, that they contain a great number of articles in a small space. These consist of a gridiron; a tea and coffee pot; three tin saucepans (one

WASHINGTON'S CAMP-CHEST.

movable handle being used for all); five small glass flasks, used for honey, salt, coffee, port-wine, and vinegar; three large tin meat dishes; sixteen plates; two knives and five forks; a candlestick and tinder-box; tin boxes for tea and sugar, and five small bottles for pepper and other materials for making soup.

Washington alluded to the tin plates in this camp-chest, in the following letter to Doctor John Cochran, surgeon-general of the northern department of the continental army, written at West Point on the 16th of August, 1779:

"DEAR DOCTOR:—I have asked Mrs. Cochran and Mrs. Livingston to dine with me to-morrow; but am I not in honor bound to apprise them of their fare? As I hate deception, even where the imagination only is concerned, I will. It is needless to premise that my table is large enough to hold the ladies. Of this they had ocular proof yesterday. To say how it is usually covered is rather more essential; and this shall be the purport of my letter.

"Since our arrival at this happy spot, we have had a ham, sometimes a shoulder of bacon, to grace the head of the table; a piece of roast beef adorns the foot; and a dish of beans, or greens, almost imperceptible, decorates the centre. When the cook has a mind to cut a figure, which I presume will be the case to-morrow, we have two beef-steak pies, or dishes of crabs, in addition, one on each side of the centre dish, dividing the space and reducing the distance between dish and dish to about six feet, which, without them, would be nearly twelve feet apart. Of late he has had the surprising sagacity to discover that apples will make pies; and it is a question if, in the violence of his efforts, we do not get one of apples, instead of having both of beef-steaks. If the ladies can put up with such entertainment, and will submit to partake of it on plates *once tin but now iron* (not become so by the labor of scouring), I shall be happy to see them; and am, dear doctor, yours, &c.,

"GEO. WASHINGTON."

Later in the war, Washington had a pair of plain silver goblets, with his crest engraven upon them, which he used in his tent. These were the only examples of a departure from that rigid economy which he exhib'ted in all his personal arrangements while in the army, not because he was parsimonious, but because he wished to set an example of plainness and self-denial to all around him. These goblets were used in the family of Robert E. Lee at Arlington House.

SILVER CAMP-GOBLET.

What a contrast do these simple table arrangements, and, indeed, all the movements and appointments of the great Republican Leader, present to those of the generals of the old world, and of those of antiquity in particular, whose achievements for the benefit of mankind, placed in the scale of just appreciation, are small compared with his.

After the victory at Yorktown, the marquée and tent used by Washington were folded up and placed in the leathern portmanteau in which they were carried, and were never again spread upon the field in camp, siege, or battle. They were made by Captain Moulder, of Philadelphia, who commanded a corps of artillery in the battle at Princeton. The marquée was used for general purposes—for the reception of visitors, consultations of officers, dining, et cetera—and the smaller tent was for more private uses. In the latter Washington retired for meditation, and wrote his letters and dispatches for his secretaries to copy; and in one part of it was a dormitory, wherein he slept. It composed the private apartment of his canvas dwelling upon the field, and few were allowed to enter it.

What a history is involved in the experience of that tent!

How many important dispatches were written within it, upon the little writing-case, or portfolio, that was presented to President Taylor by Washington's adopted son, and by him deposited, with other mementos of the great Leader, in the

WASHINGTON'S TRAVELLING WRITING-CASE.

Patent Office, where it is well preserved! How many anxious hours did that great Leader pass beneath the narrow canopy of that tent? How often, during that long war, did the forms of Reed, and Harrison, and Hamilton, and Tilghman, and Meade, and Humphreys darken the door of that tent as they passed in and out with messages and dispatches to and from the illustrious chief!

And in the large marquée, what a noble band of mighty men—mighty in moral force—among the noblest the world ever saw—were gathered in council from time to time, and determined those movements which achieved the independence of these states! In it, too, many distinguished men sat at the table of the chief—members of the old congresses; foreigners of note in diplomacy and war; and last, Cornwallis as captive and guest, after his humiliation at Yorktown. It was quite spacious, and, when fully spread, one hundred guests might conveniently dine beneath its ample roof.

That marquée and tent, wrapped in the old portmanteau, with the poles and cords as they were taken from the battle-field, were at Arlington House. The former had been spread occasionally for peaceful purposes. For several years Mr. Custis, who was much interested in the improvement of the breeds of sheep, had annual gatherings of the friends of agriculture and manufactures at a fine spring on his estate, near the banks of the Potomac, in the early days of May. On

WASHINGTON'S TENTS IN THEIR PORTMANTEAUX.

these occasions the old marquée would be erected, and sometimes nearly two hundred guests would assemble under it to partake of refreshments. These "sheep-shearings at Arlington Spring" are remembered with pleasure by the surviving participants.

When Lafayette was in this country, in 1824 and '25, as the guest of the nation, that marquée was used at Baltimore by the *Society of the Cincinnati*, for the purpose of receiving the Illustrious Friend as the guest of that fraternity—a fraternity of which he had been a member ever since its formation on the banks of the Hudson, more than forty years before. On that occasion Colonel John Eager Howard, one of the heroes of the Cowpens, presided; and Charles Carroll, who soon afterward had the proud distinction of being the last survivor of the signers of the Declaration of Independence, was a guest. And twice since that memorable reception, that war-tent, so often spread upon the line of march and on the battle-field, has been used in the service of the Prince of Peace. On these occasions it was pitched in green fields in the midst of beauty and repose, and thousands came and willingly paid liberal tribute for the privilege of sitting under the TENT OF WASHINGTON. Two churches were erected with the proceeds.

We have just alluded to the *Society of the Cincinnati*. It is a fraternity originally composed of officers of the Revolution, and was formed a little while before the disbanding and dispersion of the Continental Army. Its chief object was the perpetuation and occasional renewal of the long-cherished friendship and social intercourse which had existed between the officers of the army. The idea originated with General Knox. He communicated it to Washington, who not only approved of it, but gave the efforts to form a society upon such a basis of feeling, his cordial co-operation.

It was in the spring of 1783 that the *Society of the Cincinnati* was formed. The head-quarters of the army were then at Newburgh. A committee, composed of Generals Knox, Hand, and Huntington, and the accomplished Captain Shaw, was appointed to arrange a plan; and, on the 13th of May, at the quarters of the Baron Steuben, in Fishkill, nearly opposite Newburgh, they reported a form which was adopted as the constitutional organization of the society. After referring to the war for independence, and the separation of the colonies from Great Britain, the objects of the society were stated in the following words:

"To perpetuate, therefore, as well the remembrance of this vast event, as the mutual friendships which have been formed under the pressure of common danger, and in many instances cemented by the blood of the parties, the officers of the American army do hereby, in the most solemn manner, associate, constitute, and combine themselves into one society of friends, to endure so long as they shall endure, or any of their eldest male posterity, and in failure thereof, the collateral branches, who may be judged worthy of becoming its supporters and members."

As the officers of the army were chiefly Americans, and were about to return to their citizenship, they appropriately named the society, in honor of the illustrious Roman, Lucius Quintius Cincinnatus, whose example they were about to imitate. They resolved that the following principles should form the basis of the society:

1. "An incessant attention to preserve inviolate those exalted rights and liberties of human nature for which they have fought and bled, and without which the high rank of a rational being is a curse instead of a blessing.

2. "An unalterable determination to promote and cherish, between the respective states, that unison and national honor so essentially necessary to their happiness and the future dignity of the American empire.

3. "To render permanent the cordial affection subsisting among the officers, this spirit will dictate brotherly kindness in all things, and particularly extend to the most substantial acts of beneficence, according to the ability of the society, toward those officers and their families who unfortunately may be under the necessity of receiving it."

For the sake of frequent communication, the association was divided into state societies, to meet annually on the 4th of July, or oftener if they should find it expedient. The society also adopted an *Order* by which its members should be known and distinguished. It is composed of a medal of gold with proper emblems, "suspended by a deep-blue ribbon two inches wide, edged with white, descriptive of the union of America with France."

A representation of the *Order*, full size, is seen in the engraving. The leaves of the olive branches are of gold and green enamel; the head and tail of the eagle gold and white enamel; and the sky in the centre device (which is a fac-simile of one of the medallions on the certificate of membership), is blue enamel.

The French officers who served in the continental army presented to Washington an elegant *Order*, studded with precious stones, about two hundred in number. The leaves of the olive branches and wreaths are composed of emeralds, the berries of ruby, and the beak of the eagle amethyst. Above the eagle is a group of military emblems—flags, drums, and cannon—surrounding a

ORDER OF THE CINCINNATI.

ribbon, upon which are inscribed the words: "PRESENTED, IN THE NAME OF THE FRENCH SOLDIERS, TO HIS EXCELLENCY THE GENERAL WASHINGTON." This also is studded with precious stones. Above it is a bow of *moire antique* ribbon, of light-blue color, with white edges. This jewel is at present [1881] in the possession of the Honorable Hamilton Fish, of New York, president of the Society of the Cincinnati.

ORDER PRESENTED BY FRENCH OFFICERS.

The Society had a certificate of membership engraved in France, by J. J. Le Veau, from a drawing by Aug. Le Belle. It occupies a space thirteen and a half inches in width and twenty inches in length, and was printed on fine vellum. The engraving upon the next page is a fac-simile on a reduced scale. The design represents American liberty as a strong man armed, bearing in one hand the Union flag, and in the other a naked sword. Beneath his feet are British flags, and a broken spear, shield, and chain. Hovering by his side is the eagle, our national emblem, from whose talons the lightning of destruction is flashing upon the British lion. Britannia, with the crown falling from her head, is hastening toward a boat to escape to a fleet, which denotes the departure of British

CINCINNATI SOCIETY—MEMBER'S CERTIFICATE

power from our shores. Upon a cloud, on the right, is an angel blowing a trumpet, from which flutters a loose scroll. Upon the scroll are the sentences: *Palam nuntiata libertas, A. D.* 1776. *Fœdus sociale cum Gallia, A. D.* 1778. *Pax: libertas parta, A. D.* 1783—"Independence declared, A. D. 1776. Treaty of alliance with France declared, A. D. 1778. Peace! independence obtained, A. D. 1783."

Upon the medallion on the right is a device representing Cincinnatus at his plow, a ship on the sea, and a walled town in the distance. Over his head is a flying angel, holding a ribbon inscribed: *Virtutis præmium;* "Reward of virtue." Below is a heart, with the words: *Esto perpetua;* "Be thou perpetual." Upon the rim is the legend: *Societas Cincinnatorum Instituta A. D. MDCCLXXXIII.;* "Society of the Cincinnati, instituted 1783." The device upon the medallion on the left is Cincinnatus, with his family, near his house. He is receiving a sword and shield from three senators: an army is seen in the distance. Upon the rim are the words: *Omnia relinqui tservare rempublicam;* "He abandons every thing to serve his country" (referring to Cincinnatus).

Washington was chosen the first president-general of the Society of the Cincinnati, and General Henry Knox the secretary. The former remained in office until his death, a period of sixteen years, and was succeeded by General Alexander Hamilton. All of the certificates given to the original members, like the one delineated in the engraving, were filled up and signed by Washington, at Mount Vernon.

We have observed that it was Christmas eve when Washington arrived at Mount Vernon from Annapolis, once more a private citizen. What a glad Christmas was that for all in that pleasant home on the banks of the Potomac! It was a Christmas to be specially remembered by the retired soldier. It was a day long hoped for by him when engaged in the mighty labors of his official station. Rest, rest he often sighed for, and now the elements seemed to sympathize in his great desire. An intensely severe winter closed almost every avenue to Mount Vernon, and even neighborly intercourse was suspended. Washington had rest in abundance. To Lafayette he wrote on the first of February following his retirement: "On the eve of Christmas I entered these doors an older man by near nine years, than when I left them. Since that period, we have been fast locked up in frost and snow, and excluded in a manner from all kinds of intercourse."

"I have not only retired from all public employments," he added, "but I am retiring within myself, and shall be able to view the solitary walks, and tread the paths of private life with heartfelt satisfaction. Envious of none, I am determined to be pleased with all; and this, my dear friend, being the order of my march, I will move gently down the stream of life, until I sleep with my fathers."

And yet, even in that perfect retirement, it was several weeks before Washington could entirely divest his mind of the burden of solicitude for public affairs. To General Knox he wrote on the 20th of February: "I am just beginning to experience that ease and freedom from public cares, which, however desirable, takes some time to realize; for strange as it may seem, it is nevertheless true, that it was not till lately I could get the better of my usual custom of ruminating, as soon as I waked in the morning, on the business of the ensuing day; and of my surprise at finding, after revolving many things in my mind, that I was no longer a public man, nor had any thing to do with public transactions.

"I feel now, however, as I conceive a wearied traveller must do, who, after treading many a painful step with a heavy burden on his shoulders, is eased of the latter, having reached the haven to which all the former were directed; and from his house-top is looking back, and tracing with an eager eye the meanders by which he escaped the quicksands and mires which lay in his way; and into which none but the all-powerful Guide and Dispenser of human events could have prevented his falling."

Never had a traveller more cause for serenity of mind and perfect gratitude, in the hour of calm retrospection, than George Washington at that time; and also twelve years later, when he resigned the helm of the vessel of state into other hands, and sought repose for the last time in the shades of Mount Vernon. And when he fully realized his relief, his social desires, so long repressed, came into full play, and renewals of old acquaintance and friendly correspondence took place. "Freed from the clangor of arms and the bustle of a camp," he wrote to the wife of Lafayette, in April, after receiving information that the marquis intended to visit America soon—"Freed from the cares of public employment and the responsibility of office, I am now enjoying domestic ease under the shadow of my own vine and my own fig-tree; and in a small villa, with the implements of husbandry and lambkins around me, I expect to glide gently down the stream of life, till I am entombed in the mansion of my fathers. * * * Come, then, let me entreat you, and call my cottage your home; for your own doors do not open to you with more readiness than mine would. You will see the plain manner in which we live, and meet with rustic civility; and you shall taste the simplicity of rural life. It will diversify the scene, and may give you a higher relish for the gaieties of the court, when you return to Versailles."

"My manner of living is plain," he wrote to a friend, "and I do not mean to be put out by it. A glass of wine and a bit of mutton are always ready, and such as will be content to partake of them are always welcome. Those who expect more will be disappointed."

But this modest dream of quietude and simplicity of life was not realized. Washington was the central figure of the group of great men who had laid the foundations of the republic. To him the eyes of the nation were speedily turned for counsel and action, for that republic and all its dependent interests were soon in peril. He was too great to remain an isolated citizen, and men of every degree, his own countrymen and strangers, were soon seen upon pilgrimages to Mount Vernon; and the little "villa" was too small to shelter in comfort the many guests that often assembled under its roof.

Washington now took a general survey of all his affairs, and turned his thoughts to the improvement of his farms, the enlargement of his mansion, and the adornment of the grounds around it. These improvements were commenced in the spring of 1784, and then the construction of the house, in its present form was resolved upon. The mansion built by Lawrence Washington, and called a "villa" by the general, was of the old gable-roofed style, with only four rooms upon each floor, as we have observed. It was about one-third the size of the present building, and in the alteration, it was made to occupy the central portion, the two ends having been built at the same time. The mansion, when completed by General Washington, (and as it now appears) was of the most substantial framework, two stories in height, ninety-six feet in length, thirty feet in depth, with a piazza fifteen feet in width, extending along the entire eastern or river front, supported by sixteen square columns, twenty-five feet in height. Over this piazza is a balustrade of a light and pleasing design; and in the centre of the roof is an observatory with a small spire. There are seven dormer windows in the roof, three on the eastern side, one on each end, and two on the western or lawn side.

The ground floor of the house contains six rooms, with a spacious passage in the centre of the building, extending through it from east to west. From it a massive staircase ascends to the chambers. The rooms and the passage are all wainscoted, and have large worked cornices; and they present to the eye the appearance of great solidity. On the south side of the passage is a parlor, and the library and breakfast-room of Washington, from which a narrow staircase ascends to his private study on the second floor. On the north side of the passage are a reception-room and parlor, and a large drawing-room, in which, when there was much company, the guests were sometimes entertained at table. These apartments and their present appearance and uses we will consider elsewhere.

Near the mansion, a substantial kitchen on one side, and store-room and laundry on the other, were built, and these were connected with the dwelling by very neat open colonnades, each with roof and pavement; and, at a little distance from them, two other strong buildings were erected for house-

WESTERN FRONT OF MOUNT VERNON, AS IT APPEARED IN 1875.

servants' quarters. The mansion, the kitchen and store-house, with the connecting colonnades, and the servants' quarters, all remain, and exhibit the same external appearance which they bore when Washington left them. These may be best seen from the lawn that spreads out before the western front of the mansion, which is first approached by visitors in carriages, there being no road for horses upon the grounds before the river-front.

In the prosecution of these improvements Washington was his own architect, and drew every plan and specification for the workmen with his own hand. Every measurement was calculated and indicated with exactness; and in every arrangement for his home, he appears to have made *convenience* and *durability* the prime objects of his care. The following letter to Mr. William Rumney, of Alexandria (who had been an aide to General Charles Lee at one time during the Revolution), will give an idea of the carefulness and forethought of Washington in the management of his affairs. Mr. Rumney was then about to leave for England:

"General Washington presents his compliments to Mr. Rumney—would esteem it as a particular favor if Mr. Rumney would make the following enquiries as soon as convenient after his arrival in England, and communicate the result of them by the Packet, or any other safe and expeditious conveyance to this country.

"1st. The terms upon which the best kind of Whitehaven flag-stone—black and white in equal quantities—could be delivered at the Port of Alexandria, by the superficial foot,—workmanship, freight, and every other incidental charge included. The stone to be $2\frac{1}{2}$ Inches, or thereabouts, thick; and exactly a foot square—each kind. To have a rich polished face, and good joints so as that a neat floor may be made therewith.

"2nd. Upon what terms the common Irish Marble (black and white if to be had)—same dimensions, could be delivered as above.

"3rd. As the General has been informed of a very cheap kind of Marble, good in quality, at or in the neighborhood of Ostend, he would thank Mr. Rumney, if it should fall in his way, to institute an enquiry into this also.

"On the Report of Mr. Rumney, the General will take his

ultimate determination; for which reason he prays him to be precise and exact. The Piazza or Colonnade, for which this is wanted as a floor, is ninety-two feet eight inches, by twelve feet eight inches within the margin, or border that surrounds it. Over and above the quantity here mentioned, if the above Flags are cheap—or a cheaper kind of hard Stone could be had, he would get as much as would lay floors in the Circular Colonnades, or covered ways at the wings of the House—each of which at the outer curve, is 38 feet in length by 7 feet 2 Inches in breadth, within the margin or border as aforesaid.

"The General being in want of a House Joiner & Bricklayer who understand their respective trades perfectly, would thank Mr. Rumney for enquiring into the terms upon which such workmen might be engaged for two or three years (the time of service to commence upon the ship's arrival at Alexandria); a shorter term than two years would not answer, because foreigners generally have a seasoning, which with other interruptions too frequently waste the greater part of the first year —more to the disadvantage of the employer than the Employed.—Bed, board & Tools to be found by the former, clothing by the latter.

"If two men of the above Trades and of orderly and quiet deportment could be obtained for twenty-five or even thirty pounds sterling per annum each (estimating the dollar at 4s. 6d.), the General, rather than sustain the loss of Time necessary for communication would be obliged to Mr. Rumney for entering into proper obligatory articles of agreement on his behalf with them and sending them by the first vessel bound to this Port. "GEO. WASHINGTON.

"MOUNT VERNON, *July* 5, 1784."

The pavement-stone procured through Mr. Rumney, in accordance with the foregoing order, still exists beneath the grand piazza and the colonnades, but in a dilapidated state. Many of the blocks are gone, others are broken, and all show abrasion by footsteps and the elements. Many of the carpenter's tools, imported from England at that time by Washington, for the use of his workmen, are preserved.

Washington was very fond of planting trees and shrubbery; and his diaries show that he was much engaged in that business in 1784 and 1785. He went to the woods almost every day to select and mark young trees for transplanting to the grounds around the mansion, and he generally superintended their removal.

In the rear of the mansion, Washington laid out a fine lawn, upon a level surface, which comprises about

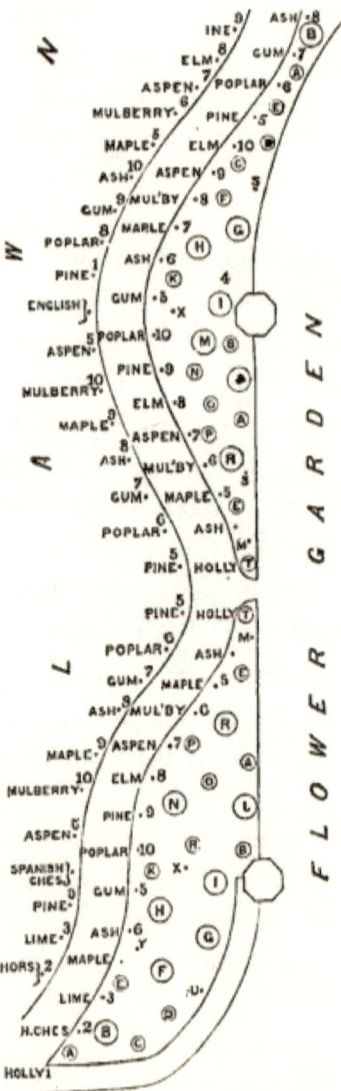

SECTION OF SHADED CARRIAGE-WAY.

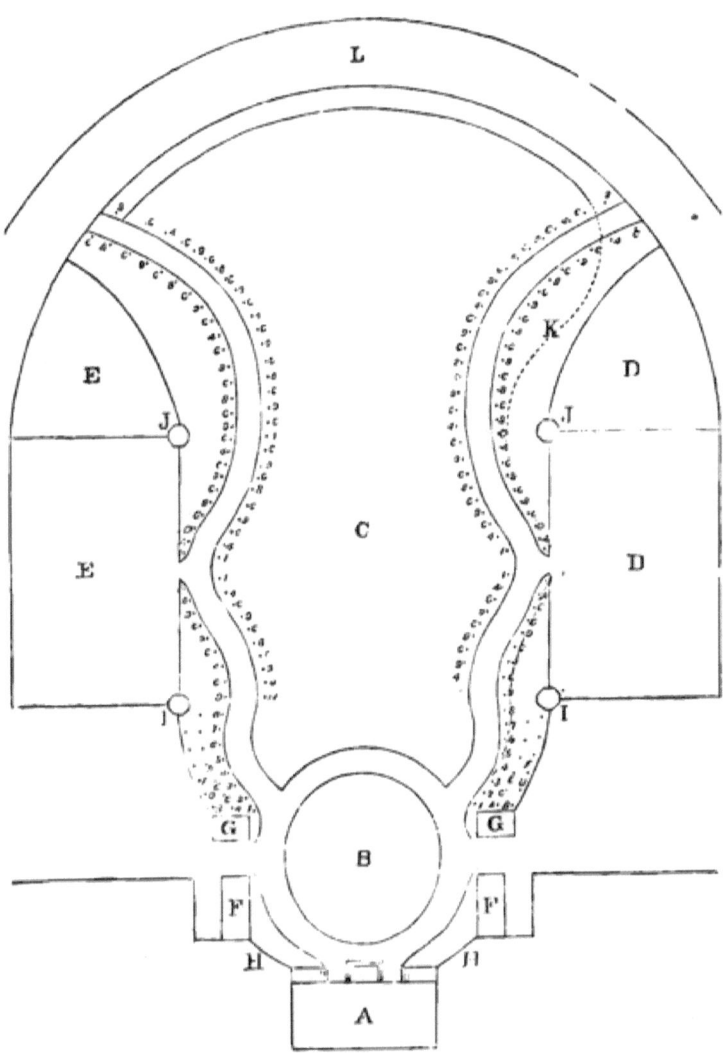

GENERAL PLAN OF THE MANSION AND GROUNDS AT MOUNT VERNON.

A The Mansion.
B Oval Grass-plot.
C The Lawn.
D D Flower-garden.
E E Vegetable Garden.
F F Kitchen and Laundry.
G G House-servants' Quarters.
H H Circular Colonnades.
I I Water closets.
J J Seed-houses.
K Carriage-way as finally laid out.
L Outside Road.

twenty acres. Around it he made a serpentine carriage-way; and he planted a great variety of shade trees upon each side of it. Upon one side of the lawn he formed a spacious flower-garden, and upon the other an equally spacious vegetable garden, and these were planted with the greatest care, according to the minute directions of the master. I have before me the original plan of these grounds, made by Washington's own hands. It is very carefully drawn. The exact position and the name of every tree to be planted, are laid down. With it is a section-drawing, on a larger scale, showing the proposed carriage-way around the lawn, the names of a large number of trees that were to adorn it, and the places of others indicated by letters and numerals, which are explained by a memorandum. Directly before the western front an oval grass-plot was designed, with a dial-post in the centre, and a carriage-way around it.

The lawn, the oval grass-plot, and the gardens were laid out according to the plan drawn by Washington, and remain unchanged in form. Quite a large number of trees, planted along the margins of the carriage-way, at that time, are yet there, and are noble specimens of their kind. Many others have decayed and passed away; and, in some instances, quite large trees now stand where others were planted by the hand of Washington three-quarters of a century ago.

In each garden Washington erected small houses, of octagonal form, for the storage of seeds and implements of horticulture. These are yet standing. The lower portion of each is of brick, and the remainder of plank, wrought so as to resemble blocks of stone. These garden-houses, and water-closets of similar form and dimensions, standing on the borders of the garden near the mansion, are now [1859] fallen into

GARDEN-HOUSE.

almost hopeless decay. The massive brick walls around both gardens remain in perfect preservation.

On the north side of the flower-garden Washington erected quite an extensive conservatory for plants, into which he collected many rare exotics. Some of them were presented to him as testimonials of esteem, and others were purchased at the garden of John Bartram, near Philadelphia. Bartram was a member of the Society of Friends, and an eminent botanist. He had died during the Revolution, leaving his business in the able hands of his son William, who, in 1791, published a most interesting account of his botanical explorations through the Southern states of our Union.

A few tropical plants found their way to the Potomac occasionally, upon vessels from the West Indies. Among the latter, on one occasion, were some fine lemon-trees of large

CENTURY PLANT AND LEMON-TREE.

growth, and from them Washington selected two or three. Others were propagated from these by cuttings, until, at the time of his death, they had become quite a grove in one end of the conservatory. Only one of these remained twenty years ago. It was standing in the flower-garden when I was there in 1858, by the side of a fine century-plant, which was sent to Washington by a gentleman at Porto Rico, in 1798. The tree was about fifteen feet in height; and, though bearing fruit in abundance, showed signs of decay.

At the junction of two of the principal avenues in the

VIEW IN THE FLOWER-GARDEN AT MOUNT VERNON—THE SAGO PALM.

flower-garden, I saw one other plant—and only one—that had experienced the fostering care of Washington. It was a Sago Palm, an East India production, from which is obtained the article of domestic use known as pearl sago, a species of fecula or starch. It stood in a large tub in which flowers were blooming; and its tufted leaves, like immense feathers, growing from the heavy stem seven feet from the ground, were fresh and beautiful.

The *Lemon Tree,* the *Century Plant,* and the *Sago Palm,* are all that remain of the movable plants which belonged to Washington, and were taken from the green-house when it was destroyed by fire in December, 1835, the same night when the destructive element consumed more than five hundred buildings and other property valued at more than twenty millions of dollars, in the city of New York. The fire originated in a defective flue connected with the conservatory, and

RUINS OF THE CONSERVATORY AT MOUNT VERNON.

that building, with the servants' quarters adjoining it, was laid in ashes in the course of a few hours. What plants were saved from the flames were mostly destroyed by the frost, for it was one of the coldest nights on record.

The conservatory was never rebuilt nor the ruins removed. These, soon overgrown with vines and shrubs, formed a picturesque garden wall, but lost some of their attractiveness to the eye of taste, by the presence of two tall, perpendicular chimneys, which were seen above the shrubbery from every point of view in the garden. These broken walls, too, struck the visitor unpleasantly. They were at the modern carriage entrance to Mount Vernon, and were the first objects associated with Washington that met the eye on approaching the mansion from the public road.

ICE HOUSE AT MOUNT VERNON.

Eastward of the flower-garden, and on the opposite side of the chief entrance to Mount Vernon, Washington constructed an ice-house, after his retirement from public life, at the close of his presidency. It was something new in Virginia; indeed, ice-houses were not in very common use elsewhere at that time. It was well preserved a few years ago, and was finely shaded by tall trees, which formed a beautiful grove on the north side of the mansion.

Previous to the erection of this ice-house, Washington had used, for the purpose of keeping meat, butter, and vegetables cool in summer, a large dry-well at the south-east corner of the lawn in front of the mansion, just on the brink of the high precipitous bank of the river. Into this a descent was made by a flight of steps, and over it he erected an elegant summer-house, with a spire and iron vane in the form of a crescent. The well and a summer-house are there, but the latter is not the original built by Washington. When I last visited the

SUMMER HOUSE AT MOUNT VERNON.

spot, the staircase leading up to the summer-house was nearly rotted away, and a part of the wall of the well had fallen in. There was some danger in climbing over this chasm, on the feeble steps. There was a fine view of the Potomac from the summer-house, and from it the sketch of the mansion which appears as a frontispiece of this book, was made. The summer-house has been rebuilt in the original form.

I have before me a manuscript memorandum from the hand of Washington, in which he notes, in minute detail, the distances and directions in feet and inches, and by points of compass, of various objects, such as the garden-houses, the dial-post, and the dry-well, from the "front door of the mansion." It is interesting, as showing the extreme minuteness and accuracy with which Washington kept a record of all his operations, and would serve those who might wish to restore Mount Vernon to its original form and perfection, as an indicator of points now lost through neglect and decay.

During the spring and summer of 1784, visitors flocked to Mount Vernon in great numbers. Many of the companions in arms of the beloved chief, of all grades, from general officers to private soldiers, went there to pay their respects, and enjoy once again sweet intercourse with him under whom they had always delighted to serve.

At length one came who was specially a man after Washington's own heart—a young man whom he loved as a son or a younger brother. He had been a friend to the Americans in their struggle for freedom, and was a friend of mankind. That visitor was the Marquis de Lafayette, a distinguished scion of an ancient noble family, who, in the summer of 1776, while at the table of the commandant of Mentz, in Germany, with other French officers, heard the Duke of Gloucester, brother to the King of England, speak of the Declaration of Independence just put forth by the Anglo-American colonies, and of the strong measures adopted by the British ministry to crush the rising rebellion. The marquis was then just past eighteen years of age, slender in form, and a boy in personal appearance. But the heart of a patriot and hero beat beneath his coat of green, and his imagination and zeal were tired by the recital of the story of a people fighting for liberty. He returned to Paris full of high resolves, and leaving there an equally enthusiastic and a cheerfully consenting young wife —the rich and beautiful daughter of the Duke de Noailles— he came to America, volunteered to fight in the cause of colonial emancipation, and, throughout the war, performed services in the field here, and at the court of France, of inestimable benefit to the country. Life, youth, fortune, the endearments of home, were all freely devoted to the cause, and he made the aspirations of the Americans emphatically his own, with an enthusiasm that scorned all obstacles. "It is fortunate for the king," said the old Count Maurepas, "that Lafayette does not take it into his head to strip Versailles of its furniture to send to his dear Americans, as his majesty would be unable to refuse it."

Washington, governed by his intuitive perception of character, which never deceived him, took Lafayette to his bosom on his first arrival at Philadelphia, in 1777; and from that hour until death severed the bond, they were friends of truest character. And now, the intelligence that this dear friend was about to visit him in his quiet home at Mount Vernon gave Washington a most exquisite pleasure. The portrait of the marquis, painted by Charles Willson Peale, in 1778, was then hanging upon the wall of his parlor: it afterwards occupied a place among the works of art at Arlington House.

Lafayette arrived at New York on the 4th of August, 1784, after a passage of thirty-four days from France. There he received the congratulations of the citizens for a few days, and then hastened toward Mount Vernon. He was detained in Philadelphia two or three days, and there wrote as follows:

"PHILADELPHIA, *Tuesday Evening.*

"MY DEAR GENERAL:—I have already had the pleasure to acquaint you with my arrival in America, and am endeavoring to reach Mount Vernon as soon as possible. My first plan was only to stay here two days, but the affectionate reception I have met with in this city, and the returning some compliments to the Assembly, render it necessary for me to stay one day longer. On Friday I will be at the head of Elk, the next day at Baltimore, and by Sunday or Monday I hope at last to be blessed with a sight of my dear General. There is no rest for me until I go to Mount Vernon. I long for the pleasure to embrace you, my dear General, and the happiness of being once more with you will be so great that no words can ever express it. In a few days I will be at Mount Vernon, and I do already feel delighted with so charming a prospect. My best respects wait upon Mrs. Washington, and not long after you receive this I shall tell you myself how respectfully and affectionately I have the honor to be, my dear General,

"Your most obedient, humble servant,

"LAFAYETTE.

"In case your affairs call you to the Springs, I beg leave either to go there after you, or to accompany you in your journey."

Lafayette arrived at Mount Vernon on the 17th, and remained twelve days in the enjoyment of the most sincere friendship and genuine hospitality. During that time Mount Vernon was crowded with other guests, who came to meet the great benefactor of America; and when he departed for Balti-

LAFAYETTE—PAINTED BY C. W. PEALE, IN 1778.

more, quite a cavalcade of gentlemen accompanied him far on his way.

There was a bond of union, of peculiar strength, between Washington and Lafayette other than that of mere personal friendship. They were members of the fraternity of Free and Accepted Masons, and both loved the mystic brotherhood sincerely. Madame Lafayette was deeply interested in every thing that engaged the attention of her husband; and she had learned to reverence Washington with a feeling closely allied to that of devotion. She had corresponded with him, and received from him cordial invitations to the simple delights of rural life at Mount Vernon. She had, no doubt, earnestly desired to present some visible testimonial of her regard to the great patriot of the New World; and when her husband resolved to visit him in his retirement at Mount Vernon, she prepared, with her own hands, an apron of white satin, upon

MASONIC APRON, WROUGHT BY MADAME THE MARCHIONESS LAFAYETTE.

which she wrought, in needlework, the various emblems of the Masonic order. This apron Lafayette brought with him, and presented to his distinguished brother at Mount Vernon. It was kept by Washington as a cherished memorial of a noble woman; and, after his death, his legatees formally presented it to the Washington Benevolent Society of Philadelphia, in the following words:

"TO THE WASHINGTON BENEVOLENT SOCIETY.

"The legatees of General Washington, impressed with the most profound sentiments of respect for the noble institution which they have the honor to address, beg leave to present to them the enclosed relic of the revered and lamented Father of his Country. They are persuaded that the apron, which was once possessed by the man whom Philadelphians always delighted to honor, will be considered most precious to the society distinguished by his name, and by the benevolent and grateful feelings to which it owes its foundation. That this perishable memento of a hero, whose fame is more durable than brass, may confer as much pleasure upon those to whom it is presented as is experienced by the donors, is the sincere wish of the legatees.

"*October 26th*, 1816."

When the society to which this apron was presented was dissolved, the precious memento of Washington and his fair friend was presented to the Grand Lodge of Pennsylvania, and now occupies a conspicuous place upon the walls of the Grand Master's room in Masonic Hall, Philadelphia, carefully preserved under glass, in a frame.

More than two years previous to the visit of Lafayette, Washington received from the late Elkanah Watson, and his business partner, M. Cossoul, several Masonic ornaments, accompanied by the following letter:

"To his Excellency, General Washington, America.

'*Most Illustrious and Respected Brother:*

"In the moment when all Europe admire and feel the effects of your glorious efforts in support of American liberty, we hasten to offer for your acceptance a small pledge of our homage. Zealous lovers of liberty and its institutions, we have experienced the most refined joy in seeing our chief and brother stand forth in defence of a new-born nation of republicans.

"Your glorious career will not be confined to the protection of American liberty, but its ultimate effect will extend to the whole human family, since Providence has evidently selected you as an instrument in His hands to fulfil His eternal decrees.

"It is to you, therefore, the glorious orb of America, we presume to offer Masonic ornaments, as an emblem of your virtues. May the Grand Architect of the universe be the guardian of your precious days, for the glory of the western hemisphere and the entire universe. Such are the vows of those who have the favor to be by all the known numbers,

"Your affectionate brothers,

"Watson & Cossoul.

"East of Nantes, 23*d* 1*st Month*, 5782."

Washington replied as follows, from his head-quarters at Newburgh:

"State of New York, *August* 10*th*, 1782.

"Gentlemen:—The Masonic ornaments which accompanied your brotherly address of the 23d of January last, though elegant in themselves, were rendered more valuable by the flattering sentiments and affectionate manner in which they were presented.

"If my endeavors to avert the evil with which the country was threatened, by a deliberate plan of tyranny, should be crowned with the success that is wished, the praise is due to the Grand Architect of the universe, who did not see fit to suffer His superstructure of justice to be subjected to the ambition of the princes of this world, or to the rod of oppression in the hands of any power upon earth.

"For your affectionate vows permit me to be grateful, and offer mine for true brothers in all parts of the world, and to assure you of the sincerity with which I am,

"Yours,

"GEO. WASHINGTON.

"Messrs. WATSON & COSSOUL, East of Nantes."

Watson says, in relation to this gift: "Wishing to pay some mark of respect to our beloved Washington, I employed, in conjunction with my friend M. Cossoul, nuns in one of the convents at Nantes, to prepare some elegant Masonic ornaments, and gave them a plan for combining the American and French flags on the apron designed for his use." They were executed in a superior and expensive style, being wrought in gold and silver tissue.

This regalia was sent by Washington to Mount Vernon, and was afterward worn by him when he met his brethren in the lodge at Alexandria. The apron and collar are now in possession of Washington Lodge, Alexandria, to which they were presented by the late George Washington Parke Custis.

The reverence which was felt for the person of Washington by individuals was expressed by public bodies, even, as in the example just given, before the close of the struggle which he conducted so nobly. The National Congress took the initiative in voting him honors, such as the senate of old Rome was wont to decree for their heroes and sages. That body was in session at Princeton, in the summer of 1783, when arrangements for the consummation of the declared peace with Great Britain was in progress, and Washington, having been requested to make his head-quarters near, took post at Rocky Hill, a few miles off. Before his arrival, the Congress, on the 7th of August,

"*Resolved* (unanimously, ten states being present), That an equestrian statue of General Washington be erected at the place where the residence of Congress shall be established;" and appointed Arthur Lee, Oliver Ellsworth, and Thomas Mifflin, a committee to propose a plan for the same.

The committee recommended a statue of bronze, the general to be represented in a Roman dress, holding a truncheon in his right hand, and his head encircled with a laurel wreath. The statue was to be supported by a marble pedestal, on which were to be represented—the evacuation of Boston, the capture of the Hessians at Trenton, the battle of Princeton, the action of Monmouth, and the surrender of York. On the upper part of the pedestal was to be the following inscription:

"The United States, in Congress assembled, ordered this statue to be erected in the year of our Lord, 1783, in honor of GEORGE WASHINGTON, the illustrious commander-in-chief of the armies of the United States of America. during the war which vindicated and secured their liberty, sovereignty, and independence."

It was resolved that this statue should be executed by the best artist in Europe, under the superintendence of the minister of the United States at Versailles (Doctor Franklin), at the expense of the government, and that Congress should transmit to the minister the best likeness of Washington that could be procured.

A few months after the passage of these resolutions, two young artists arrived at Rocky Hill. These were Joseph Wright and William Dunlap. The former bore a letter from Dr. Franklin to Washington, and he was permitted to paint the portraits of the general and his wife. Dunlap, then a mere lad, also painted a portrait of the chief.

Young Wright was a son of Mrs. Patience Wright, who had then acquired much eminence in Europe and America for her models in wax of living men, and he inherited some of his mother's peculiar faculty. Some members of the Congress, aware of this, conceived the idea of having him make a plaster cast from the face of Washington, to be sent to Europe for the use of the sculptor who should execute the bronze statue. It was proposed, and Washington consented to submit to the unpleasant operation of lying upon his back and having the wet plaster laid upon his face. What a spectacle did the great Republican leader present at that moment!

The operation was a most disagreeable one, for the manipulator was inexperienced and unskilful. He was very anxious too, to relieve Washington from his position, and, in his haste and trepidation, an accident occurred which made his labor fruitless. After the plaster had sufficiently hardened, the artist proceeded, as quickly as possible, to remove it, when he let it fall upon the floor, and it was dashed in pieces. The desires of Congress, strongly expressed, to have another trial, were of no avail. Washington would not consent, and the statue voted by that body was never made.

Young Wright appears to have been unfortunate in his efforts to acquire fame and fortune in connection with the likeness of Washington. He afterward cut a die for a medallion profile of the chief, which was declared by all to be an exceedingly faithful picture. After striking a few impressions the die was broken, and the artist's labor was lost. An engraving on copper, of larger size, was afterward made from one of these impressions. A broadside edition of Washington's Farewell Address, printed in 1796, in possession of the writer, is embellished with an impression from that engraving.

When Washington had become a private citizen—a plain farmer on the banks of the Potomac—neither desiring nor expecting further public employment, the hearts of his countrymen, beating warmly with gratitude for his services, yearned to honor him with some testimonial of their profound regard. Virginia, his native state, proud to own him as her son, took the lead in the manifestation of this sentiment. On the 22d of June, 1784, the legislature of Virginia—

"*Resolved*, That the Executive be requested to take measures for procuring a statue of General Washington, to be of the finest marble and best workmanship, with the following inscription on its pedestal:

"'The General Assembly of the Commonwealth of Virginia have caused this Statue to be erected as a Monument of Affection and Gratitude to GEORGE WASHINGTON, who, uniting to the Endowments of the Hero the Virtues of the Patriot, and exerting both in establishing the Liberties of his Country, has rendered his Name dear to his Fellow Citizens, and given the World an immortal Example of true Glory.'"

This inscription was written by James Madison. On the day when this resolution was adopted, the General Assembly also voted an address to General Washington, and a joint committee of the two houses was appointed to prepare one and present it. The committee, with Mr. Madison at the head, waited upon Washington, at Mount Vernon, a few days afterward, presented the address, and received the following reply:

"GENTLEMEN:—With feelings which are more easy to be conceived than expressed, I meet and reciprocate the congratulations of the representatives of this commonwealth on the final establishment of peace.

"Nothing can add more to the pleasure which arises from a conscious discharge of public trust, than the approbation of one's country. To have been so happy, under a vicissitude of fortune, amidst the difficult and trying scenes of an arduous conflict, as to meet this, is, in my mind, to have attained the highest honor; and the consideration of it, in my present peaceful retirement, will heighten all my domestic joys, and constitute my greatest felicity.

"I should have been truly wanting in duty, and must have frustrated the great and important object for which we resorted to arms, if, seduced by a temporary regard for fame, I had suffered the paltry love of it to interfere with my country's welfare; the interest of which was the only inducement which carried me into the field, or permitted the sacred rights of civil authority, though but for a moment, to be violated and infringed by a power meant originally to rescue and confirm them.

"For those rewards and blessings which you have invoked for me in this world, and for the fruition of that happiness which you pray for in that which is to come, you have, gentlemen, all my thanks and all my gratitude. I wish I could insure them to you, and the state you represent, a hundredfold."

Benjamin Harrison was governor of Virginia when the General Assembly requested the executive to take measures for procuring a statue of Washington; and a little more than a month after the date of that resolution, he wrote to Doctor Franklin and Mr. Jefferson, then in Paris, on the subject, requesting them to attend to the matter, and acquainting them that he had ordered Mr. Peale to send them a full-length portrait of the general, to be used as a model for the sculptor.

The only method by which a perfect likeness of the great patriot might be secured, was to have the artist make a model from the living face; and Messrs. Franklin and Jefferson accordingly engaged Houdon, a portrait sculptor, then without a rival in the world, to go to America for the purpose. Houdon was a small, active, and exceedingly industrious Frenchman; careful and prudent, and disposed to make an excellent bargain for himself. "The terms," Mr. Jefferson wrote, "are twenty-five thousand livres [about $4,620], one thousand English guineas (the English guinea being worth twenty-five livres), for the statue and pedestal. Besides this, we pay his expenses going and returning, which we expect will be between four and five thousand livres; and if he dies on the voyage, we pay his family ten thousand livres. This latter proposition was disagreeable to us; but he has a father, mother, and sisters, who have no resource but in his labor; and he is himself one of the best men in the world." To insure the state against loss in case of his death, Mr. Jefferson, through Mr. Adams, procured an insurance upon Houdon's life, in London, at an additional expense of five hundred livres, or about ninety-two dollars.

It was more than a year after the order for the statue was given before Houdon arrived. He came over in the same vessel that brought Doctor Franklin home. On the 20th of September, 1785, the Doctor gave Houdon a letter of introduction to Washington, and, at the same time, he wrote to the general to apprise him of the sculptor's arrival. Washington immediately wrote to Houdon, saying, "It will give me pleasure, sir, to welcome you to this seat of my retirement; and whatever I have or can procure that is necessary to your purposes, or convenient and agreeable to your wishes, you must freely command, as inclination to oblige you will be among the last things in which I shall be deficient, either on your arrival or during your stay."

Houdon arrived at Mount Vernon on the 3d of October, furnished with all necessary materials for making a bust of Washington. He remained there a fortnight, and made, on the living face of our illustrious Friend, a plaster mould, preparatory for the clay impression, which was then modelled into the form of a bust, and immediately, before it could shrink from drying, moulded and cast in plaster, to be afterward copied in marble, in Paris. That clay model was left at

HOUDON'S BUST OF WASHINGTON.

Mount Vernon, where it may be seen upon a bracket in the library, white-washed, so as to resemble marble or plaster of Paris.

In the presence of Mr. Madison, Houdon made exact measurements of the person of Washington, and with ample memoranda concerning costume, et cetera, he returned to France. The statue was not completed until 1789, when to the inscription upon the pedestal were added the words: "Done in the year of Christ one thousand seven hundred and eighty-eight, and in the year of the commonwealth, twelve."

Houdon's statue stands in the rotunda of the capitol at Richmond. It is of fine Italian marble, size of life. The costume is the military dress of the Revolution. The right

HOUDON'S STATUE OF WASHINGTON

hand of the general rests upon a staff; the left is upon the folds of a military cloak thrown over the end of a bundle of fasces, with which are connected a sword and plough. Gouverneur Morris, who was in Paris when the statue was executed, stood as a model for the person of Washington. "Of what use," says Dunlap, "his person could be to the artist I cannot conceive, as there was no likeness, in form or manner, between him and the hero, except that they were both tall men." Yet such was the fact. Morris, in his diary, under date of "June 5, 1789," says: "Go to M. Houdon's. He's been waiting for me a long time. I stand for his statue of General Washington, being the humble employment of a manikin. This is literally taking the advice of St. Paul, to be all things to all men."

The foregoing facts are presented in contrast with the creations of fancy which a Virginia orator put forth as the forms of real history, in the following words: "Houdon, after taking a mould of Washington's face, persisted to make a cast of his entire person. * * * * The hero and the sage—the man of supreme dignity, of spotless purity and the most veiled modesty, laid his sacred person bare and prone before the eyes of art and affection! * * * * The cast of the body was left to the care of his workmen, but that of the head was reserved in his own hands." All this is utterly untrue. The workmen of Houdon, it is known, never joined him, and no such scene as above described ever occurred at Mount Vernon.

Six months before Houdon's arrival at Mount Vernon, another artist was domiciled there. It was Robert Edge Pine, a very small, morbidly irritable Englishman, who came to America in 1784, with the rare reputation of "king's painter," and with the lofty design of procuring portraits of the most distinguished men of the Revolution, as materials for a series of historical paintings of the war then just ended. His wife and daughters, who came with him, were as diminutive as himself, and the family appeared almost like pigmies.

Pine had been a student of art under Sir Joshua Reynolds. He was highly esteemed by that artist, and was popular with a large number of influential men in England. He brought letters of introduction to Francis Hopkinson, of Philadelphia; and the first portrait that he painted after his arrival in this country, was of that gentleman. It was finished early in 1785, and was first well engraved by Longacre, and published in the *American Portrait Gallery*. Robert Morris also patronized him, and built a studio for him in Eighth street, in Philadelphia.

Pine's republican proclivities made him unpopular with the ministerial party at home, and gave him corresponding sympathy in America. He found constant employment for his pencil in Philadelphia, Baltimore, Annapolis, and in several places in Virginia. He went to Mount Vernon in May, 1785, with a letter of introduction to Washington from Francis Hopkinson, in which the chief was requested to give the painter sittings, in furtherance of his grand design of composing scenes of the War for Independence. He was cordially received, and remained there three weeks. During that time Washington wrote as follows to Mr. Hopkinson, dated at Mount Vernon, May 16, 1785:

"DEAR SIR: 'In for a penny in for a pound,' is an old adage. I am so hackneyed to the touches of the painter's pencil, that I am now altogether at their beck, and sit, like

Patience on a monument, whilst they are delineating the lines of my face.

"It is a proof among many others of what habit and custom can effect. At first I was as impatient at the request, and as restive under the operation, as a colt is of the saddle. The next time I submitted very reluctantly, but with less flouncing. Now no dray moves more readily to the thill than I do to the painter's chair. It may easily be conceived, therefore, that I yielded a ready obedience to your request, and to the views of Mr. Pine.

"Letters from England, recommendatory of this gentleman, came to my hand previous to his arrival in America, not only as an artist of acknowledged eminence, but as one who had discovered a friendly disposition toward this country, for which it seems he had been marked."

While at Mount Vernon Pine painted the portraits of two of Mrs. Washington's grandchildren. These were Elizabeth Parke Custis, then about nine years of age, who afterward married Mr. Law, a wealthy English gentleman; and George Washington Parke Custis, the last survivor of his family, who died at Arlington House, on the Potomac, in the autumn of 1857. The pictures are exquisitely painted, and, like all of Pine's productions, the colors retain their original vividness.

Elizabeth is represented as a beautiful girl, with rich brown hair lying in careless curls, and in great profusion, upon her head and neck, her bosom covered with very light drapery, and having lying upon it the miniature of her father, John Parke Custis (printed on page 84 of this volume), suspended by a ribbon around her neck

ELIZABETH PARKE CUSTIS.

The brother was then between four and five years of age. He is represented as a fair-haired child, with loose summer garments, and carrying in his hand a branch with two or three leaves upon it. These pictures occupied a conspicuous place upon the walls of the drawing-room at Arlington House.

Pine's grand design was never carried out. He died four or five years after his visit to Mount Vernon, and his family returned to England. The portraits which he had painted were sold and scattered. That of Washington was afterward found in Montreal, and purchased by the late Henry Brevoort, of Bedford, Long Island, and is now in possession of his son, J. Carson Brevoort.

G. W. P. CUSTIS WHEN A CHILD.

A few weeks after Pine left Mount Vernon, and while the plasterers were at work ornamenting the ceiling of the great drawing-room of the mansion, then just completed, there was an arrival at the home of Washington of an extraordinary character. It was a pack of French hounds, sent to him by Lafayette. On the 1st of September Washington wrote to the marquis, saying: "The hounds which you were so obliging as to send, arrived safe, and are of promising appearance. To Monsieur le Comte Doilliamson (if I miscall him, your handwriting is to blame, and in honor you are bound to rectify the error), and in an especial manner to his fair Comtesse, my thanks are due for this favor. The enclosed letter, which I give you the trouble of forwarding, contains my acknowledgment of their obliging attention to me on this occasion."

While Washington thanked Lafayette and his friends for their kindly offices, he certainly did not feel specially thankful for the hounds. During the war, his hunting establishment, which had been perfect, had been almost broken up, and he felt no disposition to renew it. His kennel, which was situated very near the site of the present tomb of Washington, was quite dilapidated; and the paling which enclosed it and a fine spring of water, had almost disappeared. Vulcan and Truelove, Ringwood and Sweetlips, Singer and Forester, Music and Rockwood—hounds of note on the master's register when he left Mount Vernon for the senate—were missing or were too old for service when he returned, and for only about three years afterward did he keep any hounds at all. Those sent by Lafayette were of great size and strength. Because of their fierce disposition they were kept closely confined; and, a few months after their arrival, Washington broke up his kennel, gave away his hounds, bade adieu to the chase forever, and, for his amusement, formed a fine deer-park below the mansion, upon a beautiful slope extending to the river.

The late Mr. Custis has left on record the following anecdote: "Of the French hounds, there was one named *Vulcan*, and we bear him the better in reminiscence, from having often bestrid his ample back in the days of our juvenility. It happened that upon a large company sitting down to dinner at Mount Vernon one day, the lady of the mansion (my grandmother) discovered that the ham, the pride of every Virginia housewife's table, was missing from its accustomed post of honor. Upon questioning Frank, the butler, this portly, and at the same time the most polite and accomplished of all butlers, observed that a ham, yes, a very fine ham, had been prepared, agreeably to the Madam's orders, but lo and behold! who should come into the kitchen, while the savory ham was smoking in its dish, but old *Vulcan* the hound, and without more ado fastened his fangs into it; and although they of the kitchen had stood to such arms as they could get, and had fought the old spoiler desperately, yet *Vulcan* had finally triumphed, and bore off the prize, aye, 'cleanly, under the keeper's nose.' The lady by no means relished the loss of a dish which formed the pride of her table, and uttered some remarks by no means favorable to old *Vulcan*, or indeed to dogs in general; while the Chief, having heard the story, communicated it to his guests, and, with them, laughed heartily at the exploit of the *stag-hound*."

Almost simultaneously with the arrival of the French hounds, came a magnificent present from Samuel Vaughan, a wealthy resident of London, who had conceived a passionate admiration for the character of Washington. The object presented was a very beautiful chimney-piece, wrought in Italy, from the finest white and Sienite marbles, for Mr. Vaughan's own use. At the time of its arrival in England that gentleman was informed of the improvements in the mansion then in progress at Mount Vernon, and, without unpacking it, he sent it directly to Washington. It is exquisitely wrought in every part. Upon three tablets of the frieze, under the highly ornamented mantel, are sculptured, in very high relief, in white marble, pleasant domestic scenes in agricultural life. Upon the centre tablet, which is the largest, is an evening scene. A husbandman, with his wife and little child, is returning from the

ITALIAN CHIMNEY-PIECE.

fields, driving a cow and a flock of sheep. Many of the latter are seen going into a fold for the night, and beyond the enclosure is seen the setting sun. On the left of the central tablet is represented a boy, harnessing a span of horses, to be attached to a plough. On the right is a cottage. The housewife, having just drawn a bucket of water from the well, is pouring it into a tub for the cleansing of vegetables, which are seen lying by the side of it. Her little girl has her apron full,

TABLET ON THE LEFT.

CENTRE TABLET.

TABLET ON THE RIGHT.

and is eating a turnip, while a pig is coming out of a rickety sty near by.

The fireplace is an enormous iron grate, capable of containing several bushels of coal; and the hearth is of white marble, inlaid with ornaments of polished maroon-colored marble, or encaustic tile. Upon the shelf are two small dark-blue vases, covered with flowers, delicately painted; and between these are two bronze candelabra. The whole present a most pleasing picture to the eye; and the interest is increased by the associations which cluster around these objects, for they were there sixty years ago, when Washington received his guests in the spacious drawing-room, of which that chimney-piece is the greatest ornament.

PORCELAIN VASES.

With the elegant chimney-piece Mr. Vaughan sent three larger and more beautiful porcelain vases, than those which now stand upon the shelf. They were made in India, and ornamented in London. The ground is a dark blue, with delicate gilt scroll and leaf ornaments, with landscapes painted upon one side and animals upon the other.

Washington appears to have received other presents from Mr. Vaughan. On the 30th of November, 1785, he wrote to his London friend, saying: "I have lately received a letter from Mr. Vaughan (your son), of Jamaica, accompanied by a puncheon of rum, which he informs me was sent by your order as a present for me. Indeed, my dear sir, you overwhelm me with your favors, and lay me under too many obligations to leave a hope remaining of discharging them." He had attempted to do so in a degree, for in the same letter, he says: "Hearing of the distress in which that island, with others in the West Indies, is involved by the late hurricane, I have taken the liberty of requesting Mr. Vaughan's acceptance, for his own use, of a few barrels of superfine flour of my own manufacturing."

Two or three months later than the date of this letter, another present for Washington reached Mount Vernon, of more intrinsic value than all that he had received since his retirement from the army. It consisted of three asses, a jack and two jennies, selected from the royal stud at Madrid, and sent to him as a compliment from the king of Spain. His "Catholic Majesty" having been informed that Washington was endeavoring to procure these animals of the best breed in Europe, for the purpose of rearing mules on his estates, made him this present, and sent over with them a person acquainted with the mode of treating them, who arrived at Portsmouth, in New Hampshire, and journeyed to Mount Vernon by land.

According to a statement of the late Mr. Custis, the jack, called the *Royal Gift*, was sixteen hands high, of a gray color, heavily made, and of a sluggish disposition. "At the same time," says Mr. Custis, "the Marquis de Lafayette sent out a jack and jennies from the island of Malta. This jack, called the *Knight of Malta*, was a superb animal, black color, with the form of a stag and the ferocity of a tiger. Washington availed himself of the best qualities of the two jacks by crossing the breeds, and hence obtained a favorite jack, called *Compound*, which animal united the size and strength of the *Gift* with the high courage and activity of the *Knight*. The General bred some very superior mules from his coach mares. In a few years the estate of Mount Vernon became stocked with mules of a superior order, some of them rising to the height of sixteen hands, and of great power and usefulness. One wagon team of four mules sold at the sale of the General's effects for eight hundred dollars."

Washington, through Florida Blanca, the prime minister of Spain, most sincerely thanked his majesty for a present so truly valuable, in connection with his country's industrial operations; and in answer, that functionary replied, "It will give pleasure to his majesty, that opportunities of a higher nature may offer, to prove the great esteem he entertains for your Excellency's personal merit, singular virtues, and character."

At the close of 1785, Washington had completed the enlargement of his house, and was prepared for the accommodation of the increasing number of his visitors. He found his time so much occupied with these, and his equally increasing correspondence, that he resolved to employ a secretary, who should, at the same time, perform the duties of instructor of his adopted children. He addressed General Lincoln on the subject, who warmly recommended Tobias Lear, a young gentleman of Portsmouth, in New Hampshire, who had recently graduated at Harvard University. In reply, Washington said:

"Mr. Lear, or any other who may come into my family in the blended character of preceptor to the children and clerk or private secretary to me, will sit at my table, will live as I live, will mix with the company who resort to the house, and will be treated in every respect with civility and proper attention."

A satisfactory arrangement was made, which proved a happy one. Mr. Lear went to Mount Vernon, and resided there much of the time afterward, until death removed the master. Washington became very fond of him. He married, and lost his wife there; and in his will, Washington wrote: "To Tobias Lear I give the use of the farm which he now holds, in virtue of a lease from me to him and his deceased wife (for and during their natural lives), free from rent during his life." We shall meet Mr. Lear again under solemn circumstances beneath the roof of Mount Vernon mansion.

In his letter to General Lincoln respecting Mr. Lear, Washington expressed his expectation that his correspondence would decline, for he had resolved to remain strictly a private citizen. On the contrary, circumstances which speedily arose, caused his correspondence to greatly increase, and the retired soldier soon found himself borne out upon the turbulent waves of political life. He was too patriotic to shrink from duty when his country demanded his services, and therefore events soon drew him from the coveted pleasures of his quiet home.

Washington, with other sagacious men, had watched the

course of public affairs since the close of the war with the deepest solicitude, for he perceived imminent dangers on every side. The country had become impoverished by the struggle, and was burdened with an enormous debt, domestic and foreign; and the Congress possessed no executive powers adequate to a provision of means for the liquidation of those debts by direct taxation.

For a long time it had been clearly perceived that, while the *Articles of Confederation*, entered into by the respective states, formed a sufficient constitution of government during the progress of the war, they were not adapted to the public wants in the new condition of an independent sovereignty in which the people found themselves. There appeared abundant necessity for a greater centralization of power, by which the general government could act more efficiently for the public good.

As early as the summer of 1782, the legislature of New York, on the suggestion of Alexander Hamilton, had recommended to each state "to adopt the measure of assembling a GENERAL CONVENTION OF THE STATES, specially authorized to revise and amend the *Confederation;*" and in the spring of 1786 a strong desire was felt in many parts of the country to have such convention.

To a great extent the people had lost all regard for the authority of Congress, and the commercial affairs of the country had become wretchedly deranged. Every thing seemed to be tending toward utter chaos; and many were the anxious councils held by Washington and others under the roof of Mount Vernon, when the buds and the birds first appeared in Virginia in the spring of 1786. His correspondence with his compatriots in other states on the subject became quite extended; and his letters at this time, full of the important topic, are remarkable for their words of wisdom and tone of caution.

"I often think of our situation, and view it with concern," he wrote to John Jay in May. "From the high ground we stood upon, from the plain path which invited our footsteps, to be so fallen, so lost, is really mortifying." He saw the tendency toward ruin of the fair fabric which his wisdom and prowess had helped to raise, and his faith in public men had become weakened. "My fear is," he said, "that the people are not sufficiently *misled* to retract from error. To be plainer, I think there is more wickedness than ignorance mixed in our councils. Under this impression I scarcely know what opinion to entertain of a general convention."

Time and circumstances work out many changes in human opinions. Washington's were modified by the logic of events, and he soon favored a convention of the states. He received letters from all parts of the country upon the subject of public affairs, and his answers, widely circulated, had a commanding influence. In his quiet home at Mount Vernon he was silently wielding the powers of a statesman, and his opinions were eagerly sought.

In 1785, commissioners appointed by Virginia and Maryland, to form a compact relative to the navigation of the waters belonging to them in common, had visited Mount Vernon to consult with the retired soldier; and suggestions were then made and discussed concerning a stronger federal government, which led to important results. It led, primarily, to a general discussion by the people of the subject of the inefficiency of the federal government; then to a convention of delegates from a few states at Annapolis, in Maryland, in September, 1786; and, finally, to a more important convention the following year, on the recommendation of the Congress. The latter convention, composed of delegates from every state in the union except New Hampshire and Rhode Island, commenced its session in Philadelphia toward the close of May, 1787.

Washington was put at the head of the Virginia delegation, but for some time he refused to accept the position, having solemnly declared that he would never appear in public life again. But on all occasions that great man yielded private considerations to the public good. After consultations with friends he consented to serve, and on the 9th of May he set out in his carriage from Mount Vernon on a journey to Philadelphia. He was chosen president of the convention by unanimous vote, and for nearly four months he presided over the deliberations of that august assembly with great dignity. The convention adjourned on the 12th of September. On that day the present CONSTITUTION OF THE UNITED STATES was adopted, as a substitute for the ARTICLES OF CONFEDERATION. That constitution was submitted to the people for ratification. Toward the close of 1788 the majority of the states having signified their approval of it, the people proceeded to choose a chief magistrate of the republic.

For more than two years Washington kept a vigilant and anxious eye upon the movements of the public mind in relation to the national constitution. Day by day his correspondence increased, and he found himself again upon the sea of political life. Meanwhile the hospitable mansion at Mount

Vernon was frequently filled with visitors; and one whom Washington loved, as a soldier and as a friend, was invited there as a guest, with a request that he should remain as long

COLONEL DAVID HUMPHREYS.

as the house should be agreeable to him. That guest was David Humphreys, a native of Derby, Connecticut, and then about thirty-five years of age. He had received the diploma of Bachelor of Arts at Yale College in 1771, when the eminent Doctor Daggett was president. His cotemporaries there were Dwight, Trumbull, and Barlow, a triad of poets, with whom he was associated in paying court to the muse of song. Humphreys was a tutor in the family of the lord of Phillipse's manor, on the Hudson, for awhile, and then entered the continental army as a captain. He rose to the rank of lieutenant-colonel during the war, and toward the close became one of Washington's favorite aides. He went abroad in 1784, as secretary to the commission for negotiating treaties of commerce with foreign powers. He was abroad two years, and on his return made quite a protracted visit at Mount Vernon. That was in 1786; and one evening in August, while reclining on the bank of the river, in the shadows of its wooded slopes, he began the composition of an ode entitled "*Mount Vernon,*" commencing with the following stanza:

> "By broad Potowmack's azure tide,
> Where Vernon's Mount, in sylvan pride
> Displays its beauties far,
> Great WASHINGTON, to peaceful shades,
> Where no unhallow'd wish invades,
> Retir'd from fields of war."

Humphreys brought with him from France, at the special request of the king, a token of his "most Christian majesty's" regard for Washington. It was an engraving of a full-length portrait of the king, Louis XVI., in his state robes, enclosed in a superb gilt frame, made expressly for the occasion. At the top, surrounded by appropriate emblems, are the royal arms of France, and, at the bottom, the arms of the Washington family. In the corners are the monograms of the king and Washington—"L. L. XVI." and "G. W." These—the arms and the emblematic ornaments—are in relief. The picture, in its original frame, is at Mount Vernon, dimmed and darkened by age and neglect.

In 1788, Humphreys, as we have just observed, became a resident at Mount Vernon; and there he wrote a *Life of General Israel Putnam.* Humphreys had been a member of that officer's military family in the war for independence; and

ENGRAVING OF LOUIS XVI.

just before his departure for Mount Vernon, he visited the veteran at his home in Connecticut, and received from his own lips many of the stirring narratives recorded in that biography.

At Mount Vernon Humphreys translated, from the French of M. Le Mierre, the tragedy of *The Widow of Malabar*, which was first brought out at the theatre in Philadelphia, by Hallam and Wignel (heads of the old American company of players), in May, 1790. The prologue, written by John Trumbull, author of *M'Fingall*, was spoken on that occasion by Mr. Hallam, and the epilogue, written by Humphreys, was spoken by Mrs. Henry.

While Colonel Humphreys was at Mount Vernon in the autumn of 1788, distinguished visitors were entertained there for a few days. These were the Count de Moustier, the French minister, a handsome and polite man; his sister, the Marchioness de Brienne—who was illnaturedly described by General Armstrong as a "little, singular, whimsical, hysterical old woman, whose delight is in playing with a negro child and caressing a monkey"—and her son, M. Dupont. They had made a long journey from New Hampshire, by way of Fort Schuyler (now Utica) on the Mohawk River, where they enjoyed the spectacle of an Indian treaty.

The Marchioness de Brienne was quite an accomplished writer and skilful amateur artist; and in the evening of the day when Washington was inaugurated the first President of the United States, the following year, the front of her brother's house was beautifully decorated with paintings by her own hand, suggestive of the past, the present, and the future in American history. These were illuminated by borderings of lamps upon the doors and windows.

In the autumn of that year the marchioness persuaded President Washington to sit to her for his portrait in miniature. In his diary, on Saturday, the 3d of October, he recorded:

"Walked in the afternoon, and sat about two o'clock for Madam de Brehan [Brienne] to complete a miniature profile of me, which she had begun from memory, and which she had made exceedingly like the original."

The marchioness made several copies of this picture, one of which Washington presented to Mrs. Bingham, of Philadelphia. From another, an engraving was afterward made in Paris, and several impressions were sent to Washington. She

WASHINGTON AND LAFAYETTE.

also painted on copper, in medallion form, the profiles of Washington and Lafayette, in miniature, within the same circumference, and presented the picture to Washington. This was preserved at Arlington House.

Another foreign lady, the wife of Peter J. Von Berckel, of Rotterdam, the first embassador from Holland to the United States, was a great admirer of the character of Washington, and painted an allegorical picture in testimony of her reverence for the Liberator of his country. It was executed upon copper, eighteen by twenty inches in size. The design, intending to be complimentary to Washington, was well conceived. Upon the top of a short, fluted column, was a bust of Washington, crowned

WASHINGTON'S DESTINY.

with a military and civic wreath. This stood near the entrance to a cave where the Parcæ or Fates—Clotho the *Spinster*, Lachesis the *Allotter*, and Atropos the *Unchangeable*—were seen, busy with the destinies of the patriot. Clotho was sitting with her distaff, spinning the thread of his life, and Lachesis was receiving it. Atropos was just stepping forward with open shears to cut it, when Immortality, represented as a beautiful youth, seized the precious thread, and gave it to Fame, a winged female, with a trumpet, in the skies, who bore it on to future ages. The latter thought was beautifully expressed by Thomas Moore, many years later, when he thus sang of a poet's immortality:

> "Even so, though thy memory should now die away,
> 'Twill be caught up again in some happier day,
> And the hearts and the voices of Erin prolong,
> Through the answering Future, thy name and thy song."

This picture was presented to Washington by Mr. Von Berckel, with the following lines, composed by the fair artist:

> "In vain the sisters ply their busy care,
> To reel off years from Glory's deathless heir:
> Frail things shall pass, his fame shall never die
> Rescued from Fate by Immortality."

After the death of Mrs. Washington, the painting became the property of the late G. W. P. Custis, who presented it to the venerable General C. C. Pinckney, of South Carolina, to whose military family he had belonged. While on a visit at Arlington House, many years ago, Mr. Custis described the picture to the writer, at the same time illustrating his description by a rude pencil sketch, of which the accompanying engraving is a fac-simile on a smaller scale. Such was the impression of the picture upon the memory of that venerable man, after a lapse of fifty years.

Soon after the departure of the French minister and his party from Mount Vernon, two other French gentlemen, with letters of introduction, visited Washington. These were M. de Warville, and M. St. Frie, who, Washington said, were "intelligent, discreet, and disposed to receive favorable impressions of America." Brissot de Warville was young, handsome, and full of enthusiasm. In his letter of introduction, Lafayette said, "He is very clever, and wishes much to be presented to you. He intends to write a history of America, and is, of course, desirous to have a peep into your papers, which appears to me a deserved condescension, as he is fond of America, writes pretty well, and will set matters in a proper light."

Brissot de Warville did not write a history of America, but during the French revolution that soon followed this visit, he became quite a conspicuous object in the history of his own country. He was intensely democratic, and when he returned to France, he appeared in the streets of Paris in the garb of a Philadelphia Quaker, with which he was enamored. In the French revolution he became a Girondist leader. He finally made himself obnoxious to Robespierre and his party by refusing to vote for the execution of the king, and was doomed to suffer death on the guillotine. He fell on the 30th of October, 1793, and the surviving Girondists were called Brissotins.

In his letters, Brissot de Warville spoke with enthusiasm of America, and after his visit at Mount Vernon, he wrote of Mrs. Washington, saying, "Every thing about the house has an air of simplicity; the table is good, but not ostentatious, and no deviation is seen from regularity and domestic economy. She superintends the whole, and joins to the qualities of an excellent housewife, the simple dignity which ought to characterize a woman whose husband has acted the greatest part on the theatre of human affairs, while possessing that amiability and manifesting that attention to strangers which makes hospitality so charming."

As the year 1788 drew to a close, Washington felt well assured that he would be called by the voice of the nation to the important position of Chief Magistrate of the Republic.

Early in September it had been ascertained that a sufficient number of states had ratified the National Constitution, to make it the organic law of the land, and on the 13th, Congress passed an act, appointing the first Wednesday in January, 1789, for the people to choose electors of a President, according to the provisions of that constitution; the first Wednesday in February following for the electors to meet and make a choice; and the first Wednesday in March for the new government to be organized in the city of New York.

The hearts of all were now turned toward Washington as the man to whom the helm of state should be given, and his friends, well knowing his reluctance to re-enter public life, commenced writing persuasive letters to him. To all of them he expressed sentiments such as he wrote to Lafayette, when he said of the proffered office—"It has no fascinating allurement for me. At my time of life and under my circumstances, the increasing infirmities of nature and the growing love of retirement do not permit me to entertain a wish beyond that of living and dying an honest man on my own farm. Let those follow the pursuits of ambition and fame who have a keener relish for them, or who may have more years in store for the enjoyment of them."

The election was held at the appointed time, and Washington was chosen President of the United States for four years from the 4th of March ensuing. He now again yielded his own wishes to the claims of his country, and prepared to leave his beloved home. Meanwhile, office-seekers were sending him letters by scores, and sometimes they came in person to solicit favor for themselves or friends. He had already expressed his fixed determination to enter upon the duties of his office "not only unfettered by promises, but even unchargeable with creating or feeding the expectation of any man living" for his "assistance to office." By this declaration applicants soon learned the wisdom of silence.

But there were men who sought the influence of his position, upon whom he not only looked with favor but with delight. These were they who had schemes which, though cherished by themselves for selfish purposes, would be of great advantage to the industrial interests of the country. One of these visited Mount Vernon at the close of March, 1789, to lay before the President elect some facts concerning the introduction of the manufacture of glass into America. A gentleman of Alexandria, in a letter to a friend, thus describes the event:

"I am just returned from Mount Vernon, where I was present at a scene which made every patriotic pulse vibrate with the most pleasurable sensations.

"This, sir, was a tribute of a new citizen of the United States to their illustrious President. Mr. John F. Amelung, a native of Germany, and an artist of considerable eminence, emigrated to this country with a large family and extensive fortune, and having contemplated the said commerce, etc., he selected, with great prudence, a central situation for the establishment of a manufactory of the first magnitude and importance, in which he has succeeded beyond all hope and expectation. Through his vast exertions he is now enabled to supply the United States with every species of glass, the quality of which is equal, if not superior, to that imported, while he actually undersells all foreign traders in that article in our own markets. To the testimony of the ablest connoisseurs and characters of taste and respectability, it only remained for Mr. Amelung to court the patronage of the great patriot; and I had the good fortune to be present at an offering to his excellency of two capacious goblets of flint glass, exhibiting the general's coat-of-arms, etc.

"The conversation naturally embraced and discussed our manufacturing interests, and was managed with such delicate address, as to pay a compliment to the ingenuity and labors of this celebrated artist, who has supported, without intermission, three hundred hands these three years past, with the utmost order and character. New Bremen, which gives appellation to this manufactory, is situated on Monococy, contiguous to the waters of the Potomac, by which he may in time supply the seaport towns of the eastern and southern states, and thus give domestic circulation to an immense quantity of specie remitted annually for this article alone to the foreign merchants."

Washington had already been apprised of the existence of this establishment, for in a letter to Jefferson, in February preceding, he said: "A factory of glass is established upon a large scale on Monococy river, near Fredericktown, in Maryland. I am informed it will this year produce glass of various kinds, nearly to the amount of ten thousand pounds value."

So tardily did the members of the National Congress assemble, that a quorum was not present at the capital in New York until the beginning of April, when the votes of the electoral college were counted, and Washington was declared to be elected President of the United States by the unanimous voice of the people. That delay was a source of pleasure to him. In a letter to General Knox, he compared it to a reprieve: "for," he said, "in confidence I tell you (with the *world* it would obtain little credit), that my movements to the chair of government will be accompanied by feelings not unlike those of a culprit who is going to the place of his execution." "I am sensible," he continued, "that I am embarking the voice of the people, and a good name of my own on this voyage, but what returns will be made for them heaven alone can foretell. Integrity and firmness are all I can promise. These, be the voyage long or short, shall never forsake me, although I may be deserted by all men; for of the consolations which are to be derived from these, under any circumstances, the world cannot deprive me."

The Senate of the United States was organized on the 6th of April, and John Langdon, a representative therein from New Hampshire, was chosen its president *pro tempore*. As soon as the votes of the electoral college were opened and counted, he wrote a letter to the illustrious farmer at Mount Vernon, notifying him of the fact of his election. This letter, with an official certificate, was conveyed to the chief magistrate elect by the venerable Secretary Thomson, who arrived at Mount Vernon on Tuesday, the 14th, between ten and eleven o'clock in the morning. Washington was making the usual tour of his farms, and the secretary was cordially received by Mrs. Washington, who had enjoyed his friendship and the hospitalities of his house at Philadelphia.

On his return from the fields at a quarter before one, Washington greeted Mr. Thomson with much warmth, for their friendship was most sincere. They had gone through a long struggle for their country's liberation hand in hand, one in the field, the other in the senate; and the bond of sympathy, strengthened by retrospection, was powerful. Thomson was soon invited to the library, where he revealed the object of his visit, and delivered the letter of President Langdon. Public affairs at once became the topic of conversation, and long did

CHARLES THOMSON.

the two patriots linger at the table that day, after Mrs. Washington, Colonel Humphreys, Mr. Lear, and two or three guests had withdrawn. Only for a few minutes were they separated, when Washington, in his private study in an upper room, wrote the following letter to Mr. Langdon, and placed it in the hands of a servant to be conveyed to the post-office at Alexandria:

"MOUNT VERNON, 14*th April*, 1789.

"SIR: I had the honor to receive your official communication, by the hand of Mr. Secretary Thomson, about one o'clock this day. Having concluded to obey the important and flattering call of my country, and having been impressed with the idea of the expediency of my being with Congress at as early a period as possible, I propose to commence my journey on Thursday morning, which will be the day after to-morrow."

Toward evening Washington left Mount Vernon on horseback, accompanied by Billy, and rode rapidly toward Fredericksburg, where his aged and invalid mother resided. He went to embrace her and bid her farewell before leaving for the distant seat of government. She was suffering from an acute disease, and the weight of more than fourscore years was upon her. The interview between the matron and her illustrious son was full of the most touching sublimity. "The people, madam," said Washington, "have been pleased, with the most flattering unanimity, to elect me to the chief magistracy of the United States; but before I can assume the functions of that office, I have come to bid you an affectionate farewell. So soon as the public business which must necessarily be encountered in arranging a new government can be disposed of, I shall hasten to Virginia, and —" Here she interrupted him, saying, "You will see me no more. My great age, and the disease that is rapidly approaching my vitals, warn me that I shall not be long in this world. I trust in God I am somewhat prepared for a better. But go, George, fulfil the high destinies which Heaven appears to assign you; go, my son, and may that Heaven's and your mother's blessing be with you always."

The mother and son embraced for the last time, for before he could return to Virginia, she was laid in the grave.

Washington returned to Mount Vernon on the evening of the 15th, and found every thing in preparation for the journey toward New York the following morning. Nothing essential to the master's comfort and convenience was omitted by the faithful Billy.

There was a great stir at Mount Vernon on the morning of the 16th. Before sunrise a messenger had come from Alexandria, and departed; and that evening Washington wrote in his diary: "About ten o'clock I bade adieu to Mount Vernon, to private life, and to domestic felicity, and with a mind oppressed with more anxious and painful sensations than I have words to express, set out for New York, in company with Mr. Thomson and Colonel Humphreys, with the best disposition to render service to my country in obedience to its call, but with less hope of answering its expectations."

TRAVELLING BOOT-JACK.

Washington's neighbors and friends at Alexandria, had invited him to halt and partake of a public dinner on the way. This manifestation of friendship touched his heart; but still deeper were his tenderest emotions awakened, when, as he and his travelling companions ascended a little hill about a mile from his home, and came in view of the lodges at his gate, he saw a cavalcade of those friends, waiting to escort him to the town. The scene was one of marvellous interest. It was the first of a series of ovations that awaited him on his journey. The sun was shining with all the warmth and brightness of mid-April in Virginia, the smiles of cultivation were on every hand, and the song of birds and the perfume of early flowers fell gratefully upon the senses.

Alas! how changed is now the aspect of that ancient entrance

14

ANCIENT ENTRANCE TO MOUNT VERNON, IN 1858.

to Mount Vernon! Stately trees are near as in the days of old, but the voices of labor are no more heard. All is silence and desolation, except when the bird sings, the squirrel chirps, or the echo of the huntsman's gun startles the solitary pedestrian, for the road, filled or gullied by the winds and rains, is scarcely passable for beast or vehicle. The old lodges, wherein once rang the merry laugh of children, are utterly deserted, and fast falling into hopeless decay; and all around them a thick forest stands, where the wheat, the corn, and the tobacco once bloomed.

Washington was anxious to proceed to New York with as

little parade as possible, but the enthusiasm of the people could not be repressed. His journey was like a triumphal march. At Alexandria he partook of a public dinner, when the mayor said, "The first and best of our citizens must leave us; our aged must lose their ornament, our youth their model, our agriculture its improver, our commerce its friend, our infant academy its protector,* our poor their benefactor." * * * * * "Farewell!" he said, turning to Washington, "Go, and make a grateful people happy; a people who will be doubly grateful when they contemplate this new sacrifice for their interests."

Washington's feelings were deeply touched. He could say but little. "Words fail me," he said, "unutterable sensations must, then, be left to more expressive silence, while from an aching heart I bid all my affectionate friends and kind neighbors—farewell."

The president was greeted by the Marylanders at Georgetown; and at Baltimore he was entertained by a large number of citizens at a public supper. When leaving the city the next morning, at half-past five, he was saluted by discharges of cannon, and attended by a cavalcade of gentlemen who rode seven miles with him. At the frontier of Pennsylvania, he was met early on the morning of the 19th, by two troops of cavalry, and a cavalcade of citizens, at the head of whom were Governor Mifflin and Judge Peters; and by them he was escorted to Philadelphia. Upon that frontier, Washington left his carriage, and mounting a superb white charger, he took

---

* Washington had given funds for the establishment of an academy at Alexandria, and was its patron.

position in the line of procession, with Secretary Thomson on one side, and Colonel Humphreys on the other.

At Gray's Ferry, on the Schuylkill, they were joined by an immense number of citizens, led in order by General St. Clair. A triumphal arch was erected on both sides of the river covered with laurel branches, and approached through avenues of evergreens. As Washington passed under the last arch, Angelica Peale, daughter of the eminent artist, and a child of rare beauty, who was concealed in the foliage, let down a handsomely ornamented civic crown of laurel, which rested upon the head of the patriot. The incident caused a tumultuous shout. The procession moved on into the city, its volume increasing every moment. At least twenty thousand people lined its passage-way from the Schuylkill to the city; and at every step the President was greeted with shouts of "Long live George Washington!" "Long live the Father of his country!"

The President was entertained at a sumptuous banquet, given by the authorities, at the City Tavern, and the next morning the military were paraded, to form an escort for him to Trenton But heavy rain frustrated their designs. Washington was compelled to ride in his carriage, and he would not allow an escort of friends to travel in the rain.

When the President and suite approached Trenton in the afternoon, the clouds had disappeared, and in the warm sunlight, he crossed the Delaware amid the greetings of shouts, and cannon-peals, and the *feu de joie* of musketry. His route lay across the same bridge over the little stream which flows through the town, where, twelve years before, he had been driven across by Cornwallis, on the evening previous to the battle at Princeton. Upon that bridge, where he was thus humiliated, was now a triumphal arch, twenty feet in height, supported by thirteen pillars twined with evergreens. It was the conception and work of the women of New Jersey, under the general direction of Annis Stockton; and upon the side of his approach, over the arch, were emblazoned the words:

"THE DEFENDER OF THE MOTHERS WILL BE THE PROTECTOR OF THE DAUGHTERS."

The arch was otherwise beautifully decorated, and as Washington approached, many mothers with their daughters appeared on each side of it, all dressed in white. As he passed, thirteen young girls, their heads wreathed with flowers, and holding baskets of flowers in their hands, while they scattered some in his way, sang the following ode, written for the occasion by Governor Howell:

> "Welcome, mighty chief, once more
> Welcome to this grateful shore;
> Now no mercenary foe,
> Aims again the fatal blow,
> Aims at thee the fatal blow.
>
> "Virgins fair, and mothers grave,
> Those thy conquering arm did save,
> Build for thee triumphal bowers.
> Strew, ye fair, his way with flowers!
> Strew your hero's way with flowers."

With joyous greetings at every step, Washington proceeded through New Jersey, over which he had once fled with a half starved, half-naked army, before a closely pursuing foe; and at Elizabethtown Point, he was met, on the morning of the 23d, by a committee of both houses of Congress, and several civil and military officers. They had prepared a magnificent barge for his reception, which was manned by thirteen pilots, in white uniforms, commanded by Commodore Nicholson. In New York harbor, the vessels were all decked with flags, in honor of the President, and gayly dressed small boats swarmed upon the waters, filled with gentlemen and ladies. The Spanish ship-of-war *Galveston*, lying in the harbor, was the only vessel of all nations, that did not show signs of respect. The neglect was so marked, that many words of censure were heard, when, at a given signal, just as the barge containing Washington was abreast of her, she displayed, on every part of her rigging, every flag and signal known among the nations. At the same moment she discharged thirteen heavy guns, and these were answered by the grand battery on shore. In the midst of this cannonade, and the shouts of the multitude on land and water, the President debarked, and was conducted by a military and civic procession to the residence prepared for his use, at No. 10 Cherry-street, near Franklin Square.

Such was the reception of the first President at the capital of the Union. The demonstrations of joy and loyalty were most sincere and universal, and yet the pen of wit and the pencil of caricature had been busy. As early as the 7th of April, John Armstrong wrote to General Gates, from New York, saying:

"All the world here are busy in collecting flowers and sweets of every kind to amuse and delight the President in his approach and on his arrival. Even Roger Sherman has set his head at work to devise some style of address more novel and dignified than 'Excellency.' Yet in the midst of this admiration, there are skeptics who doubt its propriety, and wits who amuse themselves at its extravagance. The first will grumble, and the last will laugh, and the President should be prepared to meet the attacks of both with firmness and good nature. A caricature has already appeared called 'THE ENTRY,' full of very disloyal and profane allusions. It represents the general mounted on an ass, and in the arms of his man Billy—Humphreys leading the Jack, and chanting hosannahs and birth-day odes. The following couplet proceeds from the mouth of the devil:

'The glorious time has come to pass,
When David shall conduct an ass.'"

On Thursday, the 30th of April, 1789, Washington was inaugurated the First President of the United States. The ceremonies were preceded by a national salute at Bowling Green, the assembling of the people in the churches to implore the blessings of Heaven on the nation and the President, and a grand procession. The august spectacle was exhibited upon the open gallery at the front of the old Federal Hall at the head of Broad-street, in the presence of a vast assemblage of people. Washington was dressed in a suit of dark-brown cloth, and white silk stockings, all of American manufacture, with silver buckles upon his shoes, and his hair powdered and dressed in the fashion of the time. Before him, when he arose to take the oath of office, stood Chancellor Livingston, in a suit of black broadcloth; and near them were Vice-President Adams, Mr. Otis, the Secretary of the Senate, who held an open Bible upon a rich crimson cushion, Generals Knox, St. Clair, Steuben, and other officers of the army, and George Clinton, the Governor of the state of New York.

BIBLE USED AT THE INAUGURATION OF WASHINGTON.

Washington laid his hand upon the page containing the fiftieth chapter of Genesis, opposite to which were two engravings, one representing *The Blessing of Zebulon*, the other *The Prophecy of Issachar*. Chancellor Livingston then waved his hand for the multitude to be silent, and in a clear voice, read the prescribed oath. The President said "I swear," then bowed his head and kissed the sacred volume, and with closed eyes as he resumed his erect position, he continued with solemn voice and devotional attitude, "So help me God!"

"It is done!" exclaimed the Chancellor, and, with a loud voice, shouted, "Long live George Washington, President of the United States!" The people echoed the shout again and again; and as the President moved toward the door, the first congratulatory hand that grasped his was that of his early and life-long friend, Richard Henry Lee, to whom in childhood, almost fifty years before, he had written:

"I am going to get a whip-top soon, and you may see it and whip it."

How many human whip-tops had these staunch patriots managed since they wrote those childish epistles!

That Bible is now in the possession of St. John's Lodge, in New York. Upon each cover is a record, in gilt letters, concerning the Lodge; and on the inside, beautifully written upon parchment, in ornamental style, by G. Thresher, surmounted by a portrait of Washington, engraved by Leney, of New York, is the following statement:

"On this Sacred Volume, on the 30th day of April, 1789, in the city of New York, was administered to GEORGE WASHINGTON, the first President of the United States of America, the oath to support the Constitution of the United States. This important ceremony was performed by the Most Worshipful Grand Master of Free and Accepted Masons of the state of New York, the honorable Robert R. Livingston, Chancellor of the state.

> "Fame stretched her wings and with her trumpet blew,
> 'Great Washington is near, what praise is due?
> 'What title shall he have?' She paused, and said,
> 'Not one—his name alone strikes every title dead.'"

Mrs. Washington did not journey to New York with her husband. Her reluctance to leave Mount Vernon and the quiet of domestic pursuits was quite equal to his. She loved her home, her family and friends, and had no taste for the excitements of fashionable society and public life. She was, in every respect, a model Virginia housekeeper. She was a very early riser, leaving her pillow at dawn at every season of the year, and engaging at once in the active duties of her household. Yet these duties never kept her from daily communion with God, in the solitude of her closet. After breakfast she invariably retired to her chamber, where she remained an hour reading the Scriptures and engaged in thanksgiving and prayer. For more than half a century she practised such devotions in secret; and visitors often remarked that when she appeared after the hour of spiritual exercises, her countenance beamed with ineffable sweetness.

All day long that careful, bustling, industrious little housewife kept her hands in motion. "Let us repair to the old lady's room," wrote the wife of Colonel Edward Carrington to her sister, a short time before Washington's death, while on a visit to Mount Vernon—"Let us repair to the old lady's room, which is precisely in the style of our good old aunt's—that is to say, nicely fixed for all sorts of work. On one side sits the chambermaid, with her knitting; on the other a little colored pet, learning to sew. An old decent woman is there, with her table and shears, cutting out the negroes' winter clothes, while the good old lady directs them all, incessantly knitting herself. She points out to me several pair of nice colored stockings and gloves she had just finished, and presents me with a pair, half done, which she begs I will finish and wear for her sake. It is wonderful, after a life spent as these good people have necessarily spent theirs, to see them, in retirement, assume those domestic habits that prevail in our country."

Mrs. Washington always spoke of the time when she was in public life, as wife of the President of the United States, as her "lost days." She was compelled to be governed by the etiquette prescribed for her, and she was very restive under it. To the wife of George A. Washington, the General's nephew, who had married her niece, and who was left in charge of domestic affairs at Mount Vernon when her husband assumed the presidency, she wrote from New York, saying:

"Mrs. Sims will give you a better account of the fashions than I can. I live a very dull life here, and know nothing that passes in the town. I never go to any public place—indeed I think I am more like a state prisoner than any thing else. There are certain bounds set for me which I must not depart from; and, as I cannot do as I like, I am obstinate and stay at home a great deal."

At that time the etiquette of the President's household was not fully determined on. In his diary, on the 15th of November, Washington wrote: "Received an invitation to attend the funeral of Mrs. Roosevelt (the wife of a senator of this state [New York], but declined complying with it—first, because the propriety of accepting any invitation of this sort appeared very questionable—and secondly (though to do it in this instance might not be improper), because it might be difficult to discriminate in cases which might thereafter happen."

The establishment of precedents and the arrangements of etiquette were of more importance than might at first thought appear. The plan of having certain days and hours when the President would receive calls, was a measure of absolute necessity, in order that the chief magistrate might have the control of his time; and yet it offended many who were of the extremely democratic school.

The precedents of monarchy might not be followed in a simple republic, and yet a certain dignity was to be preserved. The arrangement of official ceremonies, connected with the

President personally, was finally left chiefly to Colonel Humphreys, who had been abroad, and was a judicious observer of the phases of society under every aspect. The customs which were established during Washington's administration concerning the *levees*—the President not returning private visits, et cetera—have ever since prevailed; and the chief magistrate of the republic is never seen in the position of a private citizen.

In the letter just quoted, Mrs. Washington wrote: "Dear Fanny, I have, by Mrs. Sims, sent you a watch. It is one of the cargo that I have so long mentioned to you that was expected. I hope it is such a one as will please you. It is of the newest fashion, if that has any influence on your taste. The chain is Mr. Lear's choosing, and such as Mrs. Adams, the Vice-President's lady, and those in polite circles use. It will last as long as the fashion, and by that time you can get another of a fashionable kind."

The watch mentioned in this letter was a flat gold one, manufactured by Lepine, "watchmaker to the king." Washington purchased one for his own use at the same time, it being much more agreeable in the pocket than the old-fashioned bulky English watch. That watch, with the key and seals, became the property of Bushrod Washington, the General's nephew, who inherited Mount Vernon, and was by him, in the following clause in his will, given to a friend:

"My gold watch I give to my friend Robert Adams, of Philadelphia, knowing that he will appreciate the gift, not for the intrinsic value of the article, but because it was worn by the Father of our Country, and afterward by his friend. After the death of the said Robert Adams, I give the said watch to his son Bushrod."

On the 23d of March, 1830, the watch was forwarded to Mr. Adams by John A. Washington, who inherited Mount Vernon from his uncle Bushrod. It came into the possession of Bushrod Washington Adams, of Philadelphia, and is preserved with the greatest care as a precious memento of the beloved patriot. Our engraving shows the watch, ribbon, seal, and key, on a scale one-third less than the objects themselves. The picture of the impression of the seal, exhibiting the Washington arms and motto, is the size of the original. The stones of the seal and key are cornelian; the former white and the latter red, and polygonal in form. The dial is of white enamel; the seconds figures carmine red. The case is standard gold, the alloy copper, giving it the red appearance of jeweller's gold.

WASHINGTON'S LEPINE WATCH, SEAL AND KEY.

In the letter from which we have just quoted, Mrs. Washington exhibits the care and frugality which she always practised at home. To Fanny she wrote:

"I send to dear Maria a piece of *chene* to make her a frock, and a piece of muslin which I hope is long enough for an apron for you. In exchange for it, I beg you will give me a worked muslin apron you have, like my gown

WASHINGTON'S LAST WATCH-SEAL.

that I made just before I left home, of worked muslin, as I wish to make a petticoat to my gown of the two aprons."

It should be remembered that the writer was in the midst of the gay life of New York, then the federal metropolis; the wife of the presiding chief magistrate of the republic, receiving visits from the great of many lands and the most notable of her own, and having her own and her husband's large fortune at command. Some may call her practice the development of a parsimonious spirit. It was not so. Hers was the "liberal hand" that devised "liberal things" for the poor and unfortunate. It was only an exhibition of economy in the use of articles and the management of affairs, which American housewives would do well to imitate.

Mrs. Washington left Mount Vernon for New York on the 19th of May, in her chaise, accompanied by her grandchildren, Eleanor Parke and George Washington Parke Custis, and a small escort on horseback. She was clothed tidily in manufactures of our own country entirely. She lodged at Baltimore the first night of her journey. When she approached that city she was met by a cavalcade of gentlemen and escorted into the town. In the evening fireworks were displayed in her honor; and after supper she was serenaded by a band of musicians, composed of some gentlemen of the city.

When she approached Philadelphia she was met, ten miles from the town, by the president of the state and the speaker of the assembly, accompanied by two troops of dragoons and a large cavalcade of citizens. Some miles from the city she was met by a brilliant company of women, in carriages. They attended her to Gray's Ferry, on the Schuylkill, where they all partook of a collation; and from that place to the city, Mrs

Robert Morris occupied a seat by the side of the President's wife, resigning her own carriage to Master Custis, then a boy a little more than eight years of age. The procession entered the city at two o'clock, when the beloved lady was greeted by thirteen discharges of cannon, and the shouts and cheers of a great multitude. While in the city she was the guest of Mrs. Morris.

On Monday morning, the 26th of May, Mrs. Washington left Philadelphia for New York, accompanied by her hostess. The military paraded for the purpose of forming an escort as far as Trenton, but, as on the morning when her husband left the same city a month before, rain prevented the performance. After proceeding a short distance they took a respectful leave of her, and returned. She slept at Trenton that night, and on Tuesday night she and her family were guests of Governor Livingston, at Elizabethtown.

On Wednesday morning Washington proceeded, in his splendid reception-barge, to Elizabethtown Point to meet his family, accompanied by Robert Morris and several other distinguished men. The barge was manned as on the occasion of the reception of the President. When it approached Whitehall, on its return, crowds of citizens thronged the wharves; and from the grand battery the voices of thirteen cannon, in quick succession, uttered a greeting.

On the day after Mrs. Washington's arrival, the President entertained a few guests at a family dinner. These consisted of Vice-President Adams, Governor Clinton, the Count du Moustier (French minister), Don Diego Gardoqui (Spanish minister). Mr. Jay, General St. Clair, Senators Langdon, Wingate, Izard, and Few, and Mr. Muhlenburg, Speaker of the House of Representatives. The dinner was plain; and Washington, standing at the head of the table, asked a blessing. After the dessert, a single glass of wine was offered to each of the guests. The President then arose, and led the way to the drawing-room, and the company departed without ceremony.

On the following day, Mrs. Washington held her first drawing-room. It was attended by a very numerous company, of the highest respectability. Unlike the *levees* at the Presidential mansion in our time, they were attended only by persons connected with the government and their families, the foreign ministers and their families, and others who held good positions in fashionable and refined society, either on account of their own merits or their social relations. All were expected to be in full dress, on these occasions. Mrs. Washington, though averse to all ostentatious show and parade, fully appreciated the dignity of her station, and was careful to exact those courtesies to which she was entitled.

She was also careful not to allow public ceremonies to interfere with some of the life-long habits of herself and husband. He usually stood by her side, for awhile, on these occasions, and received the visitors as they were presented. But he did not consider *himself* visited. He was a private gentleman; and when the visitors were assembled, he moved among the company, conversing with one and another, with the familiarity that marked his manner in his own drawing-room at Mount Vernon. On these occasions he usually wore a brown cloth coat, with bright buttons, and had neither hat nor sword.

The reception was never allowed to last beyond the appointed hour, which was from eight to nine. When the clock

AND ITS ASSOCIATIONS. 225

in the hall was striking the latter hour, Mrs. Washington would say to those present, with a most complacent smile, "The General always retires at nine, and I usually precede him." In a few minutes the drawing-room would be closed, the lights extinguished, and the presidential mansion would be as dark and quiet before ten o'clock, as the house of any private citizen.

The President held his *levees* or receptions, on Tuesdays, from three to four o'clock in the afternoon, and these were very numerously attended, but by gentlemen only. On these occasions, after the seat of government was removed to Philadelphia, he was always dressed in a suit of black velvet, black silk stockings, silver knee and shoe buckles, and having his hair powdered, and tied in a black silk bag or queue behind. He wore yellow gloves, and held a cocked hat with a cockade upon it, the edges adorned with a black feather about an inch deep. He also wore an elegant dress-sword which he bore with the utmost grace. This sword had a finely-wrought and polished steel hilt, which appeared at the left hip. The scabbard was white polished leather. The coat was worn over the sword, the point of the scabbard only appearing below the skirt.

At his *levees* in New York the President also wore a dress-sword, but less elegant than the one worn in Philadelphia, which an eye-witness has described to me. The sword used in New York is preserved

WASHINGTON'S DRESS-SWORD.

15

at Mount Vernon, it having fallen to the lot of Bushrod Washington, in the distribution of several similar weapons, disposed of by the following clause in Washington's will:

"To each of my nephews, William Augustine Washington, George Lewis, George Steptoe Washington, Bushrod Washington, and Samuel Washington, I give one of the swords or couteaux, of which I may die possessed; and they are to choose in the order they are named. These swords are accompanied with an injunction not to unsheath them for the purpose of shedding blood, except it be for self-defence, or in defence of their country and its rights; and in the latter case to keep them unsheathed, and prefer falling with them in their hands, to the relinquishment thereof."

This sword appears in Stuart's full-length portrait of Washington, painted for the Marquis of Landsdowne. It has a fine silver-gilt hilt, and black leather scabbard, silver-gilt mounted. On one side of the blade are the words RECTI FAC ET ICE—"Do what is right;" on the other, NEMINEM TIMEAS—"Fear no man."

At his receptions in Philadelphia the President always stood, says an eye-witness, "in front of the fireplace, with his face toward the door of entrance. The visitor was conducted to him, and he required to have the name so distinctly pronounced that he could hear it. He had the very uncommon faculty of associating a man's name and personal appearance so durably in his memory as to be able to call any one by name who made him a second visit. He received his visitor with a dignified bow, while his hands were so disposed as to indicate that the salutation was not to be accompanied with shaking hands. This ceremony never occurred in these visits.

even with the most intimate friends, that no distinction might be made.

"As visitors came in, they formed a circle around the room. At a quarter past three the door was closed, and the circle was formed for that day. He then began on the right, and spoke to each visitor, calling him by name, and exchanging a few words with him. When he had completed his circuit, he resumed his first position, and the visitors approached him in succession, bowed, and retired. By four o'clock this ceremony was over."

In New York the President occupied the mansion at No. 10 Cherry-street, for about nine months, and then moved to a more spacious house on the west side of Broadway, between Trinity Church and the Bowling Green, where the French minister, M. de Moustier, had resided. It was a very pleasant house, with a garden extending to the shore of the Hudson. An English gentleman, who visited the President at that time, described the drawing-room as "lofty and spacious, but," he added, "the furniture was not beyond that found in the dwellings of opulent Americans in general, and might be called plain for its situation. The upper end of the room had glass doors, which opened upon a balcony, commanding an extensive view of the Hudson River, and the Jersey shore opposite."

Some of the furniture here alluded to, was purchased of the French minister. Under date of February 1, 1790, Washington recorded in his Diary—" Agreed, on Saturday last to take Mr. McComb's house, lately occupied by the Minister of France, for one year from and after the 1st day of May next; and would go into it immediately, if Mr. Otto, the present possessor, could be accommodated This day I sent my Secretary to examine the rooms to see how my furniture would be adapted to the respective apartments."

Two days afterward he recorded:

"Visited the apartments in the house of Mr. McCombs—made a disposition of the rooms—fixed on furniture of the Minister's (which was to be sold, and was well adapted to particular public rooms)—and directed additional stables to be built."

One piece of the French minister's furniture "fixed upon" and purchased at that time, was a writing-desk, or secretary, and also an easy chair that was used with it. These Washington took with him to Philadelphia, and afterward to Mount Vernon; and in his will they were disposed of as follows:

"To my companion in arms and old and intimate friend, Dr. Craik, I give my bureau (or as cabinet-makers call it tambour secretary), and the circular chair, an appendage of my study."

That secretary fell into the possession of a grandson of Dr. Craik, the Reverend James Craik, of Louisville, in Kentucky. The engraving is from a pencil-sketch by Mr. Alexander Casseday.

The seat of the National government was removed from New York to Philadelphia in 1790, by act of Congress. That body adjourned on the 12th of August, and Washington immediately thereafter made a voyage to Newport, Rhode Island, for the benefit of his health. Close application to public business had caused a nervous prostration, that threatened consequences almost as serious as those with which he had been menaced by a malignant carbuncle the year before. He had also suffered severely from a violent inflammation of the lungs.

WASHINGTON'S SECRETARY AND CIRCULAR CHAIR.

The sea voyage was beneficial, and on the 30th of August the President and his family set out for Mount Vernon, there to spend the few months before the next meeting of Congress at Philadelphia. They left New York for Elizabethtown in the splendid barge in which they had arrived, amid the thunders of cannon and the huzzas of a great multitude of people. Washington never saw New York again. Having no further use for his barge, he wrote to Mr. Randall, the chairman of the committee through whom he had received it, saying:

"As I am at this moment about commencing my journey to Virginia, and consequently will have no farther occasion for the use of the barge, I must now desire that you will return it, in my name, and with my best thanks, to the original proprietors; at the same time I shall be much obliged if you will have the goodness to add, on my part, that in accepting their beautiful present, I considered it as a pledge of that real urbanity which, I am happy in declaring, I have experienced on every occasion during my residence among them; that I ardently wish every species of prosperity may be the constant portion of the respectable citizens of New York; and that I shall always retain a grateful remembrance of the polite attentions of the citizens in general, and of those in particular to whom the contents of this note are addressed."

A few days after this, Washington was again beneath the roof he loved so well, at Mount Vernon, but the coveted enjoyment of his home was lessened by the weight of public cares that pressed upon him. The old feeling of deep responsibility, which it was so difficult for him to lay aside at the close of his military career, returned; and in his library, where he loved to devote his morning hours to reading and the labors of the pen in recording facts connected with his pursuits as a farmer, he might be seen with state papers, maps, plans, and every thing that indicated the weighty cares of a public man.

The Congress then just closed had been a most important one, and the labors of every conscientious officer and employee of the government had been very severe. Upon them had been laid the responsible and momentous task of putting in motion the machinery of a new government, and laying the foundations of the then present and future policy of that government, domestic and foreign. As the chief magistrate of the republic, the chief officer of the government, the chief architect of the new superstructure in progress, Washington felt the solemnity of his position, and the importance of the great trusts which the people had placed in his hands; and the sense of all this denied him needful repose, even while sitting within the quietude of his home on the banks of the Potomac.

Just before Congress adjourned, Washington received a curious present, which he carried with him to Mount Vernon. It was the key of the Bastile, that old state prison in Paris, which had become a strong arm of despotism. It was first a royal castle, completed by Charles V. of France, in 1383, for the defence of Paris against the English, but in the lapse of time it had become a fortress, devoted to the selfish purposes of tyranny. It was hated by the people.

During the preceding year, the slumbering volcano of revolution burning in the hearts of the people, upon which for a long time, royalty and the privileged classes in France had been reposing, showed frequent signs of inquietude, which prophesied of violent eruption. The abuses of the government, under the administration of the ministers of a well-meaning but weak monarch, had become unendurable, and the best friends of France had spoken out boldly against them.

Among these the boldest was Lafayette. He had made a formal demand for a National Assembly. "What!" said the Count d'Artois to him on one occasion, "Do you make a motion for the States General?" "Yes, and even more than that,"

Lafayette replied; and that *more* was nothing less than a charter from the king, by which the public and individual liberty should be acknowledged and guarantied by the future States General.

That body opened their session at Versailles in May, and soon constituted themselves a National Assembly. Their hall was closed by order of the king, on the 20th, and from that time until early in July, Paris was dreadfully agitated. Every one felt that a terrible storm was ready to burst. The king, surrounded by bad advisers, attempted to avert it by means which precipitated it. He placed a cordon of troops around Paris, to overawe the opposers of government. The Assembly, supported by the people, organized a militia within the city. The number required was forty-eight thousand. In two days, two hundred and seventy thousand citizens enrolled themselves. A state mayor was appointed by the town assembly, and the Marquis La Salle was named commander-in-chief.

The armed people intercepted the court dispatches by arresting the royal couriers; and an immense assemblage went to the Hospital of the Invalids, on the 10th of July, and demanded of the governor to deliver up to them all the arms deposited there. He refused, and they seized thirty thousand muskets and twenty pieces of cannon. They also seized all the arms in the shops of the armorers, and those of the *Garde-Meuble*. The tumult throughout the city became terrible in strength and intensity, and the National Assembly sent a deputation to the king to inform him of the disturbances, and to point to the cause—the surrounding troops. The king, under advice, refused to make a change, haughtily declaring that he alone had the right to judge of the necessity of public measures.

On the night of the 13th, Paris was comparatively quiet. It was the lull before the bursting of the storm. The dismissal of M. Necker from the post of minister of finance, had greatly exasperated the inhabitants. The streets were barricaded. The people formed themselves into a National Guard, and chose Lafayette as their commander. Each assumed some sort of military dress, and laid hold of gun, sabre, scythe, or whatever weapon first fell in their way. Multitudes of men of the same opinion, embraced each other in the streets as brothers; and in an instant, almost, a National Guard was formed, consisting of a hundred thousand determined men.

It was believed that the Bastile contained a large quantity of arms and ammunition, and thither the people repaired on the morning of the 14th. A parley ensued, the gates were opened, and about forty citizens, leaders of the people, were permitted to go in. The bridges were then drawn, and a firing was heard within!

That moment marks the opening of the terrible drama of the French revolution. The fury of the populace was excited beyond all control. That firing fell upon their ears as the death-knell of their friends who had gone within the walls of the hated prison. With demoniac yells they dragged heavy cannon before the gates, in the face of a storm of grape-shot from the fortress. They quailed not before the storm, but attacked the stronghold of Despotism with tiger-like ferocity. The alarmed governor, Delaunay, soon displayed a white flag, and the firing ceased.

A second deputation was now sent to the governor. They shared the fate of the former. With redoubled fury the people again assailed the walls, made a breach, rushed in, seized the governor and other officers, and conducting them in triumph to the Place de Grace, first cut off their hands, and then their heads. The latter were then paraded upon pikes through the streets, and the great iron key of the Bastile was carried to the *Hotel de Ville*, or town hall. The National Assembly decreed its demolition. Seven prisoners who had been confined in its dungeons since the reign of Louis the Fifteenth (three of whom had lost their reason) were set at liberty, and the old fortress was demolished soon afterward.

Upon its site is now the *Place de Bastile*, within which stands the *Column of July*, erected by order of Louis Philippe, in commemoration of the events of the memorable Three Days of July, 1830, which placed him upon the throne of France.

The National Assembly, by unanimous vote, now elected Lafayette commander-in-chief of the National Guard of all France, a corps of more than four millions of armed citizens. He accepted the appointment, but, imitating the example of Washington, he refused all remuneration for his services, notwithstanding a salary of fifty thousand dollars a year was voted. The king approved of his appointment, and the monarch, being deserted by his bad advisers, threw himself upon the National Assembly. "He has hitherto been deceived," Lafayette proclaimed to the people, "but he now sees the merit and justice of the popular cause." The people shouted "Vive le roi!" and for a moment the revolution seemed to be at an end.

The key of the Bastile was placed in the hands of Lafayette, and in March following he sent it to Thomas Paine, then in London, to be forwarded as a present to Washington, together with a neat drawing, in pencil, representing the destruction of

the prison. A copy of that sketch is given on page 221. With these Lafayette enclosed a letter to Washington, dated the 17th of March, in which he gave him a general picture of affairs in France, and added:

"After I have confessed all this, I will tell you, with the same candor, that we have made an admirable and almost incredible destruction of all abuses and prejudices; that every thing not directly useful to or coming from the people has been levelled; that in the topographical, moral, and political situation of France, we have made more changes in ten months than the most sanguine patriots could have imagined; that our internal troubles and anarchy are much exaggerated; and that, upon the whole, this revolution, in which nothing will be wanting but energy of government, as it was in America, will implant liberty and make it flourish throughout the world; while we must wait for a convention, in a few years, to mend some defects, which are not now perceived by men just escaped from aristocracy and despotism."

He then added:

"Give me leave, my dear general, to present you with a picture of the Bastile, just as it looked a few days after I ordered its demolition, with the main key of the fortress of despotism. It is a tribute which I owe as a son to my adopted father—as an aide-de-camp to my general—as a missionary of liberty to its patriarch."

After considerable delay, Paine forwarded the key and drawing to Washington, with a letter, in which he said:

"I feel myself happy in being the person through whom the Marquis has conveyed this early trophy of the spoils of despotism, and the first ripe fruits of American principles transplanted into Europe, to his great master and patron. When he mentioned to me the present he intended for you, my heart leaped with joy. It is something so truly in character, that no remarks can illustrate it, and is more happily expressive of his remembrance of his American friends than any letters can convey. That the principles of America opened the Bastile is not to be doubted, and therefore the key comes to the right place. * * * *

"I should rejoice to be the direct bearer of the marquis's present to your excellency, but I doubt I shall not be able to see my much-loved America till next spring. I shall therefore send it by some American vessel to New York.

KEY OF THE BASTILE.

I have permitted no drawing to be taken here, though it has been often requested, as I think there is a propriety that it should first be presented. But Mr. West wishes Mr. Trumbull to make a painting of the presentation of the key to you."

On the 11th of August Washington wrote to Lafayette:

"I have received your affectionate letter of the 17th of March by one conveyance, and the token of the victory gained by liberty over despotism by another, for both which testimonials of your friendship and regard I pray you to accept my sincerest thanks. In this great subject of triumph for the New World, and for humanity in general, it will never be forgotten how conspicuous a part you bore, and how much lustre you reflected on a country in which you made the first displays of your character."

The key of the Bastile, and the drawing representing the demolition of the fortress, are at Mount Vernon. The former is preserved in a glass case, and the latter hangs near it, in the same relative position in which they were originally placed by Washington, in the great passage of the mansion.

Directly opposite the key, in the great passage, hangs the spy-glass used by Washington in the Revolution, and after-

WASHINGTON'S SPY-GLASS.

ward at Mount Vernon. This was always carried by Billy, his favorite body-servant, to be used in reconnoitring at a distance. Mr. Custis, in his *Recollections of Washington*, gives the following anecdote in connection with this spy-glass, or telescope, on the field of Monmouth:

"A ludicrous occurrence varied the incidents of the 28th of June. The servants of the general officers were usually well armed and mounted. Will Lee, or Billy, the former huntsman, and favorite body-servant of the Chief, a square, muscular figure, and capital horseman, paraded a corps of valets, and, riding pompously at their head, proceeded to an eminence crowned by a large sycamore-tree, from whence could be seen an extensive portion of the field of battle. Here Billy halted, and, having unslung the large telescope that he always carried in a leathern case, with a martial air applied it to his eye, and reconnoitred the enemy. Washington having observed these manœuvres of the corps of valets, pointed them out to his officers, observing, 'See those fellows collecting on yonder height; the enemy will fire on them to a certainty.' Meanwhile the British were not unmindful of the assemblage on the height, and perceiving a burly figure well mounted, and with a telescope in hand, they determined to pay their respects to the group. A shot from a six-pounder passed through the tree, cutting away the limbs, and producing a scampering among the corps of valets, that caused even the grave countenance of the general-in-chief to relax into a smile."

The pocket telescope used by Washington throughout the war was presented to President Jackson, by the late George Washington Parke Custis, on the 1st of January, 1830. To this interesting memorial Mr. Custis had affixed a silver plate, with the following inscription:

"*Erat Auctoris, est conservatoris, Libertatis.* 1775—1783."

On presenting the gift, Mr. Custis observed that, "Although it was in itself of but little value, there was attached unto it recollections of the most interesting character. It had been raised to the eye of the departed Chief, in the most awful and momentous periods of our mighty conflict; it had been his companion from '75 to '83, amid the toils, privations, the hopes, the fears, and the final success of our glorious struggle for independence; and, as the memorial of the hero who triumphed to obtain liberty, it is now appropriately bestowed upon the hero who triumphed to preserve it. Mr. C. requested that, as he (the General) was childless, he would be pleased, at his decease, to leave the telescope as Alexander left his kingdom—'to the most worthy.'"

President Jackson accepted the present and the compliment, and made a brief response. Whether he left it "to the most worthy," at his decease, or where it is now, we have no information.

Washington carried with him to Mount Vernon, with the key of the Bastile, a pair of elegant pistols, which, with equally elegant holsters, had been presented to him by the Count de Moustier, the French minister, as a token of his personal regard. These weapons, it is believed, are the ones presented by Washington to Col. Samuel Hay, of the tenth Pennsylvanian regiment, who stood high in the esteem of his general. They bear the well-known cipher of Washington, and were purchased at the sale of Colonel Hay's effects, after his death in November, 1803, by John Y. Baldwin, of Newark, New Jersey. His son, J. O. Baldwin, presented one of them to Isaac I. Greenwood, of New York, in 1825, in whose family it remains, I believe, the other having been lost on the occasion of a fire which destroyed the residence of his mother. Our engraving represents the preserved one.

WASHINGTON'S PISTOL.

Mr. Baldwin relates the following anecdote in connection with these pistols:— "When I was a boy," he says, "my father would frequently take up the *Aurora*, a newspaper then published in Philadelphia, and marking off about twenty lines, would say, 'Now, Joseph, if you read those correctly, and without a single mistake, you shall fire off one of Washington's pistols.' Such a promise was a high incentive, and if the task was fairly accomplished, my mother would take off her thimble to measure the charge, and my father, having loaded the pistol, I would go to the backdoor with an exulting heart, and lifting the weapon on high, tightly grasped with both hands, pull the trigger."

While at Mount Vernon in the autumn of 1790, Washington received from the Count D'Estaing a small bust of M. Necker, the French minister of finance, or comptroller-general, when the French Revolution broke out in 1789. James Necker was a native of Geneva, in Switzerland. He went to France as ambassador for the republic, where, in 1765, he obtained the office of syndic to the East India Company, and in 1775 was made director of the royal treasury. He exhibited such virtue of character, and such eminent abilities, that twice, though a foreigner, he was made prime minister of France. He was popular with the people at the breaking out of the French Revolution, but that storm was so variable and fickle, that he returned to Switzerland, where he remained until his death, which occurred in 1804, at the age of seventy-two years. His daughter married Baron de Staël Holstein, a Swedish ambassador at the court of France. She was the Madame de Staël so well known in the world of letters.

The little bust of Necker sent by D'Estaing to Washington, was upon a bracket over the fireplace in the library at Mount Vernon, where the President placed it himself. Upon the tall pedestal were two brass plates, bearing inscriptions, and also a small plate upon the lower part of the bust itself. On the latter was only the name of

NECKER.

Upon the upper plate on the pedestal were the words:

QUI NOBIS RESTITUIT REM.

Upon the second or lower plate was inscribed:

PRESENTED TO

GEORGE WASHINGTON,

PRESIDENT OF THE UNITED STATES OF AMERICA,

BY HIS MOST DUTIFUL, MOST OBEDIENT, AND MOST HUMBLE SERVANT, ESTAING, A CITIZEN OF THE STATE OF GEORGIA, BY AN ACT OF 22D FEB., 1785, AND A CITIZEN OF FRANCE IN 1786.

Count D'Estaing, who had twice commanded a French fleet on our coast, in co-operation with American land forces, became a member of the Assembly of Notables in the early part of the French Revolution, and being suspected of an unfriendly feeling toward the terrorists, he was destroyed by the guillotine, on the 29th of April, 1793.

In a letter to Tobias Lear, (then in New York,) dated at Mount Vernon on the 3d of August, 1790, Washington requests him, when able to get at Count D'Estaing's letters (which, with others, had been packed for removal from New York to Philadelphia), to send him a transcript of what the Count says of a bust of M. Necker he had sent to him, together with a number of prints of Necker and Lafayette.

Upon another bracket in the library at Mount Vernon, not far from the little head of Necker, was a full-size bust of Lafayette, a copy of the one in the capitol at Richmond made by Houdon, by order of the legislature of the state of Virginia, in 1786, which was executed under the direction of Mr. Jefferson, then American minister in Paris. The legisla-

BUST OF M. NECKER.

ture of Virginia also ordered a copy to be made and presented to the city of Paris. This fact was made known to the authorities there, by Mr. Jefferson, in the following words:

"The legislature of the state of Virginia, in consideration of the services of Major-General the Marquis de Lafayette, has resolved to place his bust in their capitol. This intention of erecting a monument to his virtues, and to the sentiments with which he has inspired them, in the country to which they are indebted for his birth, has induced a hope that the city of Paris would consent to become the depository of a second proof of their gratitude. Charged by the state with the

BUST OF LAFAYETTE.

execution of this resolution, I have the honor to solicit the *Prévot des Marchands* and municipality of Paris to accept the bust of this brave officer, and give it a situation where it may continually awaken the admiration and witness the respect of the allies of France.

'THOS. JEFFERSON.

'Dated [at Paris] 17*th September*, 1786."

The *Prévot* soon received a letter from the Baron de Breteuil, minister and secretary of state for the department of Paris, informing him that the king, to whom the proposition had been submitted, approved of the bust being erected in the city. The council accordingly assembled on the 28th of September, and Mr. Short, of Virginia, representing Mr. Jefferson (who was confined to his room by illness), went to the *Hotel de Ville* to present the bust, which Houdon had satisfactorily executed. The proceedings of the meeting were opened by M. Pelletier de Morfontaine, counsellor of state and *Prévot des Marchands*, by stating its object. M. Veytard, the chief clerk, read all the documents connected with the matter, after which M. Ethit de Corny, attorney-general and knight of the order of Cincinnatus, delivered an address, in which he recounted the services of Lafayette in America, the confidence of the army in him, and the attachment of the people to him. In his official capacity he then gave the requisite instructions for the reception of the bust, agreeably to the wishes of the king. It was accordingly placed in one of the galleries of the *Hotel de Ville*, where it remains to this day.

This was a most rare honor to be paid to a young man, only twenty-nine years of age. It was as unexpected to Lafayette as it was grateful to his feelings; and it was an additional link in the bright chain of memories and sympathies which bound him to this country.

Soon after his arrival in New York to assume the duties of the presidency, Washington imported a fine coach from England, in which, toward the close of the time of his residence there, and while in Philadelphia, he often rode with his family, attended by outriders. On these occasions it was generally drawn by four, and sometimes by six fine bay horses. The first mention of a coach, in his diary, in which he evidently refers to this imported one, is under the date of December 12, 1789, where he records as follows:

"Exercised in the coach with Mrs. Washington and the two children (Master and Miss Custis) between breakfast and dinner—went the fourteen miles round." Previous to this he

WASHINGTON'S ENGLISH COACH.

mentions exercising in "*a* coach" (probably a hired one), and in "the post-chaise"—the vehicle in which he travelled from Mount Vernon to New York.

This coach was one of the best of its kind, heavy and substantial. The body and wheels were a cream color, with gilt mouldings; and the former was suspended upon heavy leathern straps which rested upon iron springs. Portions of the sides of the upper part, as well as the front and rear, were furnished with neat green Venetian blinds, and the remainder was enclosed with black leather curtains. The latter might be raised so as to make the coach quite open in fine weather.

The blinds afforded shelter from the storm while allowing ventilation. The coach was lined with bright black leather; and the driver's seat was trimmed with the same. The axles were wood, and the curved reaches iron.

Upon the door Washington's arms were handsomely emblazoned, having scroll ornaments issuing from the space between the shield and the crest; and below was a ribbon with his motto upon it.

Upon each of the four panels of the coach was an allegorical picture, emblematic of one of the seasons.

EMBLAZONING ON WASHINGTON'S COACH.

These were beautifully painted upon copper by Cipriani, an Italian artist. The ground was a very dark green—so dark that it appeared nearly black; and the allegorical figures were executed in bronze, in size nine and a half by ten inches. One of them, emblematical of spring, is represented in the engraving.

Washington and his family travelled from Elizabethtown to Philadelphia in this coach when on their way from New York to Mount Vernon, in the early autumn of 1789. Dunn, his driver, appears to have been quite incompetent to manage the six horses with which the coach was then drawn; and almost immediately after leaving Elizabethtown Point, he allowed the coach to run into a gully, by which it was injured. At Governor Livingston's, where they dined, another coachman

PICTURE ON A PANEL OF WASHINGTON'S COACH.

was employed. In a letter to Mr. Lear, written at a tavern in Maryland, while on his way to Mount Vernon, Washington said:

"Dunn has given such proof of his want of skill in driving, that I find myself under the necessity of looking out for some one to take his place. Before we reached Elizabethtown we were obliged to take him from the coach and put him on the wagon. This he turned over twice, and this morning he was found much intoxicated. He has also got the horses into the habit of stopping."

In a letter to Mr. Lear soon after arriving at Mount Vernon, Washington mentions the fact that he had left his coach and harness with Mr. Clarke, a coach-maker in Philadelphia, for repairs, and requests him to see that they are well done, when he shall reach that city, Mr. Lear being then in New York. David Clarke was an Englishman, and came over to Philadelphia about the year 1783. He constructed a travelling coach for the First President, and was sometimes called "Washington's coach-maker."

On the 31st of October, Washington again writes about his coach, in a letter to Mr. Lear. He appears to have had the emblazoning changed at that time, and instead of his entire coat-of-arms upon the doors, he had the crest only retained. He tells Mr. Lear that he thinks a wreath around the crests would better correspond with the seasons which were to remain on the panels, than the motto; and suggests that the motto might be put upon the plates of the harness. He leaves the whole matter, however, to the taste and judgment of Mr. Lear and the coach-maker.

This English coach was purchased by the late Mr. Custis, of Arlington, when the effects of the general were sold, after Mrs. Washington's death; and it finally became the property of the Right Reverend William Meade, now Bishop of the Protestant Episcopal Church in Virginia. Of this vehicle, the bishop thus writes:

"His old English coach, in which himself and Mrs. Washington not only rode in Fairfax county, but travelled through the entire length and breadth of the land, was so faithfully executed, that at the conclusion of that long journey, its builder, who came over with it, and settled in Alexandria, was proud to be told by the general, that not a nail or screw had failed. It so happened, in a way I need not state, that this coach came into my hands about fifteen years after the death of General Washington. In the course of time, from disuse, it being too heavy for these latter days, it began to decay and give away. Becoming an object of desire to those who delight in relics, I caused it to be taken to pieces and distributed among the admiring friends of Washington who visited my house, and also among a number of female associations for benevolent and religious objects, which associations, at their fairs and other occasions, made a large profit by converting the fragments into walking-sticks, picture-frames, and snuff-boxes. About two-thirds of one of the wheels thus produced one hundred and forty dollars. There can be no doubt that at its dissolution it yielded more to the cause of charity than it cost its builder at its first erection. Besides other mementos of it, I have in my study, in the form of a sofa, the hind seat, on which the general and his lady were wont to sit."*

From Mount Vernon, during the recess, Washington wrote several letters to Mr. Lear, who was charged with the removal of the effects of the President from New York, hiring a house for his residence in Philadelphia, and arranging the furniture of it. Previous to Washington's arrival in Philadelphia from New York, the corporation of the latter city had hired for his use the house of Robert Morris, in Market street, on the west side of Sixth street—the best that could be procured at that time. Washington had examined it and found it quite too

---

* Meade's *Old Churches, Ministers, and Families in Virginia*, ′I. 237

small to accommodate his household as he could wish, even with an addition that was to be made. "There are good stables," he said, "but for twelve horses only, and a coach-house which will hold all my carriages." There was a fine garden, well enclosed by a brick wall, attached to the mansion.

The state legislature, had, at about the same time, appropriated a fine building for his use on South Ninth street, on the grounds now covered by the University. But he declined accepting it, because he would not live in a house hired and furnished at the public expense.

There were other considerations, without doubt, that caused Washington to decline the liberal offers of the state and city authorities, to relieve him of any private expense for the support of his personal establishment. The question of the permanent locality of the seat of the federal government was not then fairly settled, and the Philadelphians were using every means in their power to have it fixed in their city. Washington was aware of this, and as he was more favorable to a site farther south, he was unwilling to afford a plea in favor of Philadelphia, such as the providing of a presidential mansion would afford.

This matter appears to have given Washington considerable anxiety. He was willing to rent Mr. Morris's house on his own account, and, with his accustomed prudence, he directed Mr. Lear to ascertain the price; but up to the middle of November his secretary was unsuccessful in his inquiries, though they were repeatedly made. Washington was unwilling to go into it, without first knowing what rent he had to pay. 'Mr Morris. has most assuredly," he said, "formed an idea of what ought to be the rent of the tenement in the condition he left it; and with this aid, the committee [of the Philadelphia city council] ought, I conceive, to be as little at a loss in determining what it should rent for, with the additions and alterations which are about to be made, and which ought to be done in a plain and neat and not by any means in an extravagant style; because the latter is not only contrary to my wish, but would really be detrimental to my interest and convenience, principally because it would be the means of keeping me out of the use and comforts of a home to a late period, and because the furniture and every thing else would require to be accordant therewith."

Washington was convinced that the committee was delaying with the intention of having the rent paid by the public, to which he would not consent; and he was not willing to have the place fixed and furnished in an extravagant manner, and thus be subjected to pay extortionate prices for the same.

"I do not know," he said, "nor do I believe that any thing unfair is intended by either Mr. Morris or the committee; but let us for a moment suppose that the rooms (the new ones I mean) were to be hung with tapestry, or a very rich and costly paper, neither of which would suit my present furniture; that costly ornaments for the bow windows, extravagant chimney-pieces and the like were to be provided; that workmen, from extravagance of the times, for every twenty shillings' worth of work would charge forty shillings; and that advantage would be taken of the occasion to newly paint every part of the house and buildings; would there be any propriety in adding ten or twelve-and-a-half per cent. for all this to the rent of the house in its original state, for the two years that I am to hold it? If the solution of these questions is in the negative, wherein lies the difficulty of determining that the houses and lots, when finished according to the proposed plan, ought to rent for so much.

"When all is done that can be done, the residence will not be so commodious as that I left in New York, for there (and the want of it will be found a real inconvenience at Mr. Morris's) my office was in the front room, below, where persons on business immediately entered; whereas, in the present case, they will have to ascend two pairs of stairs, and to pass by the public rooms as well as the private chambers to get to it."

In making suggestions to Mr. Lear about the proper arrangement of the furniture, even in minute detail, Washington said: "There is a small room adjoining the kitchen that might, if it is not essential for other purposes, be appropriated to the Sèvres china, and other things of that sort, which are not in common use." He undoubtedly referred to the sets of china which had been presented, one to himself, and the other to Mrs. Washington, by the officers of the French army. The former was a dull white in color, with heavy and confused scroll and leaf ornaments in bandeaux of deep blue, and having upon the sides of the cups and tureens, and in the bottoms of the plates, saucers, and meat dishes, the Order of the Cincinnati, held by Fame, personated by a winged woman with a trumpet. These designs were skilfully painted in delicate colors.

These sets of china were presented to Washington and his wife, at the time when the elegant and costly Order of the Cincinnati (delineated on page 130) was sent to him. That

Order, I omitted to mention in the proper place, cost three thousand dollars. The whole of the eagle, except the beak and eye, is composed of diamonds. So, also, is the group of military emblems above it, in which each drum-head is composed of one large diamond.

WASHINGTON'S CINCINNATI CHINA.

Several pieces of the Cincinnati china, as it is called, were preserved at Arlington House. In the engraving is shown a group composed of a large plate, a soup tureen, custard cup, and teapot.

The set of china presented at the same time by the French officers to Mrs. Washington, was of similar material, but more delicate in color than the general's. The ornamentation was also far more delicate, excepting the delineation of the figure and Cincinnati Order on the former. Around the outside of each cup and tureen, and the inside of each plate and saucer,

MRS. WASHINGTON'S CHINA.

is painted, in delicate color, a chain of thirteen large and thirteen small elliptical links. Within each large link is the name of one of the original thirteen states. On the sides of the cups and tureens, and in the bottom of each plate and saucer, is the interlaced monogram of Martha Washington—M. W.—enclosed in a beautiful green wreath, composed of the leaves of the laurel and olive. Beneath this is a ribbon, upon which is inscribed, in delicately-traced letters, DECUS ET TUTAMEN ABILLO. From the wreath are rays of gold, which give a brilliant appearance to the pieces. There is also a delicate-colored stripe around the edges of the cups, saucers, and plates. A few pieces of this set of china were preserved at Arlington House. The engraving represents a cup and saucer, and plate.

Mrs. Atkins of Germantown, granddaughter of Dr. David Stuart, who owned Washington's telescope, already mentioned, had a single piece of porcelain ware that belonged to the household goods of Mount Vernon. It was a white china butter-bowl and dish, with a cover. It was entirely white, with the exception of a gold stripe along the edges of the bowl and dish, and the knob of the lid. The bowl and dish were united.

CHINA BUTTER-BOWL AND DISH.

At that time the china like that presented by the French officers was only made at the Sèvres manufactory, the art of decorating porcelain or china-ware with enamel colors and gold being then not generally known. The colors used are all prepared from metallic oxides, which are ground with fluxes, or fusible glasses of various degrees of softness, suited to the peculiar colors with which they are used. When painted, the goods are placed in the enamel kiln, when the fluxed colors melt and fasten to the glazed surface, forming colored glasses. The gold, which is applied in the form of an amalgam, ground in turpentine, is afterward polished with steel burnishers.

The first Monday in December was the day fixed upon for the assembling of Congress. The seat of government, as we have observed, had been transferred to Philadelphia, not permanently, but temporarily. As early as December, 1788, the legislature of Virginia had offered to present to the United States a tract of land ten miles square, anywhere within the bounds of that commonwealth, for the permanent seat of government. Maryland made a similar offer. The citizens of New Jersey and Pennsylvania asked to have it upon the Delaware, within a tract of land ten miles square, to be ceded to the United States. The people of Trenton, in New Jersey, petitioned to have it there; those of Lancaster, in Pennsylvania, wished to have it there, while, as we have observed, the Philadelphians were extremely anxious to have their city remain the federal capital, as it had been most of the time since the commencement of the Revolution.

States and towns perceived great local advantages to be derived from a political metropolis in their midst, and were ready to make heavy sacrifices to obtain the boon. It is amusing to observe, in the correspondence and public proceedings of the times, how strongly local prejudices were engaged in the consideration of the matter. Dr. Rush, of Philadelphia, eager to have the Congress fix on that city as its future home, wrote to one of the Pennsylvania representatives, saying: "I rejoice in the prospect of Congress leaving New York; it is a sink of political vice;" and advised tearing it away from that city "in *any way*." A Virginian declared that, in his opinion, New York was the best situation in the Union for the national capital, it being superior to any place within his knowledge "for the orderly and decent behavior of its inhabitants;" while the South Carolinians objected to Philadelphia, on account of the Quakers, who, they declared, were "eternally dogging Southern members with their schemes of slave emancipation."

It was finally agreed by both Houses of Congress, that the national capital should be upon the "Potomac River, between the eastern branch and Conogocheague," and that Philadelphia should be the national city for ten years, until the one upon the Potomac should be laid out, and proper public buildings erected. The selection of the exact site was left to the President.

This action dissatisfied the New Yorkers, and elated the Philadelphians, for they considered a "half loaf better than no bread." Robert Morris had been chiefly instrumental in securing the residence of the government at Philadelphia for the ten years, and wit and satire pointed their keenest arrows at him. A caricature was issued "in which," says Griswold, "the stout senator from Pennsylvania was seen marching off with the federal hall upon his shoulders, its windows crowded with members of both houses, encouraging or anathematizing this novel mode of deportation, while the devil, from the roof of the Paulus' Hook ferry-house, beckoned to him in a patronizing manner, crying, 'This way, Bobby.'"

Freneau, who had written many pungent poems during the Revolution, used his pen upon the topic of the removal with considerable vigor, in prose and verse. In a political epistle, he makes a New York housemaid say to her friend in Philadelphia:

>"As for us, my dear Nanny, we're much in a pet,
>And hundreds of houses will be to be let;
>Our streets, that were just in a way to look clever,
>Will now be neglected and nasty as ever;
>Again we must fret at the Dutchified gutters
>And pebble-stone pavements, that wear out our trotters.
>   *   *   *   *   *   *   *   *   •
>This Congress unsettled is, sure, a sad thing—
>Seven years, my dear Nanny, they've been on the wing;
>My master would rather saw timber, or dig
>Than see them removing to Conogocheague—
>Where the houses and kitchens are yet to be framed,
>The trees to be felled and the streets to be named."

There were some Philadelphians who were as afflicted

because Congress was coming there, as New Yorkers were in having the government leave their city. As soon as it was ascertained that the government would reside there ten years, rents, and the prices of every kind of provisions and other necessaries of life, greatly advanced. "Some of the blessings," said a letter-writer at Philadelphia, quoted by Griswold, "anticipated from the removal of Congress to this city, are already beginning to be apparent. Rents of houses have risen, and I fear will continue to rise shamefully; even in the outskirts they have lately been increased from fourteen, sixteen, and eighteen pounds to twenty-five, twenty-eight, and thirty. This is oppression. Our markets, it is expected, will also be dearer than heretofore."

It was a view of these changes, and anticipated extortion, that made Washington so anxious to know beforehand how much rent he must pay for his house in Philadelphia, and to avoid furnishing it in an extravagant manner, as he did not expect to remain there more than two years. He was resolved to continue the unostentatious way of living he had commenced in New York, not only on his own account, but for the benefit of those connected with the government who could not afford to spend more than their salaries. And that resolution, well carried out, was most salutary in its effects. When Oliver Wolcott, of Connecticut, was appointed first auditor of the treasury, he, like a prudent man, before he would accept the office, went to New York to ascertain whether he could live upon the salary of fifteen hundred dollars a year. He came to the conclusion that he could live upon one thousand dollars a year, and he wrote to his wife, saying: "The example of the President and his family will render parade and expense improper and disreputable." This sentence speaks powerfully in illustration of the republican simplicity of Washington's household in those days.

The rent of Morris's house was fixed at three thousand dollars a year, and on the 22d of November, Washington left Mount Vernon for Philadelphia, accompanied by Mrs. Washington and Master and Miss Custis, in a chariot drawn by four horses. They were allowed to travel quietly, without any public parade, but receiving at every stopping-place the warm welcome of many private citizens and personal friends. None gave the President a heartier shake of the hand on this occasion, and none was more welcome to grasp it, than Tommy Giles, a short, thickset man, of English birth, who kept a little tavern a short distance from the Head of Elk (now Elkton), on the road from Baltimore. His tavern-sign displayed a rude portrait of Washington; and the President on his way to and from Mount Vernon, never passed by until he had greeted the worthy man.

Tommy had been a fife-major in the Continental army, and had been employed a long time by Washington as his confidential express in the transmission of money from one point to another. In this business he was most trustworthy. Mrs. Giles was a stout Englishwoman, but republican to the core. Washington always shook hands with her as heartily as with her husband, and frequently left a guinea in her palm.

On these occasions, when the President had passed, Tommy would array himself in his Continental uniform, and hasten to Hollingsworth's tavern, in Elkton (where Washington slept, or took a meal and fed his horses), to pay his respects in a formal manner to his beloved General. Washington always treated him with the greatest consideration, and for several days after such interviews, Tommy would be the greatest man in the village.

Tommy was appointed postmaster at Elkton, by Washington, and was for several years crier of the Cecil county court. He always deported himself with dignity; and, regarding his acquaintance with Washington and his official position as sufficient claim to profound personal respect, he sometimes assumed an authoritative manner quite amusing. In a recent letter to me, an old resident of Philadelphia, speaking of Tommy, remarks; "I was once obliged to attend court as a witness, and one day went home, a distance of twenty-two miles. I returned the following morning in a *snow-storm*, in the month of April, and reached the court-house a few minutes after nine o'clock, when Mr. Giles was making his proclamation for me to appear. As I dismounted from my horse, my nose commenced bleeding, and I called across the street to say I would be in court as soon as it stopped. Tommy rejoined shortly and authoritatively, 'You have no business to let your nose bleed when the court wants you!' The court was more indulgent, and readily excused me."

The President and his family reached Philadelphia on Saturday, the 28th of November, and found their house in readiness for them. Mr. Lear had brought on the furniture from New York, purchased some in Philadelphia, and arranged the house much to the satisfaction of the President and his wife. Yet it was some time before they were ready to see company, and the first of Mrs. Washington's public receptions was on Friday evening, the 25th of December—Christmas-day. It is said that the most brilliant assemblage of beautiful, well-dressed, and well-educated women that had ever been seen in

America, appeared at that *levee*. The Vice-President's wife mentioned in a letter that "the dazzling Mrs. Bingham and her beautiful sisters [Misses Willing], the Misses Allens, the Misses Chew, and in short, a constellation of beauties," were present.

The season opened very gayly, and balls, routs and dinners of the most sumptuous kind, succeeded each other in rapid succession. "I should spend a very dissipated winter," wrote Mrs. Adams, "if I were to accept one-half the invitations I receive, particularly to the routs, or tea-and-cards." Philadelphia had never seen or felt any thing like it, and the whole town was in a state of virtual intoxication for several weeks. But Washington and his wife could not be seduced from their temperate habits, by the scenes of immoderate pleasure around them. They held their respective *levees* on Tuesdays and Fridays, as they did in New York, without the least ostentation; and Congressional and official dinners were also given in a plain way, without any extravagant displays of plate, or nament, or variety of dishes.

Having furnished his house as a permanent residence while he should remain President, Washington had indulged in some things which would insure congruity, that were not seen in New York. He had ordered through Gouverneur Morris, then in Paris, some articles for his sideboard and table. Among them were some silver-plated wine-coolers, the cost of which rather startled him. He had received an invoice of them, before he left Mount Vernon, and in a letter to Mr. Lear, he wrote:

"Enclosed I send you a letter from Mr. Gouverneur Morris, with a bill of the cost of the articles he was to send me. The prices of the plated ware exceed—far exceed—the utmost bounds of my calculation; but as I am persuaded he has done what he conceives right, I am satisfied, and request you to make immediate payment to Mr. Constable, if you can raise the means."

He then spoke of *wine-coolers*, that had been sent, an article that he had never used, and says: "As these *coolers* are designed for warm weather, and will be, I presume, useless in cold, or in that in which the liquors do not require cooling, *quere*, would not a stand like that for casters, with four apertures for so many different kinds of liquors, each aperture just sufficient to hold one of the cut decanters sent by Mr. Morris, be more convenient for passing the bottles from one to another, than the handing each bottle separately, by which it often happens that *one* bottle moves, *another* stops, and *all* are in confusion? Two of them—one for each end of the table, with a flat bottom, with or without feet, open at the sides, but with a raised rim, as caster-stands have, and an upright, by way of handle, in the middle—could not cost a great deal, even if made wholly of silver. Talk to a silversmith, and ascertain the cost, and whether they could be immediately made, if required, in a handsome fashion.

"Perhaps the coolers sent by Mr. Morris may afford ideas of taste; perhaps, too (if they prove not too heavy, when examined), they may supersede the necessity of such as I have described, by answering the purpose themselves. Four double flint bottles (such as I suspect Mr. Morris has sent), will weigh, I conjecture, four pounds; the wine in them when they are filled will be eight pounds more, which, added to the weight of the coolers, will, I fear, make these latter too unwieldy to pass, especially by ladies, which induces me to think of the frame in the form of casters."

Mr. Lear was pleased with Washington's suggestions, and ordered a silversmith to make two of the caster-like frames, of solid silver, and these were used upon the President's table on the occasion of the first dinner which he gave to the officers of government and their families, foreign ministers and their families, and other distinguished guests. Their lightness and convenience commended them, and from that time they became fashionable, under the appropriate title of *coasters*. Thenceforth the wine-*cooler* was left upon the sideboard, and the *coaster* alone was used for sending the wine around the table. For more than a quarter of a century afterward, the *coaster* might be seen upon the table of every fashionable family in Philadelphia. Few persons, however, are aware that Washington was the inventor of it.

The coolers sent over by Mr. Morris, were eight in number, four large and four smaller ones, the former holding four bottles, and the latter two. Two of the larger ones were presented by Washington to General Hamilton, and were until her death in possession of Mrs. Holley, of Washington city, a daughter of the latter. The others were taken from Philadelphia to Mount Vernon, and after the death of Mrs. Washington, passed into the possession of her grandson, George Washington Park Custis, and afterwards to Mr. Custis's daughter, at Arlington House. They were both elliptical in form at top, the larger one nine inches in height, and the smaller one eight inches. The silver *coasters* were also at Arlington House. They were fourteen inches in height, and each was composed of four baskets united to a handle in the centre, made of strong wire

WINE-COOLERS AND COASTER.

There was a roller under the centre of each basket, by which the coaster was more easily sent around the table. A specimen of these articles is seen in the above engraving.

Washington took his family plate with him when he went to New York in 1789, and there had it made over into more elegant and massive forms. Several pieces were also added to it, and this service graced his table and sideboard in Philadelphia. Several pieces of this plate were in use at Arlington House. The engraving shows five of them, namely, a round salver, an elliptical tray, a coffee-pot, tea-pot, and sugar-bowl. All of these had Washington's crest neatly engraven upon them. The tray with handles, all of massive silver, was plain, except a beaded rim. It was twenty-two inches in length, and seventeen and a half inches in breadth. This with the waiter, was used at all the *levees* and drawing-rooms of the President and Mrs. Washington, during the eight years of their public life in New York and Philadelphia, and served

SPECIMENS OF WASHINGTON'S PLATE.

the purposes of hospitality afterward, at Mount Vernon. How many eyes, beaming with the light of noble souls, have looked upon the glittering planes of that tray and salver! How many hands that once wielded mighty swords, and mightier pens, in the holy cause of universal freedom, long since mouldered into native earth, have taken from them the sparkling glass, while health and long life were invoked for Washington!

Mr. Custis once related to me a pleasing circumstance connected with the use of that tray. Gushing from a rocky bank beneath the trunk of a huge oak-tree—a genuine Anak of the primeval forest—near the bank of the Potomac, on his estate, is a copious spring, and around it stands a beautiful grove, wherein parties from Alexandria, Washington city and Georgetown, have picnics in the summer months. For the accommodation of these, Mr. Custis generously erected, near the spring, a kitchen and dancing-hall; and he frequently attended the joyous gatherings, and lent servants to wait upon the ladies.

On one occasion, a party of military, accompanied by ladies, went over to Arlington spring, from Washington city, for a day's recreation. Mr. Custis sent his favorite servant, Charles, to wait upon the company at table. He also sent down the precious silver tray for their use. Placing a dozen glasses of ice cream upon it, Charles carried it to the visitors, and said, " Ladies, this waiter once belonged to General Washington, and from it all the great ladies of the Revolution took wine." The young ladies, as if actuated by one impulse, immediately arose, crowded around Charles, and each in turn, kissed the cold rim of the salver, before touching the cream.

The session of 1790–91, was the third of the first Congress, and ended by limitation on the 3d of March; but Washington did not depart from Philadelphia for Mount Vernon, until Monday the 21st. On that day, at twelve o'clock, he and his family left his residence on Market-street, in his English coach, drawn by six horses, accompanied by Mr. Jefferson and General Knox (two of the heads of departments), who escorted them as far as Delaware. Major Jackson was also of the party. He accompanied Washington to Mount Vernon, and

THE PRESIDENTIAL MANSION.

throughout an extensive tour through the Southern states, which the President commenced a few days afterward.

That tour had occupied Washington's thoughts from time to time, for several months. Many leading men of the South invited him to visit their respective states. He had made a tour eastward, and it was deemed expedient that the Southern states should be honored by his presence. Their invitations generally expressed a desire, that the President, in the event of his making such tour, should honor the writers by a residence with them, while he remained in their respective neighborhoods. Among others who proffered the hospitalities of his house was Colonel William Washington, the heroic cavalry officer in the southern campaigns under Greene, who was then residing in Charleston. But his invitation, like all others of the same kind, was declined for reasons which Washington frankly stated:

"I cannot," he said, "comply with your invitation, without involving myself in inconsistency; as I have determined to pursue the same plan in my Southern as I did in my Eastern visit, which was, not to incommode any private family by taking up my quarters with them during my journey. It leaves me unincumbered by engagements, and by a uniform adherence to it, I shall avoid giving umbrage to any, by declining all such invitations."

Washington remained at Mount Vernon only a week, making preparations for his Southern tour. On the 4th of April he wrote to the several heads of departments—Jefferson, Hamilton and Knox—giving them information concerning the time when he expected to be at certain places on his route. This information was given because the public service might require communication to be made to him.

"My journey to Savannah," he said, "unless retarded by unforeseen interruptions, will be regulated, including days of halt, in the following manner: I shall be, on the 8th of April at Fredericksburg, the 11th at Richmond, the 14th at Petersburg, the 16th at Halifax, the 18th at Tarborough, the 20th at Newbern, the 25th at Wilmington, the 29th at Georgetown, South Carolina; on the 2d of May at Charleston, halting there five days; on the 11th at Savannah, halting there two days. Thence leaving the line of mail, I shall proceed to Augusta; and according to the information which I may receive there, my return by an upper road will be regulated."

It is a singular fact that Washington was at these various places on the very days contemplated. He wrote to Jefferson from Richmond on the 13th of April, to Hamilton from Charleston on the 7th of May, and to Mr. Seagrove, collector of the port of St. Mary, Georgia, from Savannah on the 20th. He was everywhere received with demonstrations of the highest respect and veneration. At Wilmington he was met by a military and civic escort, entertained at a public dinner, and in the evening attended a ball given in his honor. At Newbern he received like homage; and when, on Monday, the 2d day of May, he arrived at Haddrell's Point, a short distance from Charleston, beyond the mouth of the Cooper River, a twelve-oared barge, manned by thirteen captains of American ships, was in readiness to receive him, and convey him to the city. The barge contained a band of vocal and instrumental performers, and was followed by a flotilla of richly decked boats, of every kind, filled with gentlemen and ladies. At the wharf he was received by Governor Charles Cotesworth Pinckney, and conducted to his lodgings by a military and civic escort.

On Monday, the 9th of May, he left Charleston for Savannah; and on his way from that city a week afterward, he stopped and dined with the widow of General Greene. He reached Augusta on the 18th, and on Saturday, the 21st, he started for home, travelling by way of Columbia, Camden, Charlotte, Salisbury, Salem, Guilford, Hillsborough, Harrisburg, Williamsburg, and Fredericksburg, to Mount Vernon. He arrived home on the 12th of June, having made a most satisfactory journey of more than seventeen hundred miles, in sixty-six days, with the same team of horses. "My return to this place is sooner than I expected," he wrote to Hamilton, "owing to the uninterruptedness of my journey by sickness, from bad weather, or accidents of any kind whatsoever," for which he had allowed eight days.

Washington remained at Mount Vernon between three and four weeks. Meanwhile, he met commissioners at Georgetown, who had been appointed to lay out the national city, Washington having selected as the site the point of land on the eastern side of the Potomac, between that river and the Anacostia, or eastern branch, which flows eastward of the capitol. It is related as an historical fact, that in the year 1663, almost two hundred years ago, the proprietor of that land, named Pope, marked out a city upon it, called it Rome, named the elevation on which the capitol now stands (and where the Indian tribes held their councils) the Capitoline Hill, and the east branch of the Potomac the Tiber!

Major L'Enfant, a Frenchman, who had served as engineer in the continental army, was employed to furnish a plan and make a survey of the national city, and he spent a week at Mount Vernon, after Washington's return from his southern tour, in consultation with the President. His plans were laid before Congress at the next session, and were approved. The national city was laid out on a magnificent scale, on a plot containing eight square miles. The states of Virginia and Maryland had already ceded to the United States a territory ten miles square, for the purpose of erecting the national city within it, and this was named the District of Columbia.

L'Enfant and the commissioners disagreed, and he was succeeded by Andrew Ellicott, in 1792. On the 2d of April that year, President Washington approved of a plan for the capitol, submitted by Dr. Thornton, and in September, 1793, he laid the corner-stone of the north wing, with Masonic honors. The commissioners, without the President's knowledge or consent, named the national metropolis the *City of Washington*, which honored name it bears.

Washington was again at the presidential mansion, in Philadelphia, on the 6th of July, where he remained until September, when he returned to Mount Vernon, to spend a few weeks previous to the assembling of the new Congress. During that recess from official labors he was part of the time employed in the instruction of a new agent, Robert Lewis, in the management of his estate, his nephew, George A. Washington, having been compelled to leave for the mountains on account of ill health. At the same time he carried on quite an extensive correspondence with officers of the government and private citizens. Every post brought him numerous letters. An Indian war, in the North-western territory, was in progress; the French Revolution was assuming an alarming shape, for the obligations of an ally still appeared to rest upon the United States, especially so long as Louis remained king; and domestic affairs, pertaining to finance and commerce, were largely occupying the public mind. These topics engaged Washington's pen very frequently during his weeks of rest at Mount Vernon.

The first session of the second Congress opened on the 24th of October, and on the 25th Washington delivered his annual message in person, in the Congress Hall, corner Sixth and Chestnut streets. About two months later he was waited upon by Archibald Robertson, a Scotch artist of considerable merit, who had been induced to come to the United States to practice his profession, by Doctor Kemp, of Columbia College, New York.

Robertson came charged with an interesting commission from the Earl of Buchan He arrived in New York in October, and in December went to Philadelphia to fulfil his special engagement. He had been charged by the Earl to deliver to Washington a box made of the celebrated oak-tree that sheltered Sir William Wallace after the battle at Falkirk. Accompanying the box was a letter from the Earl, dated at Dryburgh Abbey, Jan. 28, 1791, in which, after speaking of the box, and his having trusted it to the "care of Mr. Robertson, of Aberdeen, a painter," he said:

"This box was presented to me by the goldsmiths' company at Edinburgh, of whom—feeling my own unworthiness to receive this magnificent and significant present—I requested, and obtained leave to make it over to the man in the world to whom I thought it most justly due; into your hands I commit it, requesting you to pass it, in the event of your decease, to the man in your own country, who shall appear to your judgment to merit it best, upon the same considerations that have induced me to send it to your Excellency."

He added—

"I beg your Excellency will have the goodness to send me your portrait, that I may place it among those I most honor, and I would wish it from the pencil of Mr. Robertson."

Robertson presented the box to the President on Friday, the 13th of December. He was much embarrassed, he said, on being introduced to "the American hero," but was soon relieved by Washington, who entered into familiar conversation with him, and introduced him to Mrs. Washington. The President also made the painter happy, by consenting to sit for his portrait, in compliance with the wishes of the Earl of Buchan. He also invited Robertson to dine with him; and the painter felt quite at ease before he left the august presence. Of that dinner (a family one) Robertson thus writes:

"It was ready at three o'clock—plain, but suitable for a family in genteel circumstances. There was nothing specially remarkable at the table, but that the general and Mrs. Washington sat side by side, he on the right of his lady; the gentlemen on his right hand, and the ladies on his left. It being on Saturday, the first course was mostly of eastern cod and fresh fish. A few glasses of wine were drank during the dinner, with other beverages. The whole closed with a few glasses of sparkling champagne, in about three-quarters of an hour, when the general and Colonel Lear retired, leaving the ladies in high glee about Lord Buchan and the Wallace box."

After dinner, the President sat to Mr. Robertson, for a miniature portrait, and from it, when finished, the artist painted a larger picture, in oil, for Lord Buchan, "of a size," he said, "corresponding to the collection of portraits of the most celebrated worthies of liberal principles and of useful literature, in the possession of his lordship." This picture was painted at the close of May, 1792, when Washington wrote to Lord Buchan, thanking him for the present of the box, and saying of the portrait: "The manner of the execution of it, does no discredit, I am told, to the artist." The picture was sent to Europe by Colonel Lear, and Robertson received the thanks of the Earl of Buchan.

Mrs. Washington also sat to Robertson for her miniature. She was then sixty years of age, and still beautiful. Her complexion was fair, and her dark eye was as brilliant as ever. In person she was heavier than in her younger days, and was, in a very slight degree, inclined to corpulency. That miniature is now at Arlington House. It was first engraved for the *American Portrait Gallery*, about the year 1833. In a letter to his wife, in July of that year, Mr. Custis wrote:

"I have been requested to write a short biography of my grandmother, to be accompanied by a splendid engraving from one of my originals, for Longman's work, called the *National Gallery of Portraits*, and have consented to do it." The biography was written, and the "original" chosen was Robertson's miniature, from which our engraving was copied.

In his letter of thanks to Buchan, Washington said:

"I will, however, ask, that you will exempt me from compliance with the request relating to its eventual destination. In an attempt to execute your wish in this particular, I should feel embarrassment from a just comparison of relative pretensions, and fear to risk injustice by so marked a preference."

The box was taken to Mount Vernon at the close of the session, where it remained until Washington's death, when

MARTHA WASHINGTON.

he recommitted it to the Earl by the following clause in his will:

"To the Earl of Buchan I recommit the box made of the oak that sheltered the great Sir William Wallace, after the battle of Falkirk, presented to me by his lordship, in terms too flattering for me to repeat, with a request 'to pass it, on the event of my decease, to the man in my country who should appear to merit it best, upon the same conditions that have induced him to send it to me.' Whether easy or not to select the man who might comport with his lordship's opinion, in this respect, is not for me to say; but, conceiving that no disposition of this valuable curiosity can be more eligible than the recommitment of it to his own cabinet, agreeably to the original design of the Goldsmith's Company of Edinburgh, who presented it to him, and, at his request, consented that it should be transferred to me, I do give and bequeath the same to his lordship; and, in case of his decease, to his heir, with my grateful thanks for the distinguished honor of presenting it to me, and more especially for the favorable sentiments with which he accompanied it."

The first session of the second Congress terminated on Tuesday, the 8th of May, and on the 10th Washington set out for Mount Vernon, leaving his family in Philadelphia. He remained there about four weeks, directing the affairs of his estate, inspecting the progress of the surveys and plans for the national city, and in correspondence with friends at home and abroad. He carried home with him on that occasion several copies of the *Rights of Man*, a work from the pen of Thomas Paine, published the year before, fifty copies of which, sent by the author to the President, reached him a day or two before he left Philadelphia. One of these he gave to Richard Henry Lee, who, after thanking him for it, remarked:

"It is a performance of which any man might be proud; and I most sincerely regret that our country could not have offered sufficient inducements to have retained as a permanent citizen, a man so thoroughly republican in sentiment, and fearless in the expression of his opinions."

In his letter accompanying the books, Paine remarked:

"The work has had a run beyond any thing that has been published in this country on the subject of government, and the demand continues. In Ireland it has had a much greater. A letter I received from Dublin, 10th of May, mentioned that the fourth edition was then on sale. I know not what number of copies were printed at each edition, except the second, which was ten thousand. The same fate follows me here as I *at first* experienced in America—strong friends and violent enemies; but as I have got the ear of the country, I shall go on, and at least show them, what is a novelty here, that there can be a person beyond the reach of corruption."

This work was written in answer to Edmund Burke's famous letter to a French gentleman, in 1790, entitled *Reflections on the Revolution in France.* The government, incensed at Paine's language in the *Rights of Man*, instituted a prosecution against him for libel. He went to France, became a member of the National Assembly, fell into prison during the reign of the Terrorists, and becoming offended at Washington because he properly refused his official aid in procuring Paine's liberation, on the ground of his being an American citizen, he abused him most shamefully in a published letter, more remarkable for its scurrility than talent.

Washington returned to Philadelphia early in June, and toward the close of July journeyed with his family to Mount Vernon. He remained there until early in October, when he returned to Philadelphia, with his family, to prepare for the assembling of the Congress, which took place on the 5th of November. During that time he was in frequent correspondence with the heads of departments, for matters of great public interest required frequent communications between them and the chief magistrate. An Indian war in the west was then in progress, and symptoms of insurrectionary movements in Western Pennsylvania, on account of an excise law which the people deemed oppressive, began to appear.

Washington was also much engaged, during that time, with his agricultural operations; and he and Mrs. Washington were much distressed on account of the mortal sickness of his nephew George, who had resided at Mount Vernon much of the time since his marriage several years before. Washington's anxiety concerning him is evinced by the frequent mention of his illness to his correspondents. In a letter to Lafayette, in June, he said:

"I am afraid my nephew George, your old aide, will never have his health perfectly re-established. He has lately been attacked with the alarming symptoms of spitting large quantities of blood; and the physicians give no hopes of restoration, unless it can be effected by a change of air, and a total dereliction from business, to which he is too anxiously attentive. He will, if he should be taken from his family and friends, leave three fine children, two sons and a daughter. To the eldest of the boys he has given the name of Fayette, and a fine looking child he is."

To General Knox, he wrote: "I thank you most sincerely for the medicine you were so obliging as to send for my nephew, and for the sympathetic feeling you express for his situation. Poor fellow! neither, I believe, will be of any avail. Present appearances indicate a speedy dissolution. He has not been able to leave his bed, except for a few moments to sit in an arm-chair, since the 14th or 15th of last month. The paroxysm of the disorder seems to be upon him, and death, or a favorable turn to it, must speedily follow."

The sufferer was then residing upon a small estate in Hanover. He lingered for several weeks, and expired; and on the 24th of February, Washington wrote to his widow:

"My Dear Fanny: To you, who so well know the affectionate regard I had for our departed friend, it is unnecessary to describe the sorrow with which I was afflicted, at the news of his death, although it was an event I had expected many weeks before it happened. To express this sorrow with the force I feel it, would answer no other purpose than to revive in your breast that poignancy of anguish, which by this time, I hope, is abated. The object of this letter is to convey to your mind the warmest assurance of my love, friendship, and disposition to serve you. These I also profess to bear, in an eminent degree, for your children."

He then invites her to make Mount Vernon the home of herself and children. "You can go to no place," he said, "where you will be more welcome, nor to any where you can live at less expense or trouble." He then invites her to bring his niece, Harriet Washington, with her, to Mount Vernon, of whose conduct he had heard pleasant words. Miss Harriet remained at Mount Vernon a long time, the grateful recipient of her uncle's bounty.

The young widow appears to have declined the offer of a home at Mount Vernon, preferring to keep house in Alexandria, but offering to resign the charge of her eldest son, Fayette, into Washington's keeping. In March, the President wrote to her, saying:

"The carriage which I sent to Mount Vernon, for your use, I never intended to reclaim, and now, making you a formal present of it, it may be sent for whenever it suits your convenience, and be considered as your own. I shall, when I see you, request that Fayette may be given up to me, either at that time, or as soon after as he is old enough to go to school. This will relieve you of that portion of attention, which his education would otherwise call for."

Washington's affection for children was very great, and he was ever anxious to have young people in the mansion at Mount Vernon. He enjoyed their amusements with a keen relish, and yet the mysterious awe felt in his presence, by all who had the good fortune to know him personally, was experienced by children. His adopted daughter (Mrs. Lewis) used to say that she had seen him laugh heartily at her merry pranks, or when, a gay, joyous girl, she would give him a description of some scene in which she had taken a part; and yet she had as often seen him retire from the room in which her young companions were amusing themselves, because he perceived that his presence created a reserve which they could not overcome.

His love for his two adopted children was very strong, and he watched over their mental and moral development with great solicitude. In several of his letters to Mr. Lear, from Mount Vernon, in the autumn of 1790, when preparing for his residence in Philadelphia, he mentioned the subject of schools, expressing a great desire to have young Custis placed in one of the best character.

Mrs. Washington was always over-indulgent to her two grandchildren. The boy (George Washington Parke Custis) was always familiarly called Washington, and by that name he was always distinguished in the general's private correspondence. His beautiful sister, Nelly, used to speak of the affection which Mrs. Washington lavished upon him, and the many excuses which she offered in his defence, when the father, true to his nature and education, exacted submission to the most thorough discipline on all occasions, much as he loved the boy.

"Grandmamma always spoiled Washington," his sister would say; and his daughter, in a late memoir of him, has said—" He was the pride of her heart, while the public duties of the veteran prevented the exercise of his influence in forming the character of the boy, too softly nurtured under his roof, and gifted with talents, which, under a sterner discipline, might have been more available for his own and his country's good."

Notwithstanding her indulgent disposition, Mrs. Washington was a thorough disciplinarian in her household, and Nelly Custis experienced many a tearful hour when compelled by her grandmother to attend assiduously to her studies in letters and music. Washington made her a present of a fine harpsichord, at the cost of one thousand dollars—Schroeder's beautiful invention, the piano-forte, not being then much used in America. In England, even, where Zumpe had introduced it, with many improvements, between twenty and thirty years before, the piano had by no means supplanted its parent the harpsichord, and the latter instrument, or the spinet, might be found in almost every family of wealth in the kingdom.

The best teachers were employed to instruct Nelly in the use of the harpsichord, and her grandmother made her practise upon it four or five hours every day. "The poor girl," says her brother, the late Mr. Custis, " would play and cry, and cry and play, for long hours, under the immediate eye of her grandmother, a rigid disciplinarian in all things."

That harpsichord, according to the inscription upon a plate above the keys, was manufactured by "Longman and Broderip, musical instrument makers, No. 26 Cheapside, and No. 13 Haymarket, London." It was carefully packed and taken to Mount Vernon when Washington retired from office the last time. It was used there until his death, for Nelly and her husband resided at Mount Vernon for more than

NELLY CUSTIS'S HARPSICHORD.

a year after their marriage in February, 1779. It became the property of Mr. Custis, of Arlington House, and after his death it passed into the hands of his daughter, Mrs. Lee. When Mount Vernon became the absolute property of the *Mount Vernon Ladies' Association*, Mrs. Lee presented the harpsichord to them, and it now occupies its ancient place in the venerated mansion.

The instrument was one of the most elegant of its kind. It is about eight feet long, three and a half feet wide, and three feet in length, with two banks, containing one hundred and twenty keys in all. The case is mahogany.

On the 4th of March, 1793, Judge Cushing, of Massachusetts, administered to Washington, in the senate chamber, in Philadelphia, the oath of office as President of the United States, he having been, by unanimous vote of the electoral college, speaking the will of the people, re-elected to the exalted station of chief magistrate. It was with great reluctance that he consented to serve another prescribed term of four years. He had looked forward to retirement from office with real pleasure, and when he agreed to serve his country still longer, he endured a sacrifice which none but a disinterested patriot could have made. For himself he preferred the quiet of domestic life at his pleasant home on the Potomac, to all the honors and emoluments that the world could offer. But in this instance, as in all others, he yielded his own wishes to the more important demands of his country. He knew, as well as any man living, the dangers to which the country was then exposed from the influence of French politics and of domestic factions; and the representations of the true friends of government convinced him that his further service in public life was demanded by every consideration of patriotism.

Hamilton, in whose judgment and purity of motives Washington had the most entire confidence, had urged him, in a touching letter, to accept the high office a second term; and while his cabinet was agitated by discordant opinions upon other subjects, they all agreed that Washington's retirement from office at that time would be a serious calamity to the country. Every one felt that the affairs of the national government were not yet firmly established: that its enemies were many and inveterate, and that Washington could not retire without damaging his reputation as a patriot. "I trust, sir, and I pray God, that you will determine to make a further sacrifice of your tranquillity and happiness to the public good," said Hamilton, at the close of his letter just alluded to.

Such sacrifice was made, and for four years longer Mount Vernon was without its master, except at long intervals.

Although Washington's second inauguration was in public, there was far less parade than at the first. It had been determined by those with whom he had consulted respecting the matter, as the democratic feeling was very strong, that the President should go to the senate-chamber "without form, attended by such gentlemen as he may choose, and return without form, except that he be preceded by the marshal."

Thus he went and thus he returned, conveyed in his own beautiful cream-colored coach, drawn by six splendid bay horses. And thus he went to that senate-chamber a few months later, when he presented his annual message to the Congress, for in those days the President read the address before the assembled wisdom of the nation, and did not, as now, send it in manuscript by his private secretary.

An eye-witness on one of these occasions has left a pleasant picture of it on record. "As the President alighted," he says, "and, ascending the steps, paused upon the platform, looking over his shoulder, in an attitude that would have furnished an admirable subject for the pencil, he was preceded by two gentlemen bearing long white wands, who kept back the eager crowd that pressed on every side to get a nearer view. At that moment I stood so near that I might have touched his clothes; but I should as soon have thought of touching an electric battery. I was penetrated with a veneration amounting to the deepest awe. Nor was this the feeling of a schoolboy only; it pervaded, I believe, every human being that approached Washington; and I have been told that, even in his social and convivial hours, this feeling in those who were honored to share them never suffered intermission. I saw him a hundred times afterward, but never with any other than that same feeling. The Almighty, who raised up for our hour of need a man so peculiarly prepared for its whole dread responsibility, seems to have put an impress of sacredness upon His own instrument. The first sight of the man struck the heart with involuntary homage, and prepared every thing around him to obey. When he 'addressed himself to speak,' there was an unconscious suspension of the breath, while every eye was raised in expectation.

"The President, having seated himself, remained in silence, serenely contemplating the legislature before him, whose members now resumed their seats, waiting for the speech. No house of worship, in the most solemn pauses of devotion, was ever more profoundly still than that large and crowded chamber."

"Washington was dressed precisely as Stuart has painted him in Lord Lansdowne's full-length portrait—in a full suit of the richest black velvet, with diamond knee-buckles, and square silver buckles set upon shoes japanned with the most scrupulous neatness, black silk stockings, his shirt ruffled at the breast and wrists, a light dress-sword, his hair profusely powdered, fully dressed, so as to project at the sides, and gathered behind in a silk bag, ornamented with a large rose of black riband. He held his cocked hat, which had a large black cockade on one side of it, in his hand, as he advanced toward the chair, and, when seated, laid it on the table.

"At length, thrusting his hand within the side of his coat, he drew forth a roll of manuscript, which he opened, and rising, held it in his hand, while in a rich, deep, full, sonorous voice, he read his opening address to Congress. His enunciation was deliberate, justly emphasized, very distinct, and accompanied with an air of deep solemnity, as being the utterance of a mind profoundly impressed with the dignity of the act in which it was occupied, conscious of the whole responsibility of its position and action, but not oppressed by it."

Washington made a hurried visit to Mount Vernon in April, on account of the death of his nephew, already mentioned, some matter connected with that young man's affairs requiring his personal attention. He was again called to Mount Vernon at the close of June, on account of the sudden death of Mr. Whiting, his manager, who had taken the place of Robert Lewis. "It was a critical season," says Washington, in a letter to General Henry Lee, "for the business with which he was interested. How to supply his place I know not; of course my concerns at Mount Vernon are left as a body without a head."

Notwithstanding Congress was not in session, the pressure of public business was such that Washington remained at the seat of government all through the summer, and it was not until the yellow fever, which broke out in Philadelphia in August, had raged for two or three weeks, and the officers of government had fled, that he left his post and retired to Mount Vernon. He left Philadelphia on the 10th of September. He would have remained longer, but Mrs. Washington, alarmed for the safety of the whole family, the house in which they lived being in a manner blockaded by the disorder, prevailed on him to leave.

The fever raged with great violence until late in October, when frosts checked its progress, and in November the inhabitants who had fled from the pestilence generally returned to the city. On the 2d day of December Congress was convened there.

The progress of the disease at Philadelphia was watched by Washington, at Mount Vernon, with great solicitude, especially when September had passed away, and much of October had gone by, before it abated. It was near the time set for the assembling of a new Congress, and the public welfare demanded legislative action, upon important points, as early as possible. He therefore proposed to call the Congress together at Germantown, or some other place near Philadelphia, but at a safe distance from the pestilence; and yet he doubted his power to do so. This topic employed his pen as well as his thoughts, and of many letters from Mount Vernon it was the burden.

His agricultural affairs occupied much of his time while at home. He appears to have found a manager not much to his liking, for he needed instruction. At the middle of October we find him writing to his friend, General Henry Lee, concerning a threshing-machine that that gentleman had recommended. He seemed anxious to use all really useful improvements, but the difficulty in making his overseers understand them was a bar.

"The model [of a threshing machine] brought over by the English farmers," he said, "may also be a good one, but the utility of it among careless negroes and ignorant overseers will depend absolutely upon the simplicity of the construction; for if there is any thing complex in the machinery, it will be no longer in use than a mushroom is in existence. I have seen so much of the beginning and ending of new inventions, that I have almost resolved to go on in the old way of treading until I get settled again at home, and can attend, myself, to the management of one. As a proof in point of the almost impossibility of putting the overseers of this country out of the track they have been accustomed to walk in, I have one of the most convenient barns in this or perhaps any other country, where thirty hands may with great ease be employed in threshing. Half of the wheat of the farm was actually stowed in this barn in the straw by my order, for threshing; notwithstanding, when I came home about the middle of September, I found a treading-yard not thirty feet from the barn-door, the wheat again brought out of the barn, and horses treading it out in an open exposure, liable to the vicissitudes of weather."

Washington and his family set out for the seat of government toward the close of October. Mr. Dandridge, a relation of his wife, who had been appointed the President's private secretary, accompanied them. Philadelphia presented a most gloomy aspect. Between three and four thousand of the inhabitants had fallen before the scythe of the pestilence, and there was mourning in almost every family. There was very little gayety in the capital during the session of Congress that followed. There was also a general expectation that the scourge would reappear the ensuing summer of 1794; and when, at the middle of June, Washington made a flying visit to Mount Vernon, he removed his family to a pleasant residence at Germantown, about six miles from the city. To that place he returned at the close of July, and he seems not to have visited Mount Vernon again until April the following year, when he was there for only a short time, to give his personal attention to home duties that required them. He again visited his home early in July, 1795, but, as his correspondence on the way and at Mount Vernon shows, he carried a vast weight of public business upon his mind; for, besides the routine of official duties, he was greatly burdened with anxiety respecting a treaty lately made with England, by John Jay, which he approved, and which for a time was so unpopular as to cause great excitement throughout the country.

Washington left Mount Vernon again toward the middle of August for the seat of government, and returned early in September. He remained until the 12th of October, when he set out for Philadelphia, stopping at Georgetown for a day to attend to business with the commissioners of the federal city.

It was not until June, 1796, that the master of Mount Vernon was again under his own roof. His family accompanied him; and there, at the beginning of July, they received as a guest, Don Carlos Martinez, Marquis d'Yrujo, the newly-arrived Spanish ambassador. On the 4th of July Washington wrote to Timothy Pickering, the secretary of state, saying:

"The Spanish Minister, M. d'Yrujo, spent two days with me, and is just gone. I caused it to be intimated to him that, as I should be absent from the seat of the government until the middle or latter end of August, I was ready to receive his letter of credence at this place. He answered, as I understood it, that his credentials were with his baggage on its passage to

Philadelphia, and that his reception at that place, at the time mentioned, would be perfectly convenient and agreeable to himself. He is a young man, very free and easy in his manners, professes to be well disposed toward the United States, and, as far as a judgment can be formed on so short an acquaintance, appears to be well informed."

The Spanish minister had not been long in Philadelphia when he became enamored of Sally, the beautiful daughter of Thomas M'Kean, the chief-justice of Pennsylvania, and they were married. Their son, the Duke of Sotomayer, who was born in Philadelphia, became prime minister of Spain.

"Philadelphia," says Griswold, "furnished wives for the envoys of France, England, and Spain during Washington's administration, and a large number of foreign ministers have since been married to American women." Genet, the French minister during Washington's first term, married a daughter of Governor Clinton, of New York.

Washington remained at Mount Vernon until the middle of August. During the time of this visit to his dearly-loved home, he completed the final draft of his Farewell Address to the people of the United States, prepared in contemplation of his retiring from public life forever, at the close of his term of office the ensuing spring. That address had been the subject of deep and anxious thought for many months, and at the special request of the President, Hamilton, Jay, and Madison, and perhaps others, had given him suggestions in writing, topical and verbal. These he took with him to Mount Vernon, and in the quiet of his library he arranged his address in the form and expression in which it was published in September following. It was the noblest production of Washington's mind and heart, and has been pronounced by Alison, the eminent British historian, unequalled by any composition of uninspired wisdom. It is a political legacy which not only the countrymen of Washington, but the world ought to value, as one of the most precious gifts ever bestowed by man upon his race. It is permeated with the immortal spirit of a true MAN, a true PATRIOT, and a true CHRISTIAN.

The Farewell Address was published in the *Philadelphia Advertiser*, in September, 1796, and produced a most profound sensation. The ribald voice of party spirit, which had been for a long time uttering the most scandalous abuse concerning the President, was at once subdued in tone, if not silenced, for it was deprived of the theme of Washington's renomination, which had been a convenient excuse for partisan attacks. The address was entered at length upon the journals of several of the state legislatures; was published in every newspaper in the land, and in many of those in foreign countries; and in legislative bodies and social and diplomatic circles abroad, it was a fruitful topic of remark for some time. Of all the associations which cluster around Mount Vernon, none should be dearer to the heart of every American—to every friend of freedom and good order—than that connected with WASHINGTON'S FAREWELL ADDRESS.

And now Washington calmly looked forward to his retirement from public life with a heart full of joy and gratitude. The eight years of his administration of public affairs had been years of immense toil, anxiety, and vexation. They had been stormy years, for blasts of disturbing and dangerous sentiments came frequently from the borders of the hurricane that swept so terribly over France, the old ally of the United States; and the electric forces of party spirit, subtle and implacable, had cast down, from the black clouds of selfish hate, a copious hail of abuse. But amid all that storm—in the face of those fierce blasts and that pelting hail, Washington stood calm, dignified, and unharmed; and he approached the hour when he should be no longer a public servant, to be applauded or reviled, with that serenity of mind which nothing but a conscience void of offence toward God and man can impart. And yet he was not always unmoved by the ungenerous attacks of his enemies. To his long-tried and dearly-loved friend, General Knox, then in the far east, he wrote, two days before his retirement:

"To the wearied traveller who sees a resting-place, and is bending his body to lean thereon, I now compare myself; but to be suffered to do this in peace is too much to be endured by some. To misrepresent my motives, to reprobate my politics, and to weaken the confidence which has been reposed in my administration, are objects which cannot be relinquished by those who will be satisfied with nothing short of a change in our political system. The consolation, however, which results from conscious rectitude, and the approving voice of my country, unequivocally expressed by its representatives, deprive their sting of its poison, and place in the same point of view the weakness and malignity of their efforts."

Never since has the unscrupulous virulence of party spirit been so manifest as at the time in question. No one dared openly to charge Washington with a dishonest or dishonorable act during his long public life; and yet, by inuendos and falsehoods of the darkest aspect, disguised as insinuations, his political enemies attempted to destroy his popularity, and to send him into private life without the sweet consolations of the approval of his countrymen.

One specimen of the venom of party hate will be sufficient to illustrate the remarks just made. I quote from a correspondent of the *Aurora*, a Philadelphia paper in opposition to Washington's administration. The number containing the following article was printed three days after the President's retirement from office:

"'Lord, now lettest thou thy servant depart in peace, for mine eyes have seen thy salvation,' was the pious ejaculation of a man who beheld a flood of happiness rushing upon mankind. If ever there was a time that would license the reiteration of the exclamation, that time is now arrived; for the man who is the source of all the misfortunes of our country, is this day reduced to a level with his fellow-citizens, and is no longer possessed of power to multiply evils upon the United States. If ever there was a period for rejoicing, this is the moment; every heart in unison with the freedom and happiness of the people, ought to beat high with exultation that the name of WASHINGTON, from this day, ceases to give a currency to political iniquity, and to legalize corruption. A new era is now opening upon us, an era which promises much to the people; for public measures must now stand upon their own merits, and nefarious projects can no longer be supported by a name. When a retrospect is taken of the Washingtonian administration for eight years, it is a subject of the greatest astonishment that a single individual should have cankered the principles of republicanism in an enlightened people, just emerged from the gulf of despotism, and should have carried his designs against the public liberty so far, as to have put in jeopardy its very existence. Such however are the facts, and with these staring us in the face, this day ought to be a JUBILEE in the United States."

How utterly impotent were such attempts to injure the character of Washington, let history testify.

On the 3d of March, 1797, Washington gave a farewell dinner, to which many of the leading persons at the seat of government were invited. These were chiefly the officers of government and members of the diplomatic corps, with their wives. Bishop White, whose sister was the wife of Robert Morris, was present, and described some of the events of the banquet.

"During the dinner," wrote the bishop, "much hilarity prevailed; but on the removal of the cloth, it was put an end to by the President—certainly without design. Having filled his glass, he addressed the company, with a smile on his countenance, saying, ' Ladies and gentlemen, this is the last time I shall drink your health as a public man. I do it with sincerity, and wishing you all possible happiness.' There was an end to all hilarity; and the cheeks of Mrs. Liston, wife of the British minister, were wet with tears."

On the following day John Adams, who had been elected Washington's successor, was inaugurated the second President of the United States. The event took place in the Hall of the Representatives, which was densely crowded with spectators. At the appointed hour Washington rode to Congress Hall in his coach, drawn by six horses, and, amidst the most enthusiastic cheers, entered the room prepared for the ceremonies which were to release him from public life. He was followed by Mr. Adams, and when they were seated, perfect silence prevailed. Washington then arose, and with the most commanding dignity and self-control, introduced Mr. Adams to the assembly, and proceeded to read, in a firm, clear voice, a brief valedictory.

"The most profound silence greeted him," said an eye and ear witness of the august event, to me, "as if the great assembly desired to hear him breathe, and catch his breath in homage of their hearts. Mr. Adams covered his face with both his hands; the sleeves of his coat and his hands were covered with tears." As he pronounced his parting words, a sob was heard here and there in the assembly; and when he sat down, the whole audience were in tears. "Then," says the eye-witness just quoted, "when strong nervous sobs broke loose, when tears covered the faces, then the great man was shaken. I never took my eyes from his face. Large drops fell from his cheeks."

The late President Duer, of Columbia College, who was present on that occasion, says that when Washington left the hall, there was "a rush from the gallery that threatened the lives of those who were most eager to catch a last look of him who, among mortals, was the first object of their veneration." "Some of us," he said, "effected an escape by slipping down the pillars."

When Washington had entered his carriage, the multitude in the streets uttered long and loud huzzas, and he waved his hand in return.

"I followed him," says Duer, "in the crowd to his own door, where, as he turned to address the multitude, his countenance assumed a serious and almost melancholy expression, his voice failed him, his eyes were suffused with tears, and only by his gestures could he indicate his thanks, and convey a farewell blessing to the people."

In the evening a splendid entertainment was given to the retiring President, by the inhabitants of Philadelphia, in the Amphitheatre, which was beautifully decorated with appropriate paintings. One of the newspapers of the day thus describes a compliment that was paid to Washington on that occasion:

"Upon entering the area the General was conducted to his seat. On a signal given, the band played *Washington's March*, and a scene, which represented simple objects in the rear of the principal seat, was drawn up and discovered emblematical paintings. The principal was a female figure as large as life, representing *America*, seated on an elevation composed of sixteen marble steps. At her left side stood the federal shield and eagle, and at her feet lay the *cornucopia;* in her right hand she held the Indian calumet of peace supporting the cap of liberty; in the perspective appeared the temple of fame; and, on her left hand, an altar dedicated to public gratitude, upon which incense was burning. In her left hand she held a scroll inscribed *Valedictory;* and at the foot of the altar lay a plumed helmet and sword, from which a figure of General Washington, as large as life, appeared retiring down the steps, pointing with his right hand to the emblems of power which he had resigned, and with his left to a beautiful landscape representing Mount Vernon, in front of which oxen were seen harnessed to the plough. Over the General appeared a *genius*, placing a wreath of laurels on his head."

These pictures were from the pencil of Charles Willson Peale, who, twenty-five years before, as we have observed, had painted the portrait of Washington at Mount Vernon, in the costume of a Virginia colonel.

The heads of departments, foreign ministers, and distinguished strangers in Philadelphia, were present on this gala occasion; and with that elegant display of taste, fashion, and gayety, ended the public life of Washington. To General Knox he had written two days before:

"The remainder of my life, which in the course of nature cannot be long, will be occupied in rural amusements; and, though I shall seclude myself as much as possible from the noisy and bustling crowd, none would more than myself be regaled by the company of those I esteem, at Mount Vernon; more than twenty miles from which, after I arrive there, it is not likely that I shall ever be."

Before following Washington to his home, from which he went "twenty miles" only once afterwards, let us listen to the voice of another eye-witness of events during Washington's administration (the late Rev. Ashbel Greene), as he discourses of the table of the President. He says:

"The President ate Indian cakes for breakfast, after the Virginia fashion, although buckwheat cakes were generally on the table. Washington's dining parties were entertained in a very handsome style. His weekly dining day, for company, was Thursday, and his dining hour was always four o'clock in the afternoon. His rule was to allow five minutes for the variation of clocks and watches, and then go to the table, be present or absent whoever might. He kept his own clock in the hall, just within the outward door, and always exactly regulated. When lagging members of Congress came in, as they often did, after the guests had sat down to dinner, the President's only apology was, 'Gentlemen (or sir), we are too punctual for you. I have a cook who never asks whether the company, but whether the hour has come.' The company usually assembled in the drawing-room, about fifteen or twenty minutes before dinner, and the President spoke to every guest personally on entering the room. Mrs. Washington often, but not always, dined with the company, sat at the head of the table, and if, as was occasionally the case, there were other ladies present, they sat each side of her. The private secretary sat at the foot of the table, and was expected to be quietly attentive to all the guests. The President himself sat half-way from the head to the foot of the table, and on that side he would place Mrs. Washington, though distant from him, on his right hand. He always, unless a clergyman was present, at his own table asked a blessing, in a standing posture. If a clergyman were present, he was requested both to ask a blessing and to return thanks after dinner. The centre of the table contained five or six large silver or plated waiters, those of the ends, circular, or rather oval on one side, so as to make the arrangement correspond with the oval shape of the table. The waiters between the end pieces were in the form of parallelograms, the ends about one-third part of the length of the sides; and the whole of these waiters were filled with alabaster figures, taken from the ancient mythology, but none of them such as to offend in the smallest degree against delicacy. On the outside of the oval, formed by the waiters, were placed the various dishes, always without covers; and outside the dishes were the plates. A small roll of bread, enclosed in a napkin, was laid by the side of each plate. The President, it is believed, generally dined on one dish, and that of a very simple kind. If offered something, either in the first or second course, which was very rich, his usual reply was:

'That is too good for me.' He had a silver pint cup or mug of beer placed by his plate, which he drank while dining. He took one glass of wine during dinner, and commonly one after. He then retired (the ladies having gone a little before him), and left his secretary to superintend the table, till the wine-bibbers of Congress had satisfied themselves with drinking. His wines were always the best that could be obtained. Nothing could exceed the order with which his table was served. Every servant knew what he was to do, and did it in the most quiet and yet rapid manner. The dishes and plates were removed and changed, with a silence and speed that seemed like enchantment."

On the 9th of March Washington set out for Mount Vernon, a private citizen, accompanied by Mrs. Washington, her grand-daughter, Eleanor Parke Custis, and George Washington Lafayette, son of the marquis, who was then an exile from France, and in prison. Young Lafayette was then between seventeen and eighteen years of age, and was accompanied by his preceptor, M. Frestel, who composed a part of the family then on its way to Mount Vernon.

The misfortunes of Lafayette, whom Washington loved so devotedly, and the condition of his interesting family, had given him more painful anxiety, during the latter part of his administration, than any other circumstance.

Lafayette, as we have seen, was one of the prime leaders in the revolution in France during its first stages. He was an active advocate of civil liberty, but conservative in a country where and when representatives and constituents were alike radical. When the revolution was at its height, he was at the head of the *Constitutionalists*, who advised moderation.

GEORGE WASHINGTON LAFAYETTE.

Because of this, he, of all the leaders, was left almost alone. He was forsaken by timid friends, who trembled at the frowns of the Terrorists, and was menaced by his violent political enemies. He dared to oppose the factions, of whatever creed, and for this he drew upon his head the anathemas of the Jacobins, the emigrants, and the royalists. Even his army, hitherto faithful, had become disaffected toward him, through the machinations of his enemies, and nothing remained for him but to flee. He left his army encamped at Sedan, and, in company with a few faithful friends, set off for Holland, to seek an asylum there or in the United States.

At the first Austrian post he and his friends were at first detained, and then made prisoners. Soon afterward they were sent to the dungeons of Wesel and Magdeburg, and ultimately to those of Olmutz, by order of the allied monarchs of Austria and Prussia.

When information of this condition of his dear friend reached Washington at Philadelphia, he was deeply moved. The late venerable and distinguished Richard Rush, of Philadelphia, whose death occurred on the first of August, 1859, has left on record an account of a most interesting incident illustrative of the feelings of Washington on that occasion. Mr. Bradford, the attorney-general, was living directly opposite the President's house, and was spending an evening with Washington's family, when the conversation reverted to Lafayette. Washington spoke with great seriousness, contrasted the marquis's hitherto splendid career with his present forlorn and suffering condition, and at length became so deeply affected, that his eyes filled with tears, and his whole great soul was stirred to its very depths. "Magnanimous tears they were," says Mr. Rush, "fit for the first of heroes to shed—virtuous, honorable, sanctified!"

Mr. Bradford, who deeply sympathized with the feelings of Washington, was much affected at the spectacle, and returning to his own house, he "sat down," says Griswold, from whose *Republican Court* I quote, "and wrote the following simple, but touching verses, an impromptu effusion from the heart of a man of sensibility and genius:

"THE LAMENT OF WASHINGTON

'As beside his cheerful fire,
'Midst his happy family,
Sat a venerable sire,
Tears were starting in his eye.

Selfish blessings were forgot,
Whilst he thought on Fayette's lot,
Once so happy on our plains—
Now in poverty and chains.

" ' Fayette,' cried he—'honored name!
Dear to these far distant shores—
Fayette, fired by freedom's flame,
Bled to make that freedom ours.
What, alas! for this remains—
What, but poverty and chains!

" ' Soldiers in our fields of death—
Was not Fayette foremost there?
Cold and shivering on the heath,
Did you not his bounty share?
What reward for this remains,
What, but poverty and chains!

" ' Hapless Fayette! 'midst thine error,
How my soul thy worth reveres!
Son of freedom, tyrant's terror,
Hero of both hemispheres!
What reward for all remains,
What, but poverty and chains!

" ' Born to honors, ease, and wealth,
See him sacrifice them all;
Sacrificing also health,
At his country's glorious call.
What for thee, my friend, remains,
What, but poverty and chains!

" ' Thus with laurels on his brow
Belisarius begged for bread;
Thus, from Carthage forced to go,
Hannibal an exile fled.
Alas! Fayette at once sustains
EXILE, POVERTY, and CHAINS!' "

> "Courage, child of Washington!
> Though thy fate disastrous seems,
> We have seen the setting sun
> Rise and burn with brighter beams,
> Thy country soon shall break thy chain,
> And take thee to her arms again.
>   Thy country soon shall break thy chain,
>   And take thee to her arms again!"

In the horrid dungeon at Olmutz, in a cell three paces broad and five and a half long, containing no other ornament than two French verses which rhyme with the words to suffer and to die, the generous Lafayette was confined almost three years, and yet his great soul was not bound by suffering, nor his zeal for liberty one whit abated. Deprived of pen, ink, and paper, except a sheet that "by a miracle" he possessed, he wrote a letter with a toothpick to a princess who sympathized with him, and said, in a postscript:

"I know not what disposition has been made of my plantation at Cayenne, but I hope Madame Lafayette will take care that the negroes who cultivate it *shall preserve their liberty*."

Lafayette's noble wife, as soon as she could get permission to leave France, hastened to Olmutz, with her daughters, to share the prison with the husband and father, while their son, George Washington, came to the United States, with his tutor, consigned to the fatherly care and protection of the great patriot whose name he bore. They arrived at Boston at the close of the summer of 1795, and immediately informed Washington of the fact. The President's first impulse was to take the young man to his bosom and cherish him as a son, but grave reasons of state denied him that pleasure. "To express all the sensibility," he said, in a letter to Senator Cabot, of

Boston, "which has been excited in my breast by the receipt of young Lafayette's letter, from the recollections of his father's merits, services, and sufferings, from my friendship for him, and from my wishes to become a friend and father to his son, is unnecessary." He then declared himself the young man's friend, but intimated that great caution in the manifestation of that friendship would be necessary, considering the light in which his father was then viewed by the French government, and Washington's own situation as the executive of the United States. He desired Mr. Cabot to make young Lafayette and M. Frestel, his tutor, understand why he could not receive them as he desired, but that his support and protection, until a more auspicious moment, might be relied on. He ordered them to be provided with every thing necessary, at his expense, and advised their entrance at Harvard University.

Young Lafayette assumed the name of Motier (a family name of his father); and in November Washington wrote to him with caution, telling him that the causes which rendered it necessary for them both to be circumspect were not yet removed, and desiring him to repair to Colonel Hamilton, in New York, who would see that he was well provided for.

"How long the causes which have withheld you from me may continue," Washington said, "I am not able at this moment to decide; but be assured of my wishes to embrace you so soon as they shall have ceased, and that, whenever the period arrives, I shall do it with fervency." He then, with fatherly solicitude, advised him to attend well to his studies, that he might "be found to be a deserving son of a meritorious father."

After leaving Boston, young Lafayette lived with his tutor

for awhile in the vicinity of New York, in comparative seclusion. At length the Congress took cognizance of the presence of the young man, and on the 18th of March the House of Representatives passed the following resolution and order:

"Information having been given to this House that a son of General Lafayette is now within the United States;

"*Resolved*, That a committee be appointed to inquire into the truth of the said information, and report thereon; and what measures it would be proper to take if the same be true, to evince the grateful sense entertained by the country for the services of his father.

"Ordered that Mr. Livingston, Mr. Sherburne, and Mr. Murray be appointed a committee pursuant to the said resolution."

As chairman of the committee, Mr. Livingston wrote to young Lafayette as follows:

"SIR: Actuated by motives of gratitude to your father, and eager to seize every opportunity of showing their sense of his important services, the House of Representatives have passed the resolution which I have the pleasure to communicate. The committee being directed to inquire into the fact of your arrival within the United States, permit me to advise your immediate appearance at this place, that the legislature of America may no longer be in doubt, whether the son of Lafayette is under their protection, and within the reach of their gratitude.

"I presume to give this advice as an individual personally attached to your father, and very solicitous to be useful to any person in whose happiness he is interested. If I should have that good fortune on this occasion, it will afford me the greatest satisfaction.

"I am, etc.,

"EDWARD LIVINGSTON."

This letter and the resolutions of the House of Representatives young Lafayette forwarded to President Washington, and asked his advice as to the course he should pursue. Washington advised him to come to Philadelphia at the opening of the next session of Congress, but to avoid society as much as possible. He complied, and remained in Philadelphia until the following spring, when Washington, on becoming a private citizen, embraced the son of his friend as if he had been his own child, and bore him to his home on the Potomac. There he remained until early in October, when the joyful news having reached him of the release of his father from confinement, and his restoration to his country and friends, caused him to leave for the seaboard to depart for France. He and M. Frestel sailed from New York on the 26th of October, 1797.

As young Lafayette was about to leave Mount Vernon, Washington placed a letter in his hands for his father, in which he said:

"From the delicate and responsible situation in which I stood as a public officer, but more especially from a misconception of the manner in which your son had left France, till explained to me in a personal interview with himself, he did not come immediately into my family on his arrival in America, though he was assured in the first moments of it of my protection and support. His conduct, since he first set his feet on

American ground, has been exemplary in every point of view, such as has gained him the esteem, affection, and confidence of all who have had the pleasure of his acquaintance. His filial affection and duty, and his ardent desire to embrace his parents and sisters in the first moments of their release, would not allow him to wait the authentic account of this much desired event; but, at the same time that I suggested the propriety of this, I could not withhold my assent to the gratification of his wishes to fly to the arms of those whom he holds most dear, persuaded as he is from the information he has received, that he shall find you all in Paris.

"M. Frestel has been a true Mentor to George. No parent could have been more attentive to a favorite son; and he richly merits all that can be said of his virtues, of his good sense, and of his prudence. Both your son and he carry with them the vows and regrets of this family, and all who know them. And you may be assured that yourself never stood higher in the affections of the people of this country than at the present moment."

The profile of George Washington Lafayette, given on a preceding page, was painted in crayon, by James Sharpless, an English artist, who came to this country in 1796, and visited all the principal cities and towns in the United States, carrying letters of introduction to various distinguished persons, and requesting them to sit for their portraits. These were generally painted in crayon, upon a small scale, and finished in less than three hours from the commencement of the sitting. Sharpless usually drew them in profile, and the likenesses were generally so much admired for their faithfulness, that orders would sometimes be given for whole families.

In this way he painted immense numbers of portraits, and received fifteen dollars for each commission.

Sharpless brought with him his wife and three children. He made New York his head-quarters, and generally travelled in a four-wheeled carriage, so contrived by himself as to con-

G. W. P. CUSTIS AT THE AGE OF SEVENTEEN YEARS.

vey his whole family and all of his painting apparatus, and drawn by one stout horse. He was a plain and frugal man, and amassed a competence by his profession. He was a man of science and a mechanician, and manufactured the crayons which he used in his profession. He died suddenly in New York, at the age of about sixty years, and was buried in the cemetery attached to the Roman Catholic chapel in Barclay street. His widow and family returned to England, where they sold the portraits of the distinguished Americans whom Sharpless had painted, and settled in Bath.

While in Philadelphia Sharpless painted the profile portraits of President and Mrs. Washington; and also those of George Washington Lafayette (just mentioned) and George Washington Parke Custis. The latter was then a lad between sixteen and seventeen years of age, and he and young Lafayette became warmly attached friends. When, in 1824 and 1825, General Lafayette visited this country, as the guest of the nation, his son George accompanied him, and he and Mr. Custis were much together when opportunity allowed the privilege. The following note from George W. Lafayette to the friend of his youth, is an exhibition of the warmth of his attachment:

"WASHINGTON CITY, *January the third*, 1825.

"MY DEAR CUSTIS: My father being able to dispose of himself on Wednesday, will do himself the pleasure of going that day to dine at Arlington. It is so long since I wished for that satisfaction myself, that I most sincerely rejoice at the anticipation of it. You know, my friend, how happy I was when we met at Baltimore. Since that day I felt every day more and more how much our two hearts were calculated to understand each other. Be pleased, my dear Custis, to present my respectful homage to the ladies, and receive for yourself the expression of my most affectionate and brotherly sentiments."

The profiles of General and Mrs. Washington, by Sharpless, have been pronounced by members of the Washington family who remembered the originals, as the best likenesses extant, both in form and color. Sharpless made many copies from it. So also did Mrs. Sharpless, who painted miniatures in water colors most exquisitely. One of these was in the possession of

CRAYON PROFILE OF WASHINGTON.

Mrs. Eliza M. Evans, a daughter of General Anthony Walton White, of New Jersey. It was somewhat smaller than the usual size of miniatures, and on the back was written, by the hand of the fair artist: "General Washington, Philadelphia, 1796. E. Sharpless."

These four originals, by Sharpless, were preserved at Arlington House. Those of Mrs. Washington, and Lafayette and Custis, when lads, have never been engraved before. They hung upon the walls at Mount Vernon from the time when Washington retired from the presidency until the death of Mrs. Washington, in 1802, when they passed into the possession of her grandson, G. W. P. Custis.

When fairly seated again in private life at Mount Vernon,

Washington appeared to revel in the luxury of quiet. He was never idle, never indifferent to the progress of current events, but he loved the peacefulness of nature away from the haunts

CRAYON PROFILE OF MRS. WASHINGTON.

of men, and was delighted when working like the bee among the fruits and flowers. He was not unsocial, and yet he loved to be away from the great gathering-places of men and the tumults of public life. He was not unambitious, but he was not only indifferent but averse to the plaudits of the multitude when given in the accents of flattery. He wished to be loved as a righteous man, and he relied upon his conscience more than upon the voices of men for a knowledge of the acceptableness of his endeavors. It was his guide in all things, for he regarded it in one sense as Emanuel—God with us—the righteous judge of the thoughts and actions of men.

Washington now felt that his country had received all that

could reasonably be asked of him as a public servant, and he returned to his old pursuits with a sincere desire to mingle no more in the stirring arena of busy life. "To make and sell a little flour annually," he wrote to Oliver Wolcott, "to repair houses (going fast to ruin), to build one for the security of my papers of a public nature, and to amuse myself in agricultural and rural pursuits, will constitute employment for the few years I have to remain on this terrestrial globe. If, also, I could now and then meet the friends I esteem, it would fill the measure and add zest to my enjoyments; but, if ever this happens, it must be under my own vine and fig-tree, as I do not think it probable that I shall go twenty miles from them."

Washington enjoyed the visits of friends, but those of mere ceremony he disliked, and was sometimes annoyed by those prompted by idle curiosity.

"I might tell my friend," he said, in a letter at the close of May to Mr. McHenry, the secretary of war, "that I begin my diurnal course with the sun; that if my hirelings are not in their places at that time, I send them messages of sorrow for their indisposition; that, having put these wheels in motion, I examine the state of things further; that the more they are probed, the deeper I find the wounds which my buildings have sustained by an absence and neglect of eight years; that by the time I have accomplished these matters, breakfast (a little after seven o'clock, about the time I presume you are taking leave of Mrs. McHenry) is ready; that this being over, I mount my horse and ride round my farms, which employs me until it is time to dress for dinner, at which I rarely miss seeing strange faces, come, as they say, out of respect for me. Pray, would not the word curiosity answer as well? And how different this from having a few social friends at a cheerful board! The usual time of sitting at table, a walk, and tea, bring me within the dawn of candlelight; previous to which, if not prevented by company, I resolve that, as soon as the glimmering taper supplies the place of the great luminary, I will retire to my writing-table and acknowledge the letters I have received; but when the lights are brought, I feel tired and disinclined to engage in this work, conceiving that the next night will do as well. The next night comes, and with it the same causes for postponement, and so on.

"This will account for your letter remaining so long unacknowledged; and, having given you the history of a day, it will serve for a year, and I am persuaded you will not require a second edition of it. But it may strike you that, in this detail, no mention is made of any portion of time allotted for reading. The remark would be just, for I have not looked into a book since I came home; nor shall I be able to do it until I have discharged my workmen, probably not before the nights grow longer, when possibly I may be looking in Doomsday Book."

Washington's allusion in the foregoing letter to his writing-table, reminds me of his inkstand, which was preserved at Arlington House. It was composed wholly of silver, except three cut-glass bottles, two of them used for ink, and one (in the centre) for sand. The tray was seven and a half inches in length. It was used by Washington during the last two years of his administration, and ever afterward at Mount Vernon.

Washington found his mansion and all of the surrounding buildings much in want of repair when he returned home. "I find myself," he said, "in the situation nearly of a new

WASHINGTON'S INKSTAND.

beginner; for although I have not houses to build (except one, which I must erect for the accommodation and security of my military, civil, and private papers, which are voluminous and may be interesting), yet I have scarcely any thing else about me that does not require considerable repairs. In a word, I am already surrounded by joiners, masons, and painters; and such is my anxiety to get out of their hands, that I have scarcely a room to put a friend into or to sit in myself, without the music of hammers or the odoriferous scent of paint."

The mansion at Mount Vernon was soon thoroughly repaired, and many ornaments and pieces of furniture, not known to it before, were placed in it. Whatever had been used in the presidential mansion at Philadelphia, and could be appropriately transferred to Mount Vernon, were reserved, when Washington broke up his establishment in the national capital, and disposed of all superfluities.

Among other things brought on from Philadelphia, was a pair of mural candelabra, of elegant form and workmanship.

These were upon the walls of the dining-room at Philadelphia, which was also used for public receptions by the President and his wife. They were now placed in the large drawing-

MURAL CANDELABRA.   ANCIENT LANTERN.

room at Mount Vernon. They were each constructed of a mirror enclosed in a neat metal frame; resting upon an elaborately wrought bracket, and surmounted by flowers and festoons of leaves, all of the same material, and heavily gilt. In front of the mirror was a crystal candlestick and branches, so placed as to have a brilliant reflection produced.

These "lustres," as they were sometimes called, were imported from France, and formed a strong contrast to the ancient dingy iron lantern which hung in the great passage. That lantern, first hung up in the original cottage upon Mount Vernon by Lawrence Washington, continued its services there until the death of the general. It had then cast its dim light upon the entrance door full eighty years. It remained in service for more than fifty years afterwards, lighting the great passage at Arlington house, illuminating pictures by Vandyke and Sir Godfrey Kneller.

In the dining-room at Mount Vernon was another relic of the household of Lawrence Washington. It was a sideboard, handsomely wrought of black walnut, and was an excellent specimen of the quality of furniture in Virginia a hundred years ago. Its edges and legs were ornamented with delicate leaf-carving, and the wood was as perfect as when it was first used. It was about five feet in length, two and half feet in width, and three feet in height, and quite heavy. It was used by the family at Arlington House, and was prized as one of the most precious mementoes of Mount Vernon.

There were also a tea-table and punch-bowl at Arlington House that belonged to Washington. The former was quite small, elliptical in shape, about three feet in length, and made of mahogany. It was manufactured in New York for use in the executive mansion there, as a *tea*-table only, for the little private family of Washington, which consisted of only four persons. Food was not often set upon it. Washington seldom ate any thing after dinner until eight o'clock in the evening, when, with his family, he partook of a cup of tea served from this table, and a small slice of buttered bread.

SIDEBOARD, TEA-TABLE, AND PUNCH-BOWL.

The great porcelain punch-bowl delineated in the engraving, had a deep blue border at the rim, spangled with gilt stars and dots. It was made expressly for Washington, but when, where, and by whom is not known. In the bottom is a picture of a frigate, and on the side are the initials G. W., in gold, upon a shield with ornamental surroundings. It is supposed to have been presented to Washington by the French naval officers. If so, it was doubtless manufactured and sent over at the time when the Cincinnati china was forwarded.

WASHINGTON'S SILVER CANDLESTICK.

There were two massive silver candlesticks, with extinguishers and snuffers of the same metal, at Arlington House, that once belonged to Washington. These formed a part of his furniture after his retirement from the army, in

1783, and were a portion of his plate not remodeled afterward in New York.

How many interesting associations are made to cluster around these simple utensils of domestic use, at the suggestions of fancy and conjecture! Perhaps almost every distinguished European—Lafayette, Rochambeau, Chastellux, Houdon, Pine, Moustier, Brissot, D'Yrujo, Graham—as well as equally distinguished Americans who have spent a night at Mount Vernon—bore one of them to the bedchamber.

Perhaps they were used by Washington himself at his writing-table or by the fireside, or to light the conjugal chamber. And it is quite possible that the master bore one of them on the occasion mentioned in the following paragraph from the pen of Elkanah Watson, when describing his visit at Mount Vernon:

"The first evening I spent under the wing of Washington's hospitality, we sat a full hour at table by ourselves, without the least interruption. After the family had retired, I was extremely oppressed by a severe cold and excessive coughing, contracted by the exposure of a harsh winter journey. He pressed me to use some remedies, but I declined doing so. As usual after retiring, my coughing increased. When some time had elapsed, the door of my room was gently opened, and on drawing my bed-curtains, to my utter astonishment I beheld Washington himself standing at my bedside, with a bowl of hot tea in his hand. I was mortified and distressed beyond expression. This little incident occurring in common life with an ordinary man, would not have been noticed; but as a trait of the benevolence and private virtue of Washington, deserves to be recorded."

MORNING—A LANDSCAPE BY WINSTANLEY.

While residing in Philadelphia, Washington became acquainted with the merits of William Winstanley, an English-

EVENING—A LANDSCAPE BY WINSTANLEY.

man, and landscape painter, who came to America in 1796.

He was spoken of as "an artist of genius and reputation, whose landscapes in oil are greatly admired by the connoisseurs." Washington, pleased with some specimens of his skill which were brought to his notice, gave him a commission to paint six medium-sized pictures, representing scenery on the Hudson River. These were afterward taken to Mount Vernon, and adorned the walls of the drawing-room there. Two of these, called respectively Morning and Evening, were at Arlington House in 1860. Two others were in the family of the late Mrs. Lewis (Nelly Custis); of the remaining two we have no intelligence.

Washington was again awakened from his sweet dream of peace and quietness in his home on the Potomac, by the call of his country to lend to it once more his voice and his arm. There were signs of war in the political firmament. France, once the ally of the United States, assumed the attitude of an enemy. The king and queen of that unhappy country had been murdered at the command of a popular tribunal. Out of the anarchy that ensued, had been evolved a government, in which supreme power was vested in five men called a Directory, who ruled in connection with two chambers, the Council of Ancients and the Council of Five Hundred. It was installed at the Little Luxembourg, at Paris, on the 1st of November, 1795, and held the executive power four years.

That Directory was a most despotic tyrant, and ruled with an iron hand. Its pride disgusted the nations, and every true friend of man rejoiced when it quailed before the genius and the bayonets of Napoleon.

Before Washington had left the chair of state, the friendly

feeling between the United States and France had become greatly weakened. The French Directory assumed a tone of incomparable insolence, and the American representatives in Paris were insulted. Three judicious men had been sent to adjust all difficulties with the French government. They were refused an audience with the Directory unless they would agree to pay a large sum into the French treasury. "Millions for defence, but not one cent for tribute!" said Charles Cotesworth Pinckney, one of the American envoys; and he and John Marshall, another of the envoys, were ordered out of the country. This insult the United States did not choose to allow to pass unheeded, and all diplomatic intercourse between the two governments was suspended. Preparations were made for war; and in May, 1798, Congress authorized the formation of a large military force, to be called a Provisional Army. The movement was popular with the people, and with anxious hearts their thoughts turned instinctively to Washington as the man for the commander-in-chief.

There appeared to be a universal opinion that the weight of Washington's name and character would be necessary in order to produce unanimity among the military leaders that would be brought upon the stage, and to secure the confidence and support of the people.

Washington, though in absolute retirement, had watched the progress of affairs in France with sorrow and indignation, and had expressed his mind freely to his friends upon the subject. President Adams, in the perplexities which the progress of events produced, turned to him for advice, and looked to him for aid. "I must tax you," he said, "sometimes for advice. We must have your name, if you will in any case permit us to use it. There will be more efficacy in it than in many an army." And before Washington could reply, Adams nominated to the Senate: "George Washington, of Mount Vernon, to be lieutenant-general and commander-in-chief of all the armies raised and to be raised in the United States."

Already Mr. McHenry, the secretary of war, had written: "You see how the storm thickens, and that our vessel will soon require our ancient pilot. Will you—may we flatter ourselves that, in a crisis so awful and important, you will accept the command of all our armies? I hope you will, because you alone can unite all hearts and all hands, if it is possible that they can be united."

The Senate confirmed the nomination of the president, and Washington was appointed commander-in-chief of the Provisional Army. True to the prophecies and promises of his antecedents, he accepted the trust, for his country demanded his services, but with the provision that he should not be required to take the field until circumstances should make it absolutely necessary.

"I see, as you do," he said to McHenry, "that clouds are gathering and that a storm may ensue; and I find, too, from a variety of hints, that my quiet, under these circumstances, does not promise to be of long continuance. * * * * As my whole life has been dedicated to my country in one shape or another, for the poor remains of it it is not an object to contend for ease and quiet, when all that is valuable is at stake, further than to be satisfied that the sacrifice I should make of these is acceptable and desired by my country."

And now there were stirring times again at Mount Vernon. Washington's post-bag came filled with a score of letters sometimes, for to him had been entrusted the selection of officers for the army, and there were thousands of aspirants for places of almost every grade. He nominated Colonel Alexander Hamilton as first major-general, Charles Cotesworth Pinckney, then on his way from France, the second, and General Knox the third. The subordinate offices were frequently filled by the sons of his old companions in arms, and several of his own family received commissions. Young Custis, his adopted son, was appointed aide-de-camp to General Pinckney, and his favorite nephew, Lawrence Lewis, also received a commission.

Many were the visitors who flocked to Mount Vernon during the autumn of 1798. A large number of these were army officers, who went to head-quarters to consult with the chief about military affairs; and General Pinckney having returned, was there at Christmas time. At the same time Judge Cushing, of the Supreme Court of the United States, who administered the oath of office to Washington at his second inauguration, was also there.

"We reached Mount Vernon," wrote the wife of Judge Cushing, in February, 1799, "the evening before Christmas, and if any thing could have added to our enjoyment, it was the arrival of General and Mrs. Pinckney the next day [Tuesday], while we were dining. You may be sure it was a joyful meeting, and at the very place my wishes had pointed out. To be in the company of so many esteemed friends, to hear our good General Washington converse upon political subjects without reserve, and to hear General and Mrs. Pinckney relate what they saw and heard in France, was truly a feast to me. Thus the moments glided away for two days, when our reason pointed out the propriety of our departing and improving the good roads, as the snow and frost had made them better than they are in summer."

The attitude assumed by the United States, and the appearance of Washington at the head of the army, humbled the French Directory, and President Adams was encouraged to send representatives to France again. When they arrived, toward the close of 1799, the weak Directory were no more. Napoleon Bonaparte was at the head of the government as first consul, and soon the cloud of war that hung between France and the United States was dissipated.

We now come to consider the associations of Mount Vernon during the last year of Washington's life. It opened with joy, it closed with sorrow.

Lawrence Lewis, son of Washington's sister Elizabeth, had been a resident at Mount Vernon for some time. We have already observed, by an expression in a letter of Washington to Mr. McHenry, that the visits of strangers to Mount Vernon had become somewhat burdensome to the master. With this feeling he wrote to Lawrence, giving him a formal invitation to reside at Mount Vernon, and saying:

"As both your aunt and I are in the decline of life, and regular in our habits, especially in our hours of rising and going to bed, I require some person (fit and proper) to ease me of the trouble of entertaining company, particularly of nights, as it is my inclination to retire (and unless prevented by very particular company, I always do retire) either to bed or to my study soon after candlelight. In taking these duties (which hospitality obliges one to bestow on company) off my hands, it would render me a very acceptable service." Lawrence complied with the request of his uncle, and became an inmate of the family at Mount Vernon at the beginning of 1798.

Nelly Custis was at this time blooming into womanhood, and was exceedingly attractive in person and manners. She was a great favorite with her foster-father, and as she approached marriageable age, he had indulged many anxious thoughts respecting her. The occasional visits of Lawrence Lewis to Mount Vernon had been productive of the most intimate friendly relations between them, and when he became a resident there, his respect for Nelly grew into warm and tender attachment. Washington was pleased; but there came a rival, whose suit Mrs. Washington decidedly encouraged. That rival was a son of Charles Carroll, of Carrollton, who had just returned from Europe, and displayed all the accomplishments of a good education, adorned with the social graces derived from foreign travel.

"I find that young Mr. C—— has been at Mount Vernon, and, report says, to address my sister," wrote her brother to Washington, in April, 1798, from Annapolis, where he was at school. "It may be well to subjoin an opinion," he said, "which I believe is general in this place, viz., that he is a young man of the strictest probity and morals, discreet without closeness, temperate without excess, and modest without vanity; possessed of those amiable qualities and friendship which are so commendable, and with few of the vices of the age. In short, I think it a most desirable match, and wish that it may take place with all my heart."

Washington, who favored the suit of his nephew, closed abruptly the correspondence with young Custis on that subject, by saying, in a letter to him a fortnight afterward:

"Young Mr. C—— came here about a fortnight ago, to dinner, and left us next morning after breakfast. If his object was such as you say has been reported, it was not declared here; and therefore the less is said upon the subject, particularly by your sister's friends, the more prudent it will be until the subject develops itself more."

In his next letter, in reply to this, young Custis ventured only to say: "With respect to what I mentioned of Mr. C—— in my last, I had no other foundation but report, which has since been contradicted."*

Lawrence Lewis triumphed, yet the foster-father had some time doubted respecting the result, for other suitors came to Mount Vernon, and made their homage at the shrine of Nelly's wit and beauty.

"I was young and romantic then," she said to a lady, from whose lips Mr. Irving has quoted—"I was young and romantic then, and fond of wandering alone by moonlight in the woods of Mount Vernon. Grandmamma thought it wrong and unsafe, and scolded and coaxed me into a promise that I would not wander in the woods again unaccompanied. But I was missing one evening, and was brought home from the interdicted woods to the drawing-room, where the General was walking up and down with his hands behind him, as was his wont. Grandmamma, seated in her great arm-chair, opened a severe reproof."

---

* For very interesting correspondence between General Washington and his adopted son, G. W. P. Custis, while the latter was in college at Princeton and Annapolis, from November, 1796, to January, 1799, see *Recollections and Private Memoirs of Washington*, by his adopted son, George Washington Parke Custis edited by the author of this work.

"Poor Miss Nelly," says Mr. Irving, "was reminded of her promise, and taxed with her delinquency. She knew that she had done wrong—admitted her fault, and essayed no excuse; but, when there was a slight pause, moved to retire from the room. She was just shutting the door when she overheard the General attempting, in a low voice, to intercede in her behalf. 'My dear,' observed he, 'I would say no more—perhaps she was not alone.'

"His intercession stopped Miss Nelly in her retreat. She reopened the door and advanced up to the General with a firm step. 'Sir,' said she, 'you brought me up to speak the truth, and when I told Grandmamma I was alone, I hope you believed *I was alone.*'

"The General made one of his most magnanimous bows. 'My child,' replied he, 'I beg your pardon.'"

Lawrence and Nelly were married at Mount Vernon on Washington's birthday, 1799. It was Friday, and a bright and beautiful day. The early spring flowers were budding in the hedges, and the bluebird, making its way cautiously northward, gave a few joyous notes in the garden that morning. The occasion was one of great hilarity at Mount Vernon, for the bride was beloved by all, and Major Lewis, the bridegroom, had ever been near to the heart of his uncle, since the death of his mother, who so much resembled her illustrious brother, that when, in sport, she would place a *chapeau* on her head and throw a military cloak over her shoulders, she might easily have been mistaken for the Chief.

It was the wish of the young bride, said her brother, that the general of the armies of the United States should wear, on that occasion, the splendidly-embroidered uniform which the board of general officers had adopted, but Washington could not be persuaded to appear in a costume bedizened with tinsel. He preferred the plain old continental blue and buff, and the modest black ribbon cockade. Magnificent white plumes, which General Pinckney had presented to him, he gave to the bride; and to the Reverend Thomas Davis, rector of Christ Church, Alexandria, who performed the marriage ceremony, he presented an elegant copy of Mrs. Macaulay's *History of England*, in eight octavo volumes, saying, when he handed them to him:

"These, sir, were written by a remarkable lady, who visited America many years ago; and here is also her treatise on the *Immutability of Moral Truth*, which she sent me just before her death—read it and return it to me."

With characteristic modesty, Washington made no allusion to the fact that Mrs. Macaulay (Catharine Macaulay Graham) crossed the Atlantic in the spring of 1785, for no other purpose, as she avowed, than to see the great leader of the American armies, whom she revered as a second Moses. Washington thus alluded to her, in a letter to General Knox, written on the 18th of June, 1785:

"Mrs. Macaulay Graham, Mr. Graham, and others, have just left us, after a stay of about ten days. A visit from a lady so celebrated in the literary world could not but be very flattering to me."

The year 1799—next to the last year of the century, and the last of Washington's life—was now drawing to a close, and he appears to have made preparations for his departure, as if the fact that the summons from earth would soon be presented had been revealed to him. In March he said, in a letter to

Mr. McHenry, after alluding to business affairs: "My greatest anxiety is to have all these concerns in such a clear and distinct form, that no reproach may attach itself to me when I have taken my departure for the land of spirits."

In July he executed his last will and testament. It was written entirely by himself, and at the bottom of each page of manuscript he signed his name. During the autumn he digested a complete system of management for his estate for several succeeding years, in which were tables designating the rotation of crops. This document occupied thirty folio pages, all written in his peculiar and clear style. It was completed only four days before his death, and was accompanied by a letter, dated December 10th, 1799, to his manager or steward, giving him special directions, as if the master was about to depart on a journey.

At this time Washington was in full health and vigor, and the beautiful days of a serene old age were promised him. He had once said: "I am of a short-lived family, and cannot expect to remain very long upon the earth;" yet now, at the age of almost sixty-eight, he appeared to have full expectations of octogenarian honors.

Only a few days before his death, he had walked out, on a cold, frosty morning, with his nephew, Major Lewis, and pointed out his anticipated improvements, especially showing him the spot where he intended to build a new family vault. "This change," he said, "I shall make the first of all, for I may require it before the rest."

"When I parted from him," said Major Lewis, to James K. Paulding, "he stood on the steps of the front door, where he took leave of myself and another. He had taken his usual ride, and the clear healthy flush on his cheek and his sprightly manner, brought the remark from both of us that we had never seen the general look so well. I have sometimes thought him decidedly the handsomest man I ever saw; and when in a lively mood, so full of pleasantry, so agreeable to all with whom he associated, I could hardly realize that he was the same Washington whose dignity awed all who approached him."

On the 11th of December Washington noted in his diary that there was wind and rain, and "at night a large circle round the moon." This portent of snow was truthful, for at one o'clock the next day it began to fall. It soon changed to hail, and then to rain.

Washington had been out on horseback, as usual, since ten o'clock in the morning, and returned only in time for late dinner. Mr. Lear, who was again residing at Mount Vernon, as Washington's secretary and business manager, carried some letters to him to frank, when he observed snow hanging to the general's hair about his neck, and expressed a fear that he was wet. "No," Washington replied, "my great coat has kept me dry;" and after franking the letters, and observing that the storm was too heavy to send a servant to the post-office that evening, he sat down to dinner without changing his damp clothes.

On the following day (Friday, the 13th) the snow was three inches deep upon the ground, and still falling. Washington complained of a sore throat, and the storm continuing, he omitted his usual ride. At noon the clouds broke, the sun came out clear and warm, and he occupied himself before dinner in marking some trees, between the mansion and the river, that were to be cut down, and with compass and chain defining lines for improvements.

After dinner his hoarseness grew worse, yet he regarded it as nothing serious. He was very cheerful during the evening, and sat in the parlor with Mrs. Washington and Mr. Lear, amusing himself with the newspapers, which were brought in at seven o'clock, occasionally reading aloud something that pleased him, or asking Mr. Lear to do so, his hoarseness sometimes depriving him of his voice. Among other things, Mr. Lear read to him the report of debates in the Virginia Assembly, and Washington made comments, as well as his hoarseness would permit.

About nine o'clock Mrs. Washington left the parlor, and went to the chamber of Mrs. Lewis, who was confined, and the general and Mr. Lear continued the perusal of the papers some time afterward. When he retired, Mr. Lear suggested that he had better take something for his cold, his hoarseness appearing to increase. "No," he answered, "you know I never take any thing for a cold. Let it go as it came."

Between two and three o'clock the next morning he awoke Mrs. Washington, told her that he was very ill, and had had an ague. He was so hoarse that he could scarcely speak. He breathed with great difficulty, and Mrs. Washington proposed to get up and call a servant, but the tender husband would not permit her to do so, lest she should take cold. At daylight their chambermaid, Caroline, went into the room to make a fire, as usual, when Mrs. Washington sent her for Mr. Lear. That gentleman dressed himself quickly, and, on going to the general's room, found him breathing with great difficulty, and hardly able to utter a word intelligibly.

Washington desired Mr. Lear to send immediately for Mr. Rawlins, one of the overseers, to come and bleed him, while another servant was dispatched to Alexandria for Dr. Craik, the sufferer's life-long friend and his family physician. Some mixtures were prepared to give immediate relief, but he could not swallow a drop.

Rawlins came soon after sunrise. He was much agitated. Washington perceived it, and said, "Don't be afraid." A slight incision was made in the arm, for Mrs. Washington, doubtful whether bleeding was proper in the case, begged that not much blood might be taken. The blood ran pretty freely, but the general whispered, "The orifice is not large enough;" and when Mr. Lear was about to loosen the bandage to stop the bleeding, at the request of Mrs. Washington, he put his hand up to prevent it, and said, "More, more." About half a pint of blood was taken from him, and external applications were made, but nothing seemed to relieve the sufferer.

DR. JAMES CRAIK.

At eight o'clock Washington expressed a desire to get up. His clothes were put on, and he was led to a chair by the fire. But he found no relief in that position, and at ten o'clock he lay down again.

Mrs. Washington had become much alarmed, and before Dr.

Craik arrived, she desired Mr. Lear to send for Dr. Brown, of Port Tobacco, whom Craik had recommended to be called if any alarming sickness should occur during his absence. At about nine o'clock Dr. Craik arrived. He at once took more blood from the general, put a blister on his throat, prepared a gargle of vinegar and sage tea, and ordered some vinegar and hot water for him to inhale the steam of. The gargle almost suffocated him. A little phlegm was brought up with it, and he attempted to cough, but was unable to do so.

At eleven o'clock Dr. Craik requested Dr. Dick, with whom he often consulted, to be sent for, as Dr. Brown might not come in time. He then bled the general again, but no effect was produced by it. His inability to swallow any thing continued. At three o'clock Dr. Dick arrived, and after consultation with him, Dr. Craik again bled the sufferer. The blood was thick, and flowed very sluggishly. Dr. Brown arrived soon afterward, and after the three physicians had held a brief consultation, Dr. Craik administered calomel and tartar emetic, which the general managed to swallow. But this too was without effect.

"About half-past four o'clock," says Mr. Lear, in a narrative which he wrote at the time, "he desired me to call Mrs. Washington to his bedside, when he requested her to go down into his room, and take from his desk two wills which she would find there, and bring them to him, which she did. Upon looking at them he gave her one, which he observed was useless, as being superseded by the other, and desired her to burn it, which she did, and took the other and put it into her closet.

"After this was done, I returned to his bedside and took his hand. He said to me: 'I find I am going. My breath cannot last long. I believed from the first that the disorder would prove fatal. Do you arrange and record all my late military letters and papers. Arrange my accounts and settle my books, as you know more about them than any one else, and let Mr. Rawlins finish recording my other letters which he has begun.' I told him this should be done. He then asked if I recollected any thing which it was essential for him to do, as he had but a very short time to continue with us. I told him that I could recollect nothing, but that I hoped he was not so near his end. He observed, smiling, that he certainly was, and that, as it was a debt we must all pay, he looked to the event with perfect resignation.

"In the course of the afternoon he appeared to be in great pain and distress from the difficulty of breathing, and frequently changed his posture in the bed. On these occasions I lay upon the bed and endeavored to raise him, and turn him with as much ease as possible. He appeared penetrated with gratitude for my attentions, and often said, 'I am afraid I shall fatigue you too much;' and upon my assuring him that I could feel nothing but a wish to give him ease, he replied, 'Well, it is a debt we must pay to each other, and I hope when you want aid of this kind you will find it.'"

Washington then inquired when Mr. Lewis and Washington Custis, who were in New Kent, would return; and being told, he remained silent awhile, and then desired his servant, Christopher, who had been in the room all day, to sit down, for he had been standing most of the time. He did so. A few minutes afterward Dr. Craik came into the room, and as he approached the bedside, Washington said to him: "Doctor, I die hard, but I am not afraid to go. I believed, from my first attack, that I should not survive it. My breath cannot last long." The doctor, overcome with emotion, pressed his hand, but could not utter a word. He left the bedside, and, in deep grief, sat by the fire for some time, while all was silent in the room, except the heavy breathing of the sufferer.

Doctors Dick and Brown came into the room between five and six o'clock, when they and Dr. Craik went to the bedside and asked Washington if he could sit up in bed. He held out his hand and Mr. Lear raised him up. "I feel myself going," he said; "I thank you for your attentions; but I pray you take no more trouble about me. Let me go off quickly. I cannot last long." Then casting a look of gratitude toward Mr. Lear, he lay down, and all left the bedside except Dr. Craik.

Mr. Lear now wrote to Mr. Law and Mr. Peter, gentlemen who had married two granddaughters of Mrs. Washington (sisters of Nelly Custis), requesting them to come immediately, with their wives, to Mount Vernon. At about eight o'clock the physicians tried other outward applications to relieve the sufferer, but in vain, and they left the room without any hope.

At about ten o'clock Washington attempted to speak to Mr. Lear, but failed several times. At length he murmured: "I am just going. Have me decently buried; and do not let my body be put into the vault in less than three days after I am dead." Mr. Lear could not speak, but bowed his assent. Washington whispered, "Do you understand?" Lear replied, "Yes." "'Tis well," he said; and these were the last words he ever spoke—"*'Tis well!*"

"About ten minutes before he expired," says Mr. Lear ("which was between ten and eleven o'clock), his breathing became easier. He lay quietly; he withdrew his hand from mine and felt his own pulse. I saw his countenance change. I spoke to Dr. Craik, who sat by the fire. He came to the bedside. The general's hand fell from his wrist. I took it in mine and pressed it to my bosom. Dr. Craik put his hands over his eyes, and he expired without a struggle or a sigh.

"While we were fixed in silent grief, Mrs. Washington, who was sitting at the foot of the bed, asked, with a firm and collected voice, 'Is he gone?' I could not speak, but held up my hand as a signal that he was no more. ''Tis well,' said she, in the same voice, 'all is now over; I shall soon follow him; I have no more trials to pass through.'"

"It may be asked," says Mr. Custis, "why was the ministry of religion wanting to shed its peaceful and benign lustre upon the last hours of Washington? Why was he, to whom the observances of sacred things were ever primary duties through life, without their consolations in his last moments? We answer, circumstances did not permit. It was but for a little while that the disease assumed so threatening a character as to forbid the encouragement of hope; yet, to stay that summons which none may refuse, to give still farther length of days to him whose time-honored life was so dear to mankind, prayers were not wanting to the throne of grace. Close to the couch of the sufferer, resting her head upon that ancient book, with which she had been wont to hold pious communion a portion of every day for more than half a century, was the venerable consort, absorbed in silent prayer, and from which she only arose when the mourning group prepared to lead her from the chamber of the dead."

That chamber, ever held sacred by the Washington family,

and concealed from the eyes of the curious visitor, appears now, in form and feature, precisely as when the spirit of the Father of his Country took its departure from it. Not a vestige of the furniture that was there at the time of Washington's death, remains. The bed and bedstead on which he died were at Arlington House, where they were kept as not only precious but sacred mementoes of the great and good Washington.

BED AND BEDSTEAD ON WHICH WASHINGTON DIED.

The bedstead was made of mahogany, and was manufactured in New York in 1789. It was remarkable for its size, being six feet square. It was in constant use in the bedchamber of General and Mrs. Washington, from the time of its manufacture until his death. The bed and bedding remained at Arlington House in precisely the same condition as when Washington was borne from his chamber to his tomb.

The room in which Washington died was seldom seen by visitors at Mount Vernon. While enjoying the hospitalities of the latest owner of the mansion, named Washington, for two or three days, I was permitted to enter and sketch it. It was used as a private chamber by the heads of the family. Empty, it presented the same appearance it did at Washington's death, and so I delineated it. Two doors opened from it into other chambers, and one to stairs that led to the garret.

ROOM IN WHICH WASHINGTON DIED.

As I stood alone in that death-chamber of the illustrious Washington, fancy seemed to fill it with those who occupied it on Saturday night, the 14th of December, 1799, mentioned in a memorandum by Mr. Lear. On the bed lay the great man at the sublime moment of his death. Near the bed stood Mr. Lear and Dr. Craik. "Mrs. Washington was sitting near the foot of the bed. Christopher was standing near the bedside. Caroline, Molly, and Charlotte (house-servants) were in the room, standing near the door. Mrs. Forbes, the housekeeper, was in the room likewise." And as I stood there, delineating the simple outlines of that chamber, the words of Wallace came vividly to my memory:

> "There is an awful stillness in the sky
> When, after wondrous deeds and light supreme,
> A star goes out in golden prophecy.
> There is an awful stillness in the world,
> When, after wondrous deeds and light supreme,
> A hero dies with all the future clear
> Before him, and his voice made jubilant
> By coming glories, and his nation hush'd
> As though they heard the farewell of a god—
> A great man is to earth as God to heaven."

No one, except Mrs. Washington, mourned more sincerely at the deathbed of the great patriot than Dr. Craik, a generous, warm-hearted Scotchman, and excellent physician, who settled in Virginia in early life, was with Washington in the campaigns of the French and Indian war, and of the Revolution, and was his friend and medical adviser for more than forty years. Twice he accompanied Washington to the Ohio country, the first time in 1770, and the second time in 1785. He continued to reside in Alexandria until old age caused him to relinquish his profession, when he retired with a competent fortune to Vaucluse, a part of the Ravensworths' estate, where he died in 1814, at the age of eighty-four years. He was exceedingly vigorous, in mind and body, until the last. His grandson, the Reverend James Craik, of Louisville, Kentucky, to whom I am indebted for the silhouette likeness of Dr. Craik, printed on page 318, said in a letter to me:

"He was a stout, thickset man, perfectly erect, no stoop of the shoulders, and no appearance of debility in his carriage.

Not long before his death he ran a race with me (then about eight years old) in the front yard of the house at **Vaucluse**, before the assembled family."

At midnight the body of General Washington was brought down from the chamber of death, and laid out in the large drawing-room, in front of the superb Italian chimney-piece, delineated on page 172—a work of art which the master had feared, " by the number of cases" which contained it, would be "too elegant and costly" for his "room, and republican style of living;" and on the following day (Sunday) a plain mahogany coffin was procured from Alexandria, and mourning ordered for the family, the overseers, and the domestics. On the same day several of the relatives who had been sent for arrived, among whom was Mrs. Stuart, the mother of Mrs. Washington's grandchildren.

At the head of the coffin was placed an ornament inscribed SURGE AD JUDICUM. At about the middle were the words GLORIA DEO; and upon a silver plate was the record:

GENERAL

GEORGE WASHINGTON

DEPARTED THIS LIFE ON THE 14TH DECEMBER,

1799, ÆT. 68.

The coffin was lined with lead, and upon a cover of the same material, to be put on after the coffin was laid in the vault, was a silver shield, nearly three inches in length, inscribed:

GEORGE WASHINGTON,

BORN FEB. 22, 1732,

DIED DECEMBER 14, 1799.

The time for the funeral was fixed at twelve o'clock on Wednesday, the 18th, and the Reverend Mr. Davis, of Alexandria, was invited to perform the burial service, according to the beautiful ritual of the Protestant Episcopal Church.

Having received information from Alexandria that the military and Freemasons were desirous of showing their respect for their chief and brother, by following his body to the grave, Mr. Lear ordered provisions to be prepared for a large number of people, as some refreshment would be expected by them. And Mr. Robert Hamilton, of Alexandria, wrote to Mr. Lear, that a schooner of his would anchor off Mount Vernon to fire minute guns, while the body was passing from the mansion to the tomb.

SILVER SHIELD ON WASHINGTON'S COFFIN.

The arrangements for the procession at the funeral were made by Colonels Little, Simms, and Deneale, and Dr. Dick. The old family vault was opened and cleaned, and Mr. Lear ordered an entrance door to be made for it, that it might not be again closed with brick. Mr. Stewart, adjutant of the Alexandria regiment, of which Washington had once been colonel, went down to Mount Vernon to view the ground for the procession.

The people began to collect at Mount Vernon on Wednesday, at eleven o'clock, but owing to a delay of the military, the time for the procession was postponed until three o'clock. The coffined body of the illustrious patriot lay, meanwhile, beneath the grand piazza of the mansion, where he had so often walked and mused.

Between three and four o'clock the procession moved, and, at the same time, minute guns were fired from the schooner anchored in the Potomac. The pall-bearers were Colonels Little, Simms, Payne, Gilpin, Ramsay, and Marsteler. Colonel Blackburn preceded the corpse. Colonel Deneale marched with the military. The procession moved out through the gate at the left wing of the house, and proceeded round in front of the lawn, and down to the vault on the right wing of the house. The following was the composition and order of the procession:

The troops, horse and foot, with arms reversed.
Music.
The clergy, namely, the Rev. Messrs. Davis,
Muir, Moffat, and Addison.
The general's horse, with his saddle, holsters, and pistols,
led by two grooms (Cyrus, and Wilson), in black.
The body, borne by the Masons and officers.
Principal mourners, namely,
Mrs. Stuart and Mrs. Law,
Misses Nancy and Sally Stuart,
Miss Fairfax and Miss Dennison,
Mr. Law and Mr. Peter,
Mr. Lear and Dr. Craik,
Lord Fairfax and Ferdinando Fairfax.
Lodge No. 23.
Corporation of Alexandria.
All other persons, preceded by Mr. Anderson
and the overseers.

When the body arrived near the vault, at the bottom of the lawn, on the high bank of the Potomac, the cavalry halted; the infantry moved forward and formed the in-lining; the Masonic brethren and citizens descended to the vault, and the funeral services of the church were read by the Reverend Mr. Davis. He also pronounced a short discourse. The Masons then performed their peculiar ceremonies, and the body was deposited in the vault. Three general discharges of arms were then given by the infantry and the cavalry; and eleven pieces of artillery, which were ranged back of the vault and simultaneously discharged, "paid the last tribute to the entombed commander-in-chief of the armies of the United States." The sun was now setting, and mournfully that funeral assembly departed for their respective homes.

WASHINGTON'S BIER.

The bier upon which Washington was conveyed from the mansion to the tomb, was preserved in the museum at Alexandria. It was oak, six feet in length, and painted a lead color. The handles, which were hinged to the bier, had leather pads on the under side, fastened with brass nails.

The vault in which the remains of Washington were laid, had already become dilapidated by the action of the growing roots of the trees around it, and, as we have seen, Washington, in contemplation of the immediate construction of a new one, had chosen a place for it. In his will he left the following directions:

"The family vault at Mount Vernon requiring repairs, and being improperly situated besides, I desire that a new one, of brick, and upon a larger scale, may be built at the foot of what is called the Vineyard Enclosure, on the ground which is marked out, in which my remains, and those of my deceased relatives (now in the old vault), and such others of my family as may choose to be entombed there, may be deposited."

THE OLD VAULT IN 1858.

For thirty years the remains of Washington lay undisturbed in the old vault, when the tomb was entered and an attempt was made to carry away the bones of the illustrious dead. Others were taken by mistake, and the robber being detected, they were recovered. A new vault was soon afterward erected upon the spot designated by Washington, and the old one became a gaping ruin.

Congress was in session at Philadelphia, when information of the death of Washington reached them on the day of his funeral. On the following day the announcement of it was formally made on the floor of the House of Representatives, by the Honorable John Marshall, of Virginia (afterward chief-justice of the United States), and after some appropriate action, the House adjourned.

On Monday, the 23d of December, the Congress adopted joint resolutions—*first*, that a marble monument should be erected at the capitol; *second*, that there should be "a funeral procession from Congress Hall to the German Lutheran Church, in memory of General George Washington, on Thursday, the 26th instant," and that an oration be prepared at the request of Congress, to be delivered before both Houses that day; and that the president of the Senate, and the speaker of the House of Representatives, be desired to request one of the members of Congress to prepare and deliver the same; *third*, that the people of the United States should be recommended to wear crape on their left arm as mourning for thirty days; *fourth*, that the president of the United States should direct a copy of the resolutions to be transmitted to Mrs. Washington, with words of condolence, and a request that her husband's remains might be interred at the capitol of the republic.

On the 30th of December Congress further resolved, that it should be recommended to the people of the Union to assemble on the succeeding 22d of February, "to testify their grief by suitable eulogies, orations, and discourses, or by public prayers."

GENERAL HENRY LEE.

In accordance with one of the foregoing resolutions, General Henry Lee, of Virginia, then a member of Congress, was invited to pronounce an oration on the 26th. He consented, and the Lutheran Church in Fourth street, above Arch, in Philadelphia, the largest in the city, was crowded on that occasion. No man in the Congress could have been chosen better fitted for the service than General Lee. He had served his country nobly as an officer of cavalry during the war for independence, and from boyhood had been a special favorite of Washington. He was a son of that "Lowland Beauty" who won the heart of young Washington, and drew sentimental verses from his pen. Throughout the war he was beloved by his chief for his manly and soldierly qualities, and he was an ever welcome guest at

Mount Vernon, where he was on terms of the greatest intimacy with Washington and his family. Mr. Irving gives the following example of Lee's perfect familiarity with his chief, when on a visit at Mount Vernon after the war:

"Washington one day at table mentioned his being in want of carriage-horses, and asked Lee if he knew where he could get a pair.

"'I have a fine pair, General,' replied Lee, 'but you cannot get them.'

"'Why not?'

"'Because you will never pay more than half price for any thing; and I must have full price for my horses.'

"The bantering reply set Mrs. Washington laughing, and her parrot, perched beside her, joined in the laugh. The general took this familiar assault upon his dignity, in good part. 'Ah, Lee, you are a funny fellow,' he said—'see, that bird is laughing at you.'"

Lee's oration on the death of Washington, though hastily prepared, was an admirable production: and in it he pronounced those remarkable words of eulogy, so often quoted:

"FIRST IN WAR, FIRST IN PEACE, FIRST IN THE HEARTS OF HIS COUNTRYMEN."

On that occasion, the *McPherson's Blues*, a military corps of Philadelphia, composed of three hundred young men, the *élite* of the city, performed the duties of a guard of honor. Seven of them, who were present on that occasion, yet survived in 1860, namely: Samuel Breck, aged eighty-nine; S. Palmer, aged eighty; S. F. Smith, aged eighty; Charles

348   MOUNT VERNON

M'PHERSON'S BLUE.

N. Bancker, aged eighty-four; Quintin Campbell, aged eighty-four; Robert Carr, aged eighty-three, and Watson, the annalist of Philadelphia and New York, aged eighty-one.

President Adams transmitted the resolutions of Congress to Mrs. Washington, and in reply to their request concerning the remains of her husband, she said:

"Taught by the great example which I have so long had before me, never to oppose my private wishes to the public will, I must consent to the request made by Congress, which you have the goodness to transmit to me; and in doing this, I need not, I cannot say, what a sacrifice of individual feeling I make to a sense of public duty."

The remains of Washington have never been removed from his beloved Mount Vernon. It is well. They never should be. The HOME and the TOMB of our illustrious Friend, should be inseparable; and the glowing words of LUNT should express the sentiment of every American:—

> "Ay, leave him alone to sleep forever,
>   Till the strong archangel calls for the dead,
> By the verdant bank of that rushing river,
>   Where first they pillowed his mighty head.
>
> "Lowly may be the turf that covers
>   The sacred grave of his last repose;
> But, oh! there's a glory round it hovers,
>   Broad as the daybreak, and bright as its close.

"Though marble pillars were reared above him,
   Temples and obelisks, rich and rare—
Better he dwells in the hearts that love him,
   Cold and lone as he slumbers there.

"Why should ye gather with choral numbers?
   Why should your thronging thousands come?
Who will dare to invade his slumbers,
   Or take him away from his narrow home?

"Well he sleeps in the majesty,
   Silent and stern, of awful death!
And he who visits him there, should be
   Alone with God, and his own hushed breath.

"Revel and pomp would profane his ashes:
   And may never a sound be murmured there
But the glorious river that by him dashes,
   And the pilgrim's voice in his heartfelt prayer."

The death of her husband, so sudden and unexpected, weighed heavily upon the mind and heart of Mrs. Washington for a time, but her natural cheerfulness of disposition and habitual obedience to the will of God manifested in his dispensations, healed the wound and supported her burdened spirit. She received many letters and visits of condolence. The president of the United States and his wife (Mr. and Mrs. Adams) visited Mount Vernon for the purpose, and so also did many distinguished citizens. From every part of the land came testimonials of respect and veneration for the dead; and from beyond the Atlantic she received gratifying evidences of the profound esteem in which her beloved husband was held. On hearing of his death, Lord Bridport, who was in command of a British fleet of almost sixty sail, at Torbay, ordered every ship to lower her flag to half-mast; and Bonaparte, then First

Consul of France, announced his death to his army, and ordered black crape to be suspended from all the flags and standards in the French service for ten days.

The domestic establishment at Mount Vernon was kept up after the death of the General, upon the same liberal scale of hospitality that marked it during his lifetime; and scores of pilgrims to the tomb of the Hero, Patriot and Sage, were entertained by the widow. But her prediction at the death-bed of her husband—"I shall soon follow him"—did not remain long unfulfilled. Two years and a half afterward, her body was laid in a leaden coffin by his side, in the vault. She died of a bilious fever, on the 22d of May, 1802; and the estate of Mount Vernon passed into the possession of the General's nephew, pursuant to the following clause in his will:

"To my nephew, Bushrod Washington, and his heirs (partly in consideration of an intimation made to his deceased father, while we were bachelors, and he had kindly undertaken to superintend my estate during my military service in the former war between Great Britain and France, that if I should fall therein, Mount Vernon, then less extensive in domain than at present, should become his property), I give and bequeath all that part thereof which is comprehended within the following limits: [here the boundaries are specified] containing upward of four thousand acres, be the same more or less, together with the mansion house, and all other buildings and improvements thereon." He also bequeathed to Bushrod his "library of books and pamphlets," and all of his papers.

This principal heir of Washington (who had no children) was a son of the General's brother, George Augustine, and was at that time about forty years of age. Two years before

BUSHROD WASHINGTON.

Washington's death. President Adams had appointed Bushrod to the office of Judge of the Supreme Court of the United States, and he performed the duties of his exalted station with eminent ability until his death, thirty-two years afterward.

Judge Washington took possession of the Mount Vernon estate, immediately after the death of Mrs. Washington. Among the slaves that belonged to him, and who were taken to Mount Vernon at that time, only one was living in 1860. Although set free by the will of his master in 1829, he never left the estate, but remained a resident there, where he was regarded as a patriarch. I saw him when I visited Mount Vernon in the autumn of 1858, and received from his lips many interesting reminiscences of the place and its surroundings.

Just at evening, when returning from a stroll to the ancient entrance to Mount Vernon, I found WestFord (the name of the patriarch) engaged at the shop, near the conservatory, making a plough. He was a mulatto, very intelligent and communicative; and I enjoyed a pleasant and profitable half-hour's conversation with him. He came to Mount Vernon in August, 1802, and when I saw him and made the above sketch of him he was in the seventy-second year of his age.

WestFord well knew Billy, Washington's favorite servant during the war for independence. Billy, with all of his fellow slaves, was made free by his master's will; and he received a liberal pension and a residence for life at Mount Vernon. His means for luxurious living had a bad effect upon him, and Billy became a *bon-vivant*. *Delirium tremens* finally seized him, with its terrors. Occasionally Westford sometimes relieved him of the paroxysms by bleeding. One morning, a little more than fifty years ago, he was sent for to bleed Billy. The blood would not flow. Billy was dead, and the last but one of Washington's favorite servants passed from earth forever. The other (a woman) died at Arlington House in 1855, where I saw her one morning at family worship.

I left Westford at his plough-making, with an engagement to meet him the next morning before breakfast, for the purpose of delineating a pencil sketch of his features. I found him prepared, having on a black satin vest, a silk cravat, and his curly gray hair arranged in the best manner, "For," he said, "the artists make colored folks look bad enough anyhow." When my sketch was finished, he wrote his name under it with my pencil.

While Judge Washington was living, Lafayette came to America as the guest of the nation, and after a lapse of fifty years, he again visited Mount Vernon, the home of his dear friend. For more than twenty-five years the mortal remains of that friend had been lying in the tomb, yet the memory of his love was as fresh in the heart of the marquis, as when, in November, 1784, they parted, to see each other on earth no more.

On that occasion Lafayette was presented with a most touching memorial of the man whom he delighted to call "father." The adopted son of that father, the late Mr. Custis, with many others, accompanied the marquis to the tomb of Washington, where the tears of the venerable Frenchman flowed freely. While standing there, Mr. Custis, after a few appropriate remarks, presented to Lafayette a massive gold ring, containing a lock of Washington's hair. It was a most grateful gift; and those who were present have spoken of the occurrence as one of the most interesting and touching they had ever experienced.

Again there was a gathering before the tomb of Washington on an interesting occasion. Judge Washington was then no more. He died at Philadelphia in the autumn of 1829, at the age of seventy years, bequeathing his estate of Mount Vernon to his nephew, John Augustine Washington, a son of his brother Corbin. The latter was also lying in the family vault, having died in 1832 at the age of forty-three years, and his widow, Mrs. Jane Washington, was then mistress of the mansion and estate.

The occasion referred to, was the re-entombing of General Washington and his wife. This event occurred in October 1837. Mr. John Struthers, of Philadelphia, generously offered to present two marble coffins in which the remains of the patriot and his consort might be placed for preservation forever, for already the wooden coffins, which covered the leaden ones containing their ashes, had been three times renewed. Major Lewis, the last surviving executor of Washington's will, accepted the proposed donation, and the sarcophagi were wrought from solid blocks of Pennsylvania marble. The vestibule of the new vault was enlarged so as to permit the coffins to stand in dry air, instead of being placed in the damp vault; and on Saturday the 7th of October 1837, Mr. William Strickland, of

Philadelphia, accompanied by a number of the Washington family, assisted in placing the remains of the illustrious dead in the receptacles where they have ever since lain undisturbed.

The vault was first entered by Mr. Strickland, accompanied by Major Lewis, of whom he said: "Imagine a figure stately and erect, upward of six feet in height, with a keen, penetrating eye, a high forehead partially covered with the silvery locks of seventy winters, intelligent and bland in expression, in movement graceful and dignified, and you will have the portraiture of the companion and friend of the immortal Washington." This was the favorite nephew who married Nelly Custis on the 22d of February, 1799.

When the decayed wooden case was removed from the leaden coffin of Washington, the lid was perceived to be sunken and fractured. In the bottom of this case was found the silver shield which was placed upon that leaden lid when Washington was first entombed.

"At the request of Major Lewis," says Mr. Strickland, in his published account, "the fractured part of the lid was turned over on the lower part, exposing to view a head and breast of large dimensions, which appeared, by the dim light of the candles, to have suffered but little from the effects of time. The eye-sockets were large and deep, and the breadth across the temples, together with the forehead, appeared, of unusual size. There was no appearance of grave-clothes; the chest was broad, the color was dark, and had the appearance of dried flesh and skin adhering closely to the bones. We saw no hair, nor was there any offensive odor from the body; but we observed, when the coffin had been removed to the outside of the vault, the dripping down of a yellow liquid, which stained the marble of the sarcophagus. A hand was laid upon the head and instantly removed; the leaden lid was restored to its place; the body, raised by six men, was carried and laid in the marble coffin, and the ponderous cover being put on and set in cement, it was sealed from our sight. The relatives who were present, consisting of Major Lewis, Lorenzo Lewis, John Augustine Washington, George Washington, the Rev. Mr. Johnson and lady, and Mrs. Jane Washington, then retired to the mansion."

The remains of Mrs. Washington being placed in the other marble sarcophagus, they were both boxed, so as to prevent their being injured during the finishing of the vestibule in its present form.

WASHINGTON'S MARBLE COFFIN.

Mrs. Washington's coffin is perfectly plain. That of her husband has a sculptured lid, on which is represented the American shield suspended over the flag of the Union. The latter is hung in festoons, and the whole group is surmounted with a spread-eagle as a crest.

The new tomb, in design and structure, is offensive to good taste, and its appearance justifies the description of it by an English nobleman who said, "It is a glaring red building somewhat between a coach-house and a cage." It stands at the bottom of a steep

WASHINGTON'S TOMB.

hill, on the edge of a deep wooded glen that extends to the river, and through which flows a choked brook.

The spacious vault is built of brick, with an arched roof. It is entirely overgrown with shrubbery, brambles and vines, which gives it an antiquated appearance. Its iron door is entered from the spacious vestibule; and over it, upon a stone panel, are the words:

"I AM THE RESURRECTION AND THE LIFE; HE THAT BELIEVETH IN ME, THOUGH HE WERE DEAD, YET SHALL HE LIVE!"

The vestibule is also built of brick, and is twelve feet in height. The iron picketed gateway, through which the marble sarcophagi may be seen, is flanked by two brick pilasters, surmounted by a stone coping, which covers a gothic arch. Over this arch is a white marble tablet inscribed—

"WITHIN THIS ENCLOSURE REST THE REMAINS OF
GENERAL GEORGE WASHINGTON."

On the east side of the tomb, beneath marble monuments, lie the remains of Eleanor Parke Lewis and her daughter, Mrs. M. E. Conrad. In front of the tomb are two stately obelisks of marble. One of them was erected in memory of Judge Bushrod Washington, and the other of John Augustine Washington, father of the last proprietor of Mount Vernon of the Washington name.

Very few articles of the personal property of General Washington, except the library of books, remained at Mount Vernon. After Mrs. Washington's death, the devised personal property was distributed according to the directions of his will, and the remainder was sold. The purchasers consisted chiefly of members of the family, the grandchildren of Mrs. Washington taking nearly all of the family plate, and furniture. Many of these things have been described and delineated in these pages; and many others have been scattered over the country, and since lost.

Several years ago I received from Mr. George Livermore, of Cambridge, an account of a most precious relic of Washington's earlier life, which was then in possession of the venerable Josiah Quincy, of Boston. It was the silver gorget of General Washington, which composed a part of his uniform while in the colonial service, and is seen suspended from his neck in Peale's portrait of him, painted in 1772, and printed on page 82 of this book.

"This precious relic," said Mr. Quincy in a letter to Mr. Livermore, "came to my possession under the following circumstances: from 1805 to 1813, I was one of the representatives of the state of Massachusetts, in the Congress of the United States, from Suffolk District. During these years I had the happiness, with my wife, to form an acquaintance with Mrs. Martha Peter (formerly Custis), the wife of Thomas Peter, Esq., of Tudor Place, in the District of Columbia. There sprang up between both families—particularly between Mrs. Peter and my wife—a great intimacy, the result of mutual respect and also coincidence in political feeling and opinion, which, at that period, constituted a bond of great strength. She was a woman of great personal beauty, highly accomplished, intellectual, elevated in spirit and sentiment, and worthy of the relation which she held of granddaughter to George Washington.

"When, in 1813, on resigning my seat in Congress, I called at Tudor Place to take leave, Mrs. Peter, after stating the interest she felt in me and Mrs. Quincy, asked my acceptance of the 'gorget of Washington, with the ribbon attached to it, which' she said 'she had received at the division of her grandfather's estate.' About that time, there had been formed in Boston a political association bearing the name of the Washington Benevolent Society, having for its object the support of the views and principles of Washington, of which I was one of the vice-presidents; and I immediately suggested the propriety, and asked her leave, to present in her name that precious relic to that society. She expressed her gratification at the suggestion, saying 'that she knew of no place where the principles of Washington had been more uniformly cherished, or were likely to be more highly prized or preserved longer, than in the town of Boston.'

"Accordingly, on my return in April, 1813, I made a formal statement of the above circumstances to the Washington Benevolent Society, and presented the gorget, in her name, to that society. The gift was gratefully and cordially received and acknowledged by a vote of the society, signed by Arnold Welles, president; and William Sullivan, Josiah Quincy, Samuel Messinger, John C. Warren, and Benjamin Russell, vice-presidents. A record of the gift, of the vote of thanks, and of all the proceedings, was written upon parchment, and deposited in a box especially adapted for its preservation; and an account of the doings of the society was officially transmitted to Mrs. Peter.

"The gorget remained in that situation, under the care of the society, for five or six years, until its final dissolution, when, by a vote of the society, it was formally placed in my custody; and I immediately wrote to Mrs. Peter a statement of the circumstances, offering to return the gorget to her. She was pleased to reply, that it was her wish that I should retain it in my possession, and make such disposition of it as I saw fit."

When I last visited Mount Vernon while it was in possession of a member of the Washington family (1858) I saw there a few articles, not already mentioned, that belonged to Washington. These were a liquor-chest, two mirrors, some tissue paper, one of his ordinary address cards, several diagrams and memoranda from his pen, and a number of engravings.

The liquor-chest was in a closet adjoining the dining-room, and was used by the family when I was there. It was made of

WASHINGTON'S LIQUOR-CHEST.

mahogany; and tradition avers that it composed a part of

WASHINGTON'S MIRROR.

Washington's baggage during the Revolution. It contained twelve large white glass flasks thirteen inches in height.

One of the mirrors, highly ornamented with elaborate carvings, and bearing the arms of the Washington family, was in a small parlor adjoining the great drawing-room ; and the other, a plain one, also bearing the family arms, in gilt upon a deep blue ground, at the top, was in another parlor, adjoining the library.

WATER-MARK.

The tissue paper was made expressly for Washington's use. Each sheet bears his name and crest, and a rude figure of Liberty with the pileus and cap, forming the water-mark. The paper is quite coarse in texture compared with that manufactured at the present time. The engraving of the water-mark is half the size of the original.

WASHINGTON'S ADDRESS CARD.

The address card was coarsely engraved on copper, and was used by Washington during the war. While he was President, he had a neat invitation-to-dinner card engraved in writing. The original plate of the latter is in the possession of a gentleman in Philadelphia.

Some of the diagrams from Washington's pen, alluded to, have been delineated upon other pages of this work. The engravings that belonged to him hung in the great passage and two adjoining parlors. These are, Andromache bewailing the Death of Hector; The Death of Montgomery; The Death of Warren; two Hunting Scenes; four Landscapes; The Defence of Gibraltar, four Views; Descent from the Cross; and a St. Agnes. These were all more or less injured by some tiny destroyers, that were daily making the high lights still stronger, so that all the pictures appeared snowy. If their destructive progress has not been speedily arrested, those relics of the great Patriot's household ornaments are lost forever. With characteristic modesty, Washington allowed no pictures of scenes in which he was a participant to adorn the walls of Mount Vernon. Some fine oil paintings and family portraits that were there had been distributed among relatives; that of Lawrence Washington alone remained.

Only one more object of interest at Mount Vernon remains to be noticed. It is a portrait of Washington taken from a common English earthenware pitcher, and is known as *The Pitcher Portrait.* It is in a deep gilt frame, and upon the back is an admirable eulogy of the great Patriot in monumental form. The history of this portrait and the eulogy was communicated to me in 1860 by the venerable artist Rembrandt Peale, of Philadelphia, and is both curious and interesting.

About the year 1804, the late John R. Smith, of Philadelphia, son of the eminent Jonathan Bayard Smith, showed

Mr. Peale a copy by Sharpless himself, of that artist's crayon profile of Washington, made in 1796. On the back of it was a eulogy of Washington, written in monumental form in two columns, by an English gentleman, Mr. Smith said, whose name he had forgotten, or never knew. He told Mr. Peale that the gentleman pasted it on the back of the portrait.

PITCHER PORTRAIT.

It was at about that time that a crockery dealer in Philadelphia imported a number of earthenware pitchers from Liverpool, each bearing a portrait of Washington from an engraving of Stuart's picture painted for the Marquis of Lansdowne, which Heath had badly engraved, and Nutter had better executed for Hunter's quarto edition of Lavater. Nutter's engraving was coarsely imitated in the one upon the pitcher.

The pitchers attracted the attention of Mr. Dorsey, a sugar

refiner of Philadelphia, who had a taste for art, and he purchased several of them, as he considered the likeness of Washington a good one. Mr. Dorsey, after several unsuccessful attempts to separate the part bearing the portrait, from the rest of the pitcher, succeeded, by using the broad-faced hammer of a shoemaker, in breaking them cleanly out by a single blow, given directly upon the picture.

One of these pictures broken out by Mr. Dorsey, was handsomely framed by Mr. Smith, and sent to Judge Washington at Mount Vernon, with the eulogy on the back of the Sharpless profile belonging to his father, copied by his own hand. That copy varies materially from the original, in some of its phraseology and in large omissions. This difference may be accounted for by the supposition that Mr. Smith had not room in the space on the back of the picture to transcribe the whole of the original, and some parts were omitted and others changed. The Sharpless picture was much larger than the pitcher portrait, and there was more room on the back for the eulogy.

In the year 1819 or 1820, Mr. Smith gave Mr. Harrison Hall, the publisher of the *Port Folio*, a perfect transcript of what was, probably, the original eulogy, and to the courtesy of that gentleman I am indebted for the subjoined copy, which contains all the omissions in the one upon the back of the picture at Mount Vernon. Mr. Hall, and others of Mr. Smith's friends, had been under the impression that that accomplished gentleman was the author of the eulogy, but the explicit statement of Mr. Peale and concurring circumstances appear to remove all doubt of the truth of the common tradition in the Washington family, that it was written by an unknown English gentleman. The mutilated inscription, as it appeared upon the back of the portrait at Mount Vernon, was published in Alden's *Collections of American Epitaphs and Inscriptions*, as early as the year 1814.

The following is a copy of the original on the back of the Sharpless profile given by Mr. Smith to Mr. Hall:

WASHINGTON,
The DEFENDER of his COUNTRY,
The FOUNDER of LIBERTY,
The FRIEND of MAN.
HISTORY and TRADITION are explored in vain
For a Parallel to his Character.
In the Annals of MODERN GREATNESS,
He stands alone.
And the noblest Names of Antiquity
Lose their Lustre in his Presence.

Born the *Benefactor of Mankind*,
He was signally endowed with all the Qualities
Appropriate to his *Illustrious Career*.
Nature made him *Great*,
And, Heaven directed,
He made *himself Virtuous*.

Called by his Country to the *Defence* of her *Soil*
And the *vindication* of her Liberties,
He led to the Field
Her Patriot Armies;
And displaying in rapid and brilliant succession,

The united Powers

Of *Consummate Prudence*

And Heroic Valour,

He triumphed in Arms

Over the most powerful Nation

Of Modern Europe;

His Sword giving *Freedom to America*,

His Counsels breathing *Peace to the world*.

After a short repose

From the *tumultuous Vicissitudes*

Of a Sanguinary War,

The astounding Energies of

WASHINGTON

Were again destined to a *New Course*

Of *Glory and Usefulness*.

The Civic Wreath

Was spontaneously placed

By the *Gratitude* of the *Nation*,

On the Brow of the DELIVERER of *his* COUNTRY.

He was twice *solemnly invested*

With the Powers of *Supreme Magistracy*,

By the *Unanimous Voice* of

A Free People;

And in his EXALTED and ARDUOUS station,

His *Wisdom* in the *Cabinet*

Transcended the *Glories of the Field*.

The *Destinies* of *Washington*

Were now complete.

Having passed the Meridian of a *Devoted Life*,

Having founded on the Pillars

Of NATIONAL INDEPENDENCE
The SPLENDID FABRIC
Of a *Great Republic*,
And having firmly established
The Empire of the West,
He solemnly deposited on the *Altar of his Country*,
His *Laurels* and his *Sword*,
And retired to the *Shades*
Of PRIVATE LIFE.
A *Spectacle* so *New* and so *Sublime*
Was contemplated by *Mankind*
With the *Profoundest admiration*,
And the name of WASHINGTON,
Adding now *Lustre* to *Humanity*,
Resounded
To the remotest regions of the Earth.

Magnanimous in Youth,
Glorious through Life,
Great in Death,
His highest Ambition
The *Happiness* of *Mankind*,
His *noblest victory*
The *Conquest* of *Himself*.
Bequeathing to America
The *Inheritance* of his *Fame*,
And building his *Monument*
In the *Hearts of his Countrymen*,
He Lived,
The *Ornament* of the 18th Century;
He Died.
LAMENTED BY A MOURNING WORLD.

In 1743, Mount Vernon received its name, and from that time until 1859, when the *Mount Vernon Ladies' Association* bought it, it had been owned and occupied by a Washington.

Lawrence Washington, as we have seen, named it in honor of his gallant friend, and from him it descended to his half-brother, George, who occupied it more than forty years. By him it was bequeathed to his nephew, Bushrod, who lived there twenty-seven years. It then passed into the possession of John Augustine Washington, a son of Bushrod's brother Corbin. He died three years afterward, leaving it to his widow. At her death, in 1855, it became the property of her son, John Augustine Washington, who sold it.

For many years the Mount Vernon estate had been decaying. The ravages of time and the rust of neglect were rapidly destroying all that had received the care and culture of General Washington's mind and hand; and thoughtful and patriotic visitors often felt saddened when they saw the mansion and its dependent buildings, and other visible memorials of the great and good Father of his Country, evidently perishing.

The sad thoughts of these visitors led to patriotic action, and for a long time there was a growing desire felt throughout the Union, to have Mount Vernon become the property of the nation. The young owner, unable to keep the estate in proper order, and greatly annoyed by thousands of visitors every year, many of whom took liberties about the house and grounds, in apparently utter forgetfulness that they were private property, expressed a willingness to sell it for such a purpose. Congress was asked to buy it. The application was unsuccessful.

At length an American matron conceived the idea of appealing to her countrywomen in behalf of Mount Vernon She asked them to put forth their hands to the work of obtaining sufficient money to purchase it, that the HOME AND TOMB OF WASHINGTON might be a national possession forever. The idea was electric, and it was felt and responded to all over the land. Her invalid daughter, strengthened by the thought of being instrumental in accomplishing the great work, took the direction of the enterprise. She printed a strong appeal to her countrywomen; organized an association, and procured a charter of incorporation for it; bargained for the purchase of the mansion and appendages, and two hundred surrounding acres of the Mount Vernon estate, for two hundred thousand dollars, and began in great earnestness the work of obtaining that amount of money, and as much more for the restoration and support of the estate. By common consent she was constituted regent or chief manager, and she appointed vice-regents in every state in the Union as assistants.

The efforts of American women were successful. They were cheered and aided by the best and wisest men of their country. EDWARD EVERETT, one of our most sagacious statesmen and accomplished scholars, devoted his tongue and pen to the work. He went from city to city, like Peter the Hermit pleading for the rescue of the Holy Sepulchre, delivering an oration upon the character of Washington for the benefit of the fund; and delighted crowds who listened to his eloquent words, contributed so freely, that in less than two years he paid into the treasury of the *Ladies' Mount Vernon Association*, one quarter of the purchase money. The whole amount was obtained, and now Mount Vernon is no longer a private possession, but the property of the multitudes of men, women and children of the land, who have contributed in ever so slight a degree to its purchase. It is to be theirs and their posterity's forever. Nothing now remained for the Association to do, but to obtain a sum fully equal to that of the purchase money, for the complete restoration and future support of the estate, and a general supervision of its management. This, American women have not yet (1882) accomplished; but they have done much towards it. (See page 425).

We have now considered some of the most interesting of the past associations of Mount Vernon, connected with the illustrious man whose character has in a degree sanctified them all. But there are other associations that cluster around Washington and his home, in the presence of which these material things sink into utter insignificance. They are of a moral nature, and belong not only to the Past but to all the Future.

It is delightful to contemplate the character of Washington in its relation to the events in which he was immediately engaged, for it presents a most noble example; but far more delightful and profitable is it, to contemplate him with that broader vision which discerns his relation to all people and to all time—to regard him as the fulfilment of the heart-prophecies of earnest lovers of freedom in the past; born, nurtured, developed, disciplined, and inspired, to lead a great people out of bondage, and to be forever a sublime model of a PATRIOT for the contemplation of generations yet to appear. We should become habituated thus to think of him, and learn to love the spirit which led him to the performance of great deeds, rather than the deeds themselves.

Such contemplations of Washington are not incompatible with a sober reverence for material things with which he was intimately associated: and especially should we cherish as precious memorial treasures, the HOME that he loved, and the TOMB wherein his remains repose. These may excite the mind to loftier views of the Pater Patriæ, and inspire sentiments such as filled the soul of the Rev. William Jay, of England, who, on seeing a picture of Mount Vernon, wrote impromptu—

"There dwelt the MAN the flower of human kind,
Whose visage mild bespoke his noble mind.
There dwelt the SOLDIER who his sword ne'er drew
But in a righteous cause to freedom true.
There dwelt the *Hero*, who ne'er fought for fame,
Yet gained more glory than a Cæsar's name.
There dwelt the STATESMAN, who, devoid of art,
Gave soundest counsels from an upright heart.
And oh! Columbia, by thy sons caressed,
There dwelt THE FATHER of the realms he blessed
Who no wish felt to make his mighty praise,
Like other chiefs, the means himself to raise,
But there, retiring, breathed in pure renown,
And felt a grandeur that disdained a crown."

Professor J. R. Green, the latest and best historian of England, thus wrote of Washington:

"No nobler figure ever stood in the forefront of a nation's life. ° ° ° ° There was little in his outer bearing to reveal the grandeur of soul, which lifts his figure, with all the simple majesty of an ancient statue, out of the smaller passions the meaner impulses of the world around him. ° ° ° ° ° It was only as the weary fight went on that the colonists learned little by little the greatness of their leader—his clear judgment, his heroic endurance, his silence under difficulties, his calmness in the hour of danger or defeat, the patience with which he waited, the quickness and hardness with which he struck, the lofty and serene sense of duty that never swerved from its task through resentment or jealousy, that never through war or peace felt the touch of a meaner ambition, that knew no aim save that of guarding the freedom of his fellow-countrymen, and no personal longing save that of returning to his own fireside when their freedom was secured. It was almost unconsciously that men learned to cling to Washington with a trust and a faith such as few other men have won, and to regard him with a reverence which still hushes us in the presence of his memory."

A few other matters which, if introduced before, would have disturbed the symmetry of the work, are here presented, in order to make the reliquary of the Beloved Patriot more complete.

THE ENGLISH HOME OF WASHINGTON'S FAMILY.

On the earlier pages of this work, allusion is made to the Northamptonshire branch of the Washington family, from whom our illustrious countryman was descended. Recent investigations by the Rev. J. M. Simpkinton of Brington, England, and others, have brought to light some new and

THE WASHINGTON HOUSE, BRINGTON.

interesting facts concerning that family. Mr. Simpkinton believes that he has satisfactory evidence to show that a certain house in Brington, is the one in which lived Lawrence Washington, father of Lawrence and John who emigrated to Virginia in 1657. The family appears to have been in reduced circumstances, and went from Sulgrave to Brington because of their relationship to Lord Spencer of that County. They were also allied to the second George Villiers, Duke of Buckingham, whose half-sister and William, a brother of the emigrants to America, had been united in wedlock. Another brother, Thomas, was the "Mr. Washington" mentioned on page 28.

INSCRIPTION OVER THE DOOR OF THE WASHINGTON HOUSE.

Over the door of the ancient house in Brington, identified as that of Lawrence Washington, is a square stone bearing this inscription—"THE LORD GIVETH, THE LORD TAKETH AWAY, BLESSED BE THE NAME OF THE LORD. CONSTRUCTA, 1606." This pious inscription, quite common in such relation in those days, is accounted for by the fact which the Parish Register reveals, that Lawrence and Margaret Washington, (who had seventeen children,) had a child given to them and taken away the year when the house was built. In the Parish Church of Brington may be seen the monumental slab of Lawrence Washington, on which are the family arms, as seen in the picture of a seal on page 31.

WASHINGTON'S LIBRARY.

The Library at Mount Vernon mentioned on page 31, is no longer there. It was the private property of John A. Washington, from whom the "Mount Vernon Ladies' Association" purchased the estate, and was taken by him to his new home. Every other movable relic of Washington, pictured and described in this volume, and which then remained at Mount Vernon, was taken away at the same time, excepting the key of the Bastile (page 237), pack-saddle (page 53), bust of Lafayette (page 244), a large globe, and the original plaster-cast from Washington's face, made by Houdon, with the attached model mentioned on page 176. In the year 1860, the harpsichord presented by Washington to Nelly Custis (page 282), was sent back to Mount Vernon by Mrs. Robert E. Lee, as a gift to the proprietors. The tripod that bore Washington's Compass when he was a Surveyor in his youth and mature age, has also been deposited there.

Mr. Washington was on the Staff of General Robert E. Lee, and perished at an early period of the late Civil War. His wife is also dead; and the books of the Mount Vernon Library have been separated and scattered. To give the reader a knowledge of the contents of that Library, I subjoin a catalogue of the books, with the money value of each work attached, made at Mount Vernon by the sworn appraisers, after the death of Washington. These appraisers were Thompson Mason, Tobias Lear, Thomas Peter and William H. Foote. It is proper to state that many of the titles in the catalogue are imperfectly, and some inaccurately given; but it is here reproduced as copied from the orginal document among the public records at Alexandria.

CATALOGUE.

American Encyclopedia, 18 vols. 4to.	$150.00
Skombrand's Dictionary, 1 vol.	7.50
Memoir of a Map of Hindostan, 1 do., 4to.	8.00
Young's Travels, 1 do.	4.00
Johnson's Dictionary, 2 vols.	10.00
Guthrie's Geography, 2 do.	20.00
Elements of Rigging, 2 do.	20.00
Principles of Taxation, 1 vol.	2.00
Luzac's Oration's, 1 do.,	1.00
Mawe's Gardener, 1 do.	4.00
Jeffries Aerial Voyage, 1 do.	1.00
Beacon Hill, 1 do.	1.00
Memoirs of the American Academy, (one of which is a Pamphlet,) 2 vols.	3.00
Duhamel's Husbandry, 1 vol.	2.00
Langley on Gardening, 1 do.	2.00
Price's Carpenter, 1 do.	1.00
Count De Grasse, 1 do.	1.00
Miller's Gardener's Dictionary, 1 do.	5.00
Gibson's Diseases of Horses, 1 do.	3.00
Rumford's Essays,	3.00
Miller's Tracts, 1 vol. 8vo.	2.00
Rowley's Works, 4 vols.	12.00
Robertson's Charles V., 4 do.	16.00
Gordon's History of America, 4 do.	12.00

Gibbon's Roman Empire, 6 vols.	$18.00
Stanyan's Grecian History, 2 do.	2.00
Adams' Rome, 2 do.	4.00
Anderson's Institute, 1 vol.	2.00
Robertson's America, 2 vol.	4.00
Osian's Poem's, 1 vol.	2.00
Humphrey's Works, 1 do.	3.00
King of Prussia's Works, 13 vols.	26.00
Gillies' Frederick, 1 vol.	1.50
Goldsmith's Natural History, 8 vol.	12.00
Locke on the Understanding, 2 do.	3.00
Shipley's Works, 2 do.	4.00
Buffon's Natural History, abridged, 2 do.	4.00
Ramsay's History, 2 do.	2.00
The Bee, (thirteenth volume missing.) 18 do.	34.00
Sully's Memoirs, 6 do.	9.00
Fletcher's Appeal, 1 vol.	1.00
History of Spain, 2 vols. 8vo.	3.00
Jortin's Sermons, 2 do.	2.00
Chapman on Education, 1 vol.	.75
Smith's Wealth of Nations, 3 vols.	4.50
History of Louisiana, 2 vols.	2.00
Warren's Poems,	.50
Junius' Letters, 1 do.	1.00
City Addresses, 1 do.	1.00
Conquest of Canaan, 1 do.	1.00
Shakespeare's Works, 1 do.	2.00
Antidote to Deism, 2 vols.	1.00
Memoirs of 2500, 1 vol.	.75
Forest's Voyage, 1 do., 4to	3.00
Don Quixote, 4 vols.	12.00
Ferguson's Roman History, 3 do.	12.00
Watson's History of Philip II., 1 vol.	4.00
Barclay's Apology, 1 do.	3.00
Uniform of the Forces of Great Britain in 1742, 1 do.	20.00
Otway's Art of War, 1 do.	3.00
Political States of Europe, 8 vols. 8vo.	20.00
Winchester's Lecture's, 4 do.	6.00

Principles of Hydraulics, 2 vols.	$2.00
Leigh on Opium, 1 vol. 8vo.	.75
Heath's Memoirs, 1 do.	2.00
American Museum, 10 vols.	15.00
Vertot's Rome, 2 do.	2.00
Hart's Gustavus, 2 do.	2.00
Moore's Navigation, 1 vol.	2.00
Graham on Education, 1 do.	2.00
History of the Mission among the Indians in North America, 1 do.	2.00
French Constitution, 1 do.	1.50
Winthrop's Journal, 1 do.	1.50
American Magazine, 1 do. 8vo.	4.00
Watts' Views, 1 do. 4to.	20.00
History of Marshall Turenne, 2 vols. 8vo.	2.00
Ramsay's Revolution of South Carolina, 2 do.	2.00
History of Quadrupeds, 1 vol.	1.50
Carver's Travels, 1 do.	1.50
Moore's Italy, 2 vols.	3.00
Moore's France, 2 do.	3.00
Chastellux's Travels, 1 vol.	1.00
Chasstellux's Voyages, 1 do.	1.00
Volney's Travels, 2 vols.	3.00
Volney's Ruins, 1 vol.	1.50
Warville's Voyage, in French, 3 vols.	3.00
Warville on the Relation of France to the U. States,	1.00
Miscellanies, 1 vol. 4to.	1.00
Fulton on Small Canals and Iron Bridges, 1 do.	3.00
Liberty, a poem, 1 do.	.50
Hazard's Collection of State Papers, 2 vols.	5.00
Young's Travels, 2 do.	4.00
West's Discourse, 1 vol.	2.00
A Statement of the Representation of England, and Wales, 1 do.	.50
Miscellanies, 2 vols.	2.00
Political Pieces, 1 vol.	1.00
Treaties, 1 do.	.50
Annual Register for 1781, 1 do. 8vo.	.75

Masonic Constitution, 1 vol. 4to.	$1.00
Smith's Constitutions, 1 do.	.50
Preston's Poems, 2 vols.	1.00
History of the United States, 1796, 1 vol. 8vo.	.50
Parliamentary Debates, 12 vols.	6.00
Mair's Book Keeping, 1 vol.	1.50
Miscellanies, 1 do.	1.00
Proceedings of the East India Company, 1 do. fol.	4.00
Ladies Magazine, 2 vols. 8vo.	3.00
Parliamentary Register, 7 do.	3.50
Pryor's Documents, 2 do.	2.00
Remembrancer, 6 do.	3.00
European Magazine, 2 do.	3.00
Columbian " 5 do.	10.00
American " 1 vol.	2.00
New York " 1 do.	2.00
Christian's " 1 do.	2.00
Walker on Magnetism, 1 do.	.50
Monroe's View of the Executive, 1 do.	.75
Massachusetts Magazine, 2 vols.	4.00
A Five Minutes Answer to Paine's Letter to General Washington, 1 vol.	1.00
Political Tracts, 1 do.	2.00
Proceedings on Parliamentary Reform, 1 do.	2.00
Poems on Various Subjects, 1 do.	.50
Plays, &c., 1 do.	.75
Annual Register, 3 vols.	4.50
Botanico-Medical Dissertation, 1 vol.	.25
Oracle of Liberty, 1 do.	.25
Cadmus, 1 do.	1.00
Doctrine of Projectiles, 1 do.	.50
Patricius the Utilist, 1 do. 8vo.	.50
Ahiman Rezon, 1 do.	1.50
Sharp on the Prophecies, 1 do.	.75
Minto on Planets, 1 do.	.50
Sharp on the English Tongue, 1 do.	.50
Sharp on Limitation of Slavery, 1 do.	1.50
Sharp on the Peoples Rights, 1 do.	1.00

Sharp's Remarks, 1 vol.	$ .50
National Defence, 1 do.	.50
Sharp's Free Militia, 1 do.	.50
Sharp on Congressional Courts, 1 do.	.75
Ahiman Rezin, 1 do.	1.00
Vision of Columbus, 1 do.	.50
Wilson's Lectures, 1 do.	.75
Miscellanies, 1 do.	1.00
The Contrast, A Comedy, 1 do.	.75
Sharp, an Appendix on Slavery, 1 do.	.50
Muir's Trial, 1 do.	.75
End of Time, 1 do.	.75
Erskine's View of the War, 1 do.	1.00
Political Magazine, 3 vols.	4.50
The Law of Nature, 1 vol. 12mo.	.75
Washington's Legacy, 1 do.	1.00
Political Tracts, 1 do. 8vo.	1.00
America, 1 do.	1.00
Proofs of a Conspiracy, 1 do.	1.50
Mackintosh's defence, 1 do.	1.00
Miscellanies, 1 do.	1.00
Mirabean, 1 do.	1.00
Virginia Journal, 1 do. 4to.	1.00
Miscellanies, 1 do. 8vo.	2.25
Poems, &c., 1 do. 4to.	1.00
Morse's Geography, 1 do. 8vo.	2.00
Messages &c., 1 do.	1.00
History of Ireland, 2 vols.	2.00
Harte's Works, 1 vol.	1.25
Political Pamphlets, 1 do.	1.00
Burn's Poems, 1 do.	2.00
Political Tracts, 1 do.	.75
Miscellanies, 1 do.	1.00
Higgins on Cements, 1 do.	1.00
Repository, 2 vols.	3.00
Reign of George III., 1 vol.	1.00
Political Tracts, 1 do,	1.25
Tar Water, 1 do.	.75

Minot's History, 1 do.	$.75
Mease on the Bite of a Mad Dog, 1 do.	1.75
Political Tracts, 1 do.	1.00
Reports, 1 do.	1.50
Revolution of France, 1 do.	1.00
Essay on Property, 1 do.	1.00
Sir Henry Clinton's Narrative, 1 do.	1.00
Lord North's Administration, 1 do.	1.50
Lloyd's Rhapsody, 1 do.	1.00
Tracts, 1 do.	1.00
Inland Navigation, 1 do.	1.00
Chesterfield's Letters, 1 do.	1.50
Smith's Constitutions, 1 do. 4to.	1.00
Morse's Geography, 2 vols. 8vo.	4.00
Belknap's American Biography, 2 vols.	3.00
Belknap's History of New Hampshire, 1 vol.	2.00
" " " " 3 vols.	5.00
Minot's History of Massachusett's, 1 vol.	2.00
Jenkinson's Collection of Treaties, 3 vols.	6.00
District of Maine, 1 vol. 8vo.	1.50
Gulliver's Travels, 2 vols.	1.50
Tracts on Slavery, 1 vol.	1.00
Priestley's Evidences, 1 do.	1.00
Life of Buncle, 2 vols.	3.00
Webster's Essays, 1 vol.	1.50
Bartram's Travels, 1 vol.	2.00
Bossu's Travels, 2 vols.	3.00
Situation of America, 1 vol.	1.00
Jefferson's Notes, 1 do.	1.50
Coxe's View, 1 do.	1.50
Ossian's Poem's, 1 do.	1.50
Adams on Globes, 1 do.	2.00
Pike's Arithmetic, 1 do.	2.00
Bunaby's Sermons and Travels, 1 do.	1.00
Champion on Commerce, 1 do.	1.00
Brown's Bible, 1 vol. fol.	15.00
Bishop Wilson's Bible, 3 vols.	60.00

Bishop Wilson's Works, 1 vol.	$15.00
Laws of New York, 2 vols.	12.00
Laws of Virginia, 2 vols.	3.00
Middleton's Architecture, 1 vol.	3.00
Miller's Naval Architecture, 1 do.	4.00
The Senator's Remembrancer, 1 do.	3.00
The Origin of the Tribes or Nations in America, 1 do. 8vo.	.75
A Treatise on the Principles of Commerce between Nations, 1 do.	.50
Annual Register, 1 do.	.50
General Washington's Letters, 2 vols.	4.00
Insurrection, 1 vol.	.50
American Remembrancer, 3 vols.	1.50
Epistles for the Ladies, 1 vol.	.50
Discourses upon Common Prayer, 1 do.	.25
The Trial of the Seven Bishops, 1 do. 8vo.	.50
Lebroune's Surveyor, 1 do. fol.	1.00
Sharp's Sermons, 1 do 8vo.	.50
Muir's Discourses, 1 do.	.75
Emblems, Divine and Moral, 1 do.	1.00
Yorick's Sermons, 2 vols.	1.00
D'Ivernois on Agriculture, Colonies and Commerce, 1 vol.	.75
Pocket Dictionary, 1 do.	.25
Prayer Book, 1 do.	1.50
Royal English Grammar, 1 do.	.25
Principles of Trade compared, 1 do.	.50
Dr. Morse's Sermon, 1 do.	.50
Duché's Sermon, 1775, 1 do.	.50
Sermons, 1 do.	.50
Embassy to China, 1 do.	1.00
Warren's Poems, 1 do.	1.00
Sermons, 1 do.	.25
Humphrey Clinker, 1 do.	.25
Poems, 1 do.	.50
Swift's Works, 1 do.	.50
History of a Foundling, (3d vol. wanting,) 3 vols.	1.50
Adventures of Telemachus, 2 do.	.00

Nature Displayed, 1 vol.	$1.00
Solyman and Almenia, 1 do.	.50
Plays, 1 do.	.50
The High German Doctor, 1 do.	.25
Benezet's Discourse, 1 do.	.25
Life and Death of the Earl of Rochester, 1 do.	25
Journal of the Senate and House of Representatives, 9 vols. fol.	27.00
Laws of the United States, 7 do.	28.00
Revised Laws of Virginia, 1 vol.	10.00
Act of Virginia Assembly; 5 vols.	1 00
Cruttwell's Concordance, 1 vol.	5.00
Dallas's Reports, 1 do. 8vo.	3.00
Swift's System, 2 vols.	3.00
Journals of the Senate and House of Representatives, 3 do.	6.00
State Papers, 1 vol.	2.00
Burn's Justice, 4 vols.	12.00
Marten's Law of Nations, 1 vol.	1.50
Views of the British Customs, 1 do.	1.00
Debates of Congress, 3 vols.	4.50
Journal of Congress, 13 do.	40.00
Laws of the United States, 3 do.	6.00
Kirby's Reports, 1 vol.	2.00
Virginia Justice, do.	1.00
Virginia Laws, 1 do.	1.00
Dogge on Criminal Law, 3 vols.	4.50
Laws of the United States, 2 do.	4.00
Debates of the State of Massachusetts on the Constitution, 1 vol.	.50
Sharp on the Law of Nature, 1 do.	.25
Sharp on the Law of Retribution, 1 do.	.25
Sharp on Libels and Juries, 1 do.	.25
Acts of Congress, 1 do.	.75
Debates of the Convention of Virginia, 1 do.	.50
The Landlord's Law, 1 vol. 12mo.	.25
Attorney's Pocket Book, 2 vols. 8vo.	1.00
President's Messages, 1 vol.	2.00

Jay's Treaty, 1 vol.	$ .50
Debates of the Convention of Massachusetts, 1 do.	.50
Law against Bankrupts, 1 do.	.50
Debates in the Convention of Pennsylvania, 1 do.	.50
Debates in the Convention of Virginia, 1 do.	.50
Debates in the House of Representatives of the United States with respect to their power on Treaties, 1 do.	.50
Sundry Pamphlets, containing Messages from the President to Congress, &c.,	1.00
Orations, 1 vol. 4to.	.50
Gospel News, 1 vol. 8vo.	1.00
Mosaical Creation, 1 vol. 8vo.	.75
Original and Present State of Man, 1 vol.	.50
Sermons, 2 vols.	1.50
Political Sermons, 3 do.	2.25
Miscellanies, 1 vol.	.75
Ray on the Wisdom of God in Creation, 1 do.	1.00
Orations, 1 do.	.75
Medical Tracts, 2 vols.	1.50
Masonic Sermons, 1 vol.	.50
Miscellanies, 1 do.	.75
Backus's History, 1 do.	1.00
Sick Man Visited, 1 do.	.75
State of Man, 1 do.	.75
Churchill's Sermon, 1 do.	.75
Account of the Protestant Church, 1 do.	.75
Exposition of the Thirty-nine Articles, 1 do.	1.00
Dodington's Diary, 1 do.	1.00
Davies' Cavalry, 1 do.	1.00
Simm's Military Course, 1 do.	1.00
Gentlemen's Magazine, 3 vols.	4.50
Library Catalogue, 1 vol.	1.50
Transactions of the Royal Humane Society, 1 do.	3.00
Zimmermans' Survey, 1 do.	.75
History of Barbary, 1 do.	.75
Anson's Voyage around the World, 1 do.	1.00
Horseman and Farrier, 1 do.	1.00

Gordon's Geography, 1 vol.	$1.00
Kentucky, 1 do	.75
History of Viginia, 1 do.	1.00
American Revolution, 1 do.	1.00
Cincinnati, 1 do.	1.00
Political Tracts, 1 do.	.75
Remarks on the Encroachments of the River Thames, 1 do.	.50
Sharp on Crown Law, 1 vol. 8vo.	.50
Common Sense, &c., 1 vol.	.75
Hardy's Tables, 1 do.	.75
Beauties of Sterne, 1 do.	.75
Peregrine Pickle, 3 vols.	1.50
McFingal, 1 vol.	.50
Memoirs of the Noted Buckhouse, 2 vols.	1.50
Odyssey, (Pope's Translation of Homer,) 5 vols.	3.00
Miscellanies, 3 do.	1.50
Fitz Osborne's Letters, 1 do.	.50
Voltaire's Letters, 1 do	.50
Guardian, 2 vols.	1.00
Beauties of Swift, 1 vol .	.50
The Gleaner, 3 vols.	3.00
Miscellanies, 2 do.	1.50
Lee's Memoirs, 1 vol.	1 00
The Universalist, 1 do.	1.00
Chesterfield's Letters, 4 vols.	2.00
Louis XV.,	3.00
Bentham's Panopticon, 3 do	2.00
Reason, &c., 1 vol.	.50
Tour through Great Britain, 4 vols.	3.00
Female Fortune-Hunter, 3 do.	1.00
The Supposed Daughter, 3 do.	1.50
Gil Blas, 4 do.	3.00
Columbian Grammar, 1 vol.	.50
Frazier's Assistant, 1 do.	.50
Review of Cromwell's Life, 1 do.	.75
Seneca's Morals, 1 do.	.75
Travels of Cyrus, 1 do.	.75

Miscellanies, 1 vol.	.75
Charles XII, 1 do.	.50
Emma Corbett (the 2d volume wanting), 2 vols.	1.00
Pope's Works, 6 vols. 12mo.	2.00
Foresters, 1 vol.	.50
Adam's Defence, 1 vol. 8vo.	.75
Butler's Hudibras, 1 vol.	1.00
Spectator, 6 vols.	3.00
New Crusoe, 1 vol.	.75
Philadelphia Gazette, 1 vol. fol.	10.00
Pennsylvania Packet, 2 vols.	12.00
Gazette of the United States, 10 do.	40.00
Atlas to Guthrie's Geography, 1 vol.	40.00
Moll's Atlas, 1 do.	10.00
West India Atlas, 1 do.	20.00
General Geographer, 1 do.	30.00
Atlas of North America, 1 do	10.00
Manœuvres, 1 vol. 8vo.	1.00
Military Instruction, 1 vol.	.50
Count Saxe's Plan for New Modelling the French Army, 1 do.	.50
Military Disipline, 1 vol. 4to.	2.00
Prussian Evolutions, 1 vol.	1.50
Code of Military Standing Resolutions, 2 vols.	4.00
Field Engineer, 1 vol. 8vo.	1.50
Army List, 1 vol.	.75
Prussian Evolutions, 1 vol. 4to.	.50
LeBlond's Engineer, 2 vols. 8 vo.	3.00
Muller on Fortification, 1 vol.	2.00
Essay on Field Artillery, by Anderson, 1do.	.75
A System of Camp Disipline, 1 do.	2.00
Essay on the Art of War, 1 do.	1.00
Treatise of Military Disipline, 1 do.	1.50
List of Military Officers, British and Irish, in 1777, 1 do.	.50
Vallancey on Fortifications, 1 do.	1.50
Muller on Artillery, 1 do.	1.50
Muller on Fortifications, 1 do.	2.00

Militia, 1 vol. 8vo.	$1.00
American Atlas, 1 vol. fol.	4.00
Steuben's Regulations, 1 vol. 8 vo.	.75
Traite de Cavalerie, 1 vol. fol.	6.00
Truxton on Latitude and Longitude, 1 vol.	1.50
Ordinances of the King, 1 do.	2.00
Magnetic Atlas, 1 do.	1.00
Roads through England, 1 vol. 8vo.	1.00
Carey's War Atlas, 1 vol. fol.	.75
Colles's Survey of Roads, 1 vol. 8vo.	.50
Military Institutions for Officers, 1 vol.	.50
Norfolk Exercise, 1 do.	.25
Advice of the Officers of the British Army, 1 do.	.25
Webb's Treatise on the Appointment of the Army, 1 do.	.25
Acts of the Parliament respecting Militia. 1 do.	.25
The Partisan, 1 do.	.50
Anderson on Artillery, (in French,) 1 do.	.25
List of Officers under Sir William Howe in America, 1 do.	.25
The Military Guide, 1 do.	.50
The Duties of Soldiers in General, 3 vols.	1.50
Young's Tour, 2 do.	3.00
Young on Agriculture, (17 vols. full bound, 8 half bound, and 1 pamphlet,) 26 do.	50.00
Anderson on Agriculture, (1 vol. full bound, the others in boards,) 4 do.	8.00
Lisle's Observations on Husbandry, 2 do.	3.00
Museum Rusticum, 6 do.	10.00
Marshall's Rural Ornament, 2 do.	4.00
Barlow's Husbandry, 2 do.	3.00
Kennedy on Gardening, 2 do.	2.00
Hale on Husbandry, 4 do.	6.00
Sentimental Magazine, 5 do.	1600
Price on the Picturesque, 2 do.	4.00
Agriculture, 2 do.	2.00
Miller's Gardener's Calendar, 1 vol.	2.00
Rural Economy, 1 vol.	1.00

Agricultural Inquiries, 1 vol.	$1.00
Maxwell's Practical Husbandry, 1 do.	2.00
Boswell on Meadows, 1 do.	1.00
Gentleman Farmer, 1 do.	1.50
Practical Farmer, 1 do.	1.50
Millwright and Miller's Guide, 1 do.	2.00
Bordley on Husbandry, 1 do.	2.25
Sketches and Inquiries, 1 do.	2.00
Farmer's Complete Guide, 1 do.	1.00
The Solitary or Carthusian Gardener, 1 do.	1.00
Homer's Illiad, by Pope, (first two vols. wanting,) 4 vols.	2.00
Don Quixote, 4 do.	3.00
Federalist, 2 do.	3.00
The World Displayed, (13th vol. wanting,) 19 do. 12mo.	9.50
Search's Essays, 2 do. 8vo.	2.00
Freneau's Poems, 1 vol	1.00
Cattle Doctor, 1 do.	.75
Stephens's Directory, 1 do.	.50
New System of Agriculture, 1 do.	.50
Columbus's Discovery, 1 do.	.25
Moore's Travels, 5 vols.	4.00
Agricultural Society of New York, 1 vol. 4to.	2.00
Transactions of the Agricultural Society of New York, 1 do.	1.00
Annals of Agriculture, 1 do.	2.00
Dundonald's Connection between Agriculture and Chemistry, 1 do.	1.00
Labors in Husbandry, 1 do.	1.00
Account of different Kind of Sheep, 1 do. 8vo.	.50
The Hot-house Gardener, 1 do	1.50
Historical Memoirs of Frederick II., 3 vols.	1.00
Treatise on Peat Moss, 1 vol.	.60
Treatise on Bogs and Swampy grounds, 1 do.	.75
Complete Farmer, 1 do. fol.	6.00

Pamphlets.

Reports of the National Agricultural Society of Great Britain, 103 Nos., 4to.	25.00

Pamphlets.

Massachusetts Magazine, 41 Nos. 8vo.	$6.00
New York Magazine, 38 do.	6.00
London Magazine, 18 do.	3.00
Political Magazine, 8 do.	1.00
Universal Asylum, 9 do.	1.50
Universal Magazine, 11 do.	1.50
Country Magazine, 15 do.	2.00
Monthly and Critical Reviews, 11 do.	2.00
Gentleman's Magazine, 8 do,	1.00
Congressional Register, 9 do.	1.00
Miscellaneous Magazine, 27 do.	3.00
Tom Paine's Rights of Man, 43 do.	15.00
Miscellaneous Magazine, 27 do.	4.00

Books

Hazard's Collection of State Papers, 2 vols. 4to.	5.00
Morse's American Gazetteer, 1 vol. 8vo.	2.00
Annals of Agriculture, (20 and 21) 2 vols.	3.00
On the American Revolution, 1 vol.	1.50
15 Pamphlets, Annals of Agriculture,	2.50
Judge Peters on Plaster of Paris, 1 vol.	1.50
Belknap's Biography, 1 do.	1.50
American Remembrancer, 1 do.	.50
Federalist, 2 vols.	1.50
A Pamphlet, The Debate of Parliament on the Articles of Peace, 1 vol.	.25
History of the American War in 17 Pamphlets,	1.50
Miscellaneous Pamphlets, 26 Nos.	2.00
Washington, A Poem,	2.00
Alfieri, Bruto Primo, Italian Tragedy,	1.00
Fragment of Politics and Literature, by Mandrillon, (in French,) 1 vol. 8 vo.	.75
Revolution of France and Geneva, (in French.) 2 vols.	2.00
History of the Administration of the finances of the French Republic, 1 do.	0.50
History of the French Administration, 1 do.	.75
The Social Compact, (in French, 1 do.)	.25

Books.

Chastellux's Travels in North America, (in French.) 2 vols. 8vo.	$1.50
1 Pamphlet of the French Revolution at Geneva,	.25
America Delivered, a Poem, (in French,) 2 vols.	1.50
Sinclair's Statistics (in French,) 1 vol.	1.50
The Works of Monsieur Chamousset, (in French,) 2vols.	4.00
Letters of American Farmer, (in French,) 3 do.	4.50
Germanicus, (in French,) 1 vol.	.25
Triumph of the New World, (in French,) 2 vols.	1.50
United States of America, (in German,) 1 vol.	1.50
Chastellux, Discourse on the Advantage of the Discovery of America, 1 do.	1.00
A German Book, 1 do.	.25
The French Mercury, (in French,) 4 vols,	3.00
Essay on Weights, Measures &c.. 2 do	.75
History of England, 2 do.	.25
Political Journal, (in German,) 1 vol.	.50
Letters in French and English, 1 do.	.25
History of the Holy Scriptures, 1 do.	.25
History of Gil Blas, 2 vols.	1.00
Telemachus, 2 do.	1.00
Poems of M. Grecourt, 2 do.	.25
Court Register, 6 do. 12mo..	1.50
6 Pamphlets, Political Journal, (in German,).	.50
Description of a Monument, 1 vol..	.50
Beacon Hill, 1 do.	.25
Letters in the English and German Language, 1 do.	25
A Family House-Keeper, 1 do.	.25
Pamphlets of different descriptions,	15.00

Maps, Charts, &c.

Chart of Navigation from the Gulf of Honda to Philadelphia, by Hamilton Moore —— to Bay of Fundy, do.	40.00
Griffiths Map of Pennsylvania, and Sketch of Delaware.	8.00
Howell's Large Map of Pennsylvania,	10.00

Maps and Charts.

Henry's Map of Virginia,	$8.00
Bradley's Map of the United States,	5.00
Holland's Map of New Hampshire,	3.00
Ellicott's Map of the West End of Lake Ontario,	4.00
Hutchins's Map of the Western Part of Virginia, Maryland, Pennsylvania and North Carolina,	3.00
Adlum and Williams's Map of Pennsylvania,	2.00
Map of Kennebec River, &c.,	1.00
Andrews Military Map of the Seat of War in the Netherlands,	1.00
Howell's Small Map of Pennsylvania,	2.00
Great Canal between Forth and Clyde,	2.00
Plan of the Line between North Carolina and Virginia,	2.00
M'Murray's Map of the United States,	3.00
Military Plans of the American Revolution,	8.00
Evan's Map of Pennsylvania, New Jersey, New York, and Delaware,	1.00
Plan of the Mississippi from the River Iberville to the River Yazoo,	2.00
Map of India,	5.00
Chart of France,	1.00
Map of the World,	.50
Map of the State of Connecticut,	2.00
Spanish Maps,	.50
Table of Commerce and Population of France,	.50
Battle of the Nile, &c.,	1.00
Routes and Order of Battle of Generals St. Clair and Harmar,	1.00
Truxton on the Rigging of a Frigate,	1.00
View of the Encampment at West Point,	.50
Emblematic Prints,	4.00
Plan of the Government and House of New York,	.50
Chase and Action between the Constellation and Insurgent, (two prints,)	4.00
General Wilkinson's Map of Part of the Western Territory,	1.00
Plan of Mount Vernon, by John Vaughan,	1.00
Specimen of Penmanship,	.50

Maps and Charts.

5 Plans of the Federal City and District,	$5.00
1 Large Draft,	3.00
Plan of the City of New York, Panopticon,	.80
Hoop's Map of the State of New York,	1.00
Howell's Pocket Map of the State of Pennsylvania,	2.00
A French Map of the Carolinas,	2.00
Fry and Jefferson's Map of Virginia,	2.00
Howell's Small Map of Pennsylvania,	2.00
A Map of New England,	2.00
9 Maps of different Parts of Virginia and Carolina, and also a number of loose Maps,	52.00
Carlton's Map, (2 sets,) of the coasts of North America,	8.00
Treatise on Cavalry, with large cuts,	50.00
Walker's View in Scotland,	3.00
A large Portfolio with sundry Engravings,	40.00
Alexander's Victories, 26 prints,	100.00
8 Reams of large folio Paper,	40.00
2 Reams of small Paper,	8.00
13 Reams of Letter Paper,	39.00
5 Whole Packages of Sealing-wax,	5.00
5 Leaden Paper Presses,	5.00
6 Blank Books,	18.00
13 Small books,	2.00
1 Large Globe,	50.00
1 Trunk,	6.00

Books Omitted.

Dictionary of Arts and Sciences, 4 vols. 8vo.,	20.00
Smollet's History of England, 1 vol.	11.00
Handmaid to the Arts, 2 vols.	2.00
Bancroft on Permanent Colors, 1 vol.	1.00
1 Theodolite,	.50

Washington's Library contained above twelve hundred books and pamphlets, about one hundred Maps Charts and Plans, and a considerable number of Engravings. The whole had an appraised total money value of about two thousand six hundred dollars.

Nearly every work in the collection was of practical value to a man like Washington, and seemed to have been purchased for use as a mechanic would purchase his tools. Works of an imaginative character were comparatively few; yet there was a sufficiency of light reading for the healthful amusement and culture of the younger and less thoughtful part of the household.

It will be observed that the Library was singularly barren in the more ephemeral political literature, both English and American, of the period immediately preceding the Revolution, when pamphleteers in both hemispheres were very active. The dearth of such literature in the Library at Mount Vernon may be partly accounted for by the fact that previous to the Revolution, Washington avoided politics and public employment as much as possible, as he had a natural dislike for them. He took only a general passing interest in the political agitations of the day, and lived the easy life of a country gentleman of wealth, more interested in social enjoyments and the management of his large landed estate, than anything else.

There is one book in existence which was at Mount Vernon in the early years of Washington's married life, that does not appear in the catalogue. In a list of articles ordered by Washington, from London, for "Miss Custis, 6 years old," (see page 74,) is named a "spinet," and "books, according to the inclosed list"—books for musical instruction. One of these, an octavo, entitled "The Complete Tutor for the Harpsichord or Spinet," has upon a fly-leaf in the hand-writing of the eminent Elias Boudinot, the words, "Miss Boudinot's Book, presented by her friend, Mrs. Washington, 1780." Its frontispiece is a picture of a musician in the costume of about 1760, playing upon a Harpsichord in form precisely like the one delineated on page 282. The book is in the possession of John William Wallace, Esq., of Philadelphia, a descendant of Miss Boudinot.

THE GROUNDS ABOUT THE MANSION.

On page 156, mention is made of the lawn on the West front of the Mount Vernon Mansion, and the method observed in planting the trees. I have before me the original memorandum made by Washington, concerning distances on that Western side, or main front of the house; and also on the Eastern side or river front, where the great piazza is. The following is a copy of the memorandum:

"MEMORANDUM.

"From the middle of the front door to the centre of the line between the Garden Houses, is N. °56, 12 W.*; 111 feet to the west line of the store and Ho. opposite†—148 feet to the outer part of the circle—174 to the line between the two necessaries—178 to the line of the trees—267 to the line between the centre of the Garden Gates—360 to the centre of the line between the Garden Houses.

The line between the Store and Ho. opposite is N. °32, 15 E—132 feet.
The line between the centre of the Garden Gates, is N. °33 .. E. and
The line between the Garden Houses is N. °33. 45 E.

From the necessary in the Lower Garden to the Mulberry Tree—reckoning
   from the wall of the Garden, is 25. 9
   to the Spanish Chestnut is 63. 3
   and to the Cherry Tree is 95. 9
From the necessaries in the Upper Garden, the distance from the Garden Wall to the English Walnut, is 25, 9. to the Spanish Chestnut 63. 3. and to the Cherry Tree, 95. 9. the same as on the other side"

---

* 8½ feet to circle—29 to the grass—79 to Dial-post.
† 128 to the edge of the inner circle.

Memorandum.

From the middle of the front door to the center of the line between the garden houses is :—

72, 56, 13. N:L * 111 feet to the test line of the same & the opposite 148 feet to the outer part of the circle 174 to the line between the two recesses ——178 to the line of the center of the freed—26½ to the line between the center of the garden also—360 to the center of the Section between the garden houses

* 8½ ft to circle—29 to the graft—79 to Dial post.
$ 128 to the edge of the inner circle.

From the Gar'en House in the Lower Garden, (say from the Garden Wall)
opposite the first Cherry Tree is 18. 6
to the new planted Walnut, . 28. 9
to the other Cherry Tree. . . . 71.
From the other Garden House to y^e first Walnut, . . 27. 3
to the 2d Walnut is . . . 55.
to the 3d Walnut is . . . . 78.
From the Lower Garden Ho. (centre thereof to the centre of the Gate is 95. 6
from thence to the centre of necessary. . . . 93. 6
From the centre of the other Garden Ho. to the centre of the gate is 90. 3
from thence to the centre of N'y, ... 93.
From the centre of the front door to the English Walnut, is N. °37. 45 W.
From Ditto to the Mulberry Tree, N. °80 . W.
From the Line between the Garden Houses to the outer circle is 252 ft.
From one necessary to the other, the course is N. °32. 20 E.
From the Piazza to the descent of the Hill in a line with the spire of the dry well and the point of the Hill at the N. circle, is 130 ft., and the course between the two is N. °40. 15 E.
The course of the Wall between the lower necessary and the Garden Ho. is S. °54. 15 E.
Ditto between the N Garden House and Nes'y. is S °56.—E.
The distance between the 2 Garden Houses, is . . . 263 ft.
The semi-circles at the sides, is . . . 150 ft.
The distance between the Store and House opposite. is . . 132 ft."

WASHINGTON AS A FREE MASON.

The simple fact that Washington was a member of the fraternity of Free and Accepted Masons, is mentioned on page 166, and in succeeding pages are some notices of Masonic regalia presented to him. All that is known of Washington's Masonic Life, is given in a volume by Sidney Hayden, published in 1866, entitled "Washington and his Masonic Compeers." The frontispiece to that work, is a copy of a portrait of Washington in full Masonic Regalia, as presiding officer of Alexandria Lodge, No. 22, for which it was painted in September, 1796, by a speculating and indifferent portrait-painter named Williams. He went to Philadelphia for the purpose, and obtained the privilege of making the portrait, through an address from the officers of the Alexandria Lodge asking

Washington for it. The picture was presented to the lodge, and Mr. Williams received from that body the sum of fifty dollars " in consequence of the trouble he was at in going to and coming from Philadelphia." The artist expected to profit largely by the operation, in filling orders for copies. But the picture was so poor that copies were not called for, whereupon he asked the lodge for further compensation. It was refused.

A copy of Williams's picture is here given, from a photograph from the original, not as a likeness of the First President, for it is a caricature, but because it shows him in the full Masonic Regalia which he kept at Mount Vernon and used at Alexandria, the sash and apron of which was the one presented to him by Watson and Coussol, twelve years before, as mentioned on pages **168** and **169**. The collar and ornaments are those of a Past Master.

MASONIC PORTRAIT.

On the back of the portrait (which is yet in possession of the Lodge at Alexandria,) is the following inscription: " His Excellency, GEORGE WASHINGTON, Esq., President of the United States, aged 64. Williams. *Pinxit ad vivum* in Philadelphia, September 18, 1794."

HOUDON'S LIKENESS OF WASHINGTON.

The original plaster mold of Washington's face, by Houdon, and attached to the original clay model of the rest of the head,

CAST FROM WASHINGTON'S FACE.

neck, shoulders and breast by the same artist, mentioned on page 176, is yet (1881,) at Mount Vernon, but being kept in a private room, few persons ever see it. A careful copy of the mask was made for the United States mint at Philadelphia, several years ago, where it is preserved with great care. To James Ross Snowden, Esq., late Superintendent of that Mint, I am indebted for a Photograph of the mask from which our engraving is made. It is undoubtedly the most accurate profile likeness of Washington, ever produced, as Houdon's statue at Richmond gives us the only correct portraiture of his person and costume. As such it is invaluable.

SHADOW PORTRAIT OF WASHINGTON.

In connection with this profile I give another remarkable one which, according to well authenticated tradition, was made at Mount Vernon, from life. The story is that not long before the death of Washington, the shadow of his head in profile, and also that of his wife, was cast the natural size, by a strong light upon a wall, from which careful outlines were traced, transferred to paper and filled with color so as to produce perfect silhouette likenesses. This was doubtless done by that woman of genius, Mrs. Lawrence Lewis (Eleanor Parke Custis,) Washington's adopted daughter, in whose possession they were for more than thirty years, when she gave them to a friend. On the back of each is the following certificate:

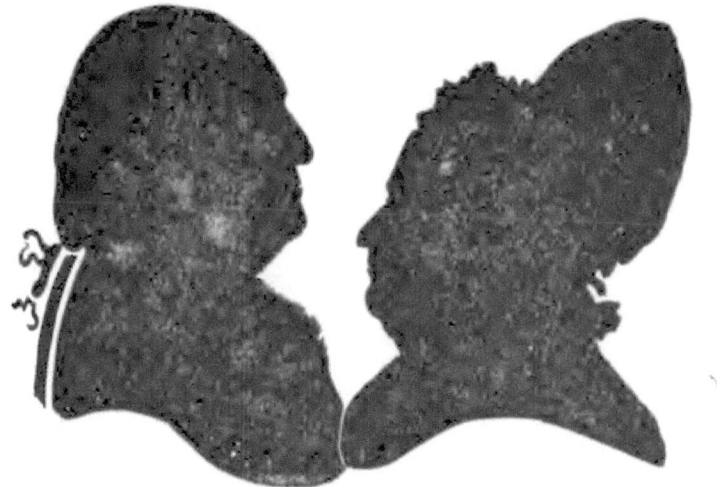

"The within are profiles of General and Mrs. Washington, taken from their shadows on a wall. They are as perfect likenesses as profiles can give. Presented to me by my friend, Mrs. Eleanor Parke Lewis. Woodland, July, 1832.
ELIZABETH BORDLEY GIBSON."

I am indebted to John A. McAllister, Esq., of Philadelphia, for photographs from the originals. It will be observed that the outline of Washington's face in this shadow profile, is almost identical with that of the plaster mask by Houdon.

HOW THE MANSION AT MOUNT VERNON WAS FURNISHED.

To gratify the natural and laudable desire of every one who reveres the character of Washington, to know all that is proper about his domestic life, I give below a list of articles with which the mansion at Mount Vernon was furnished and adorned. It is copied from the inventory made by the sworn appraisers, after the death of Washington, with their estimated value of each article.

INVENTORY.

In the New Room.

2 Large Looking-glasses,	$200.00
4 Silver-plated Lamps, &c.	60.00
6 Mahogany Knife Cases.	100.00
2 Sideboards, on each of which is an Image and China Flower-pot,	160.00
27 Mahogany Chairs at $10,	270.00
2 Candle Stands,	40.00
2 Fire Screens,	40.00
2 Elegant Lustres,	120.00
2 Large Gilt-Framed Pictures, represesting the Fall of Rivers,	160.00
4 do. representing Water Courses, &c.	240.00
1 do. Small likeness of General Washington,	100.00
1 do. Louis XVI.	50.00
2 do. Prints, Death of Montgomery.	150.00
2 do. Battle of Bunker Hill.	100.00
2 Large Gilt-framed Pictures, Dead Soldier,	45.00

1 Likeness of St. John,	$45.00
1 do. Virgin Mary,	15.00
4 Small prints, (one under each Lamp,)	8.00
1 Painting, Moonlight,	60.00
5 China Jars,	100.00
All the Images	100.00
1 Mat,	10.00
Window Curtains,	100.00
2 Round Stools,	6.00
Shovel, Tongs, Poker and Fender,	20.00

In the Little Parlor.

1 Looking-glass,	30.00
1 Tea Table,	8.00
1 Settee,	15.00
10 Windsor Chairs,	20.00
2 Prints representing Storms at Sea,	30.00
1 do. A Sea-fight between Paul Jones of the *Bon-Homme Richard* and Captain Pearson of the *Serapis*,	10.00
2 do. one the Whale Fishery of Davis's Straits, and the other of the Green Lands,	20.00
1 Likeness of General Washington in an oval Frame,	4.00
1 do. Dr. Franklin,	4.00
1 do. Lafayette,	4.00
1 Gilt Frame of wrought work, containg Chickens in a Basket,	20.00
1 do. Likeness of a Deer,	50.00
1 Painted Likeness of an Aloe,	2.00
6 Others of different Paintings,	12.00
1 Carpet,	10.00
2 Window Curtains,	5.00
Andirons, Tongs and Fender,	6.00

In the Front Parlor.

1 Elegant Looking Glass,	60.00
1 Tea Table,	15.00

1 Sofa,	$70.00
11 Mahogany Chairs,	99.00
3 Lamps, two with Mirrors,	40.00
5 China Flower-Pots,	50.00
1 Gilt Frame, Marquis Lafayette and Family,	100.00
1 do. General Washington,	50.00
1 do. Mrs. Washington,	50.00
1 do. Mrs. Lear,	80.00
1 do. Mrs. Law,	70.00
1 do. Mrs. Washington's two Children,	50.00
1 do. Mrs. Washington's Daughter when grown,	10.00
1 Small Oval Frame, (gilt) containing the likeness of Washington Custis,	10.00
1 do. George W. Lafayette,	10.00
1 do. General Washington,	10.00
1 do. Mrs. Washington,	10.00
1 Gilt Square Frame, the Likeness of Miss Custis,	10.00
1 do. Emblematic of General Washington,	16.00
2 Window Curtains,	16.00
1 Carpet,	80.00
Andirons, Shovel, Tongs &c.,	8.00

In the Dining Room.

1 Oval Looking-Glass.	15.00
1 Mahogany Sideboard,	23.00
1 Tea Table,	2.00
2 Dining Tables,	30.00
1 Large Case,	10.00
2 Knife Cases,	6.00
10 Mahogany Chairs,	50.00
1 Large Gilt Frame, Print, The Death of the Late Earl of Chatham,	50.00
1 do. General Wolfe.	15.00
1 do. Penn's Treaty with Indians,	15.00
1 do. Rittenhouse,	5.00
1 do. Dr. Franklin,	10.00

1 Large Gilt Frame, Print, General Washington,	$7.00
1 do. General Greene,	7.00
1 do. America,	6.00
1 do. General Lafayette, or Conclusion of the Late War,	7.00
1 do. General Wayne,	7.00
1 do. Washington's Family of Mount Vernon,	20.00
1 do. Alfred visiting his Noblemen,	6.00
1 do. Alfred dividing his Loaf with the Pilgrims,	9.00
1 Carpet,	2.00
Window Curtains,	2.00
Water Pitcher,	.50
Andirons, Shovel Tongs and Fender,	8.00

In the Bed Room.

1 Looking Glass,	10.00
1 Small Table,	5.00
1 Bed, Bedstead and Mattress,	50.00
4 Mahogany or Walnut Chairs,	8.00
1 Large Gilt Frame containing a Battle fought by Cavalry,	30.00
Window Curtains and Blinds,	1.50
1 Carpet,	5.00
Andirons, Shovel, Tongs and Fender,	4.00

In the Passage.

14 Mahogany Chairs,	70.00
1 Print Diana, dec'd by Venus,	5.00
1 do. Adoni's carried off by Venus,	5.00
1 do. The Dancing Shepherds,	5.00
1 do. Morning,	5.00
1 do. Evening,	8.00
1 do. View of the River Po in Italy,	8.00
1 do. Constantine's Arch,	8.00
1 do. General Washington,	25.00
1 do. Key of Bastile with its Representation,	10.00
1 Thermometer,	5.00

4 Images over the Door,	$20.00
1 Spy-Glass,	5.00

In the Closet under the Stair-case.

1 Fire Screen,	2.00
1 Machine to Scrape Shoes on,	2.00

In the Piazza.

30 Windsor Chairs,	30.00

From the foot of the Stair-case to the second Stairs.

1 Gilt Frame, Print. Musical Shepherds,	10.00
1 do. Moonlight,	10.00
1 do. Thunderstorm,	10.00
1 do. Battle of Bunker's Hill,	5.00
1 do. Death of Montgomery,	15.00

In the Passage on the second Floor.

1 Looking Glass,	4.00

In the Front Room on the second Floor.

1 Dressing Table,	8.00
6 Mahogany Chairs,	15.00
Bed, Bed-Stead and Curtains,	75.00
Window Curtains,	1.00
1 Large Looking Glass,	15.00
1 Print, Gainesboro Forest,	8.00
1 do. Nymph's Bathing,	8.00
1 do. Village,	6.00
1 do. Storm,	7.00
1 Carpet,	5.00
Wash-Basin and Pitcher,	1.00
Andirons, Shovels, Tongs and Fender,	5.00

In the Second Room.

1 Arm Chair,	6.00

Bed-Stead, Bed, Curtains and Window Curtains,	$70.00
1 Looking Glass,	15.00
1 Dressing Table,	8.00
Likeness of General Lafayette.	50.00
1 Carpet,	10.00
4 Chairs,	6.00
Wash-Basin and Pitcher,	1.00
Andirons, Shovel, Tongs and Fender,	4.00

In the Third Room.

6 Mahogany Chairs,	24.00
1 Bed, Bedstead and Curtains.	85.00
Window Curtains,	1.00
Chest of Drawers,	15.00
1 Looking Glass,	6.00
1 Wash-Basin and Pitcher,	4.00
1 Carpet,	7.00
1 Print, The Young Herdsman,	5.50
1 do. The Flight,	5.50
1 do. Morning,	5.50
1 do. Evening,	5.50
Andirons, Shovel, Tongs and Fender,	4.50

In the Fourth Room.

5 Mahogany Chairs,	16.00
1 Bed, Bed-Stead and Curtains,	77.50
Window Curtains,	2.00
1 Close Chair,	6.00
1 Pine Dressing Table,	1.00
1 Carpet,	10.00
1 Large Looking-Glass,	15.00
1 Print, Sun Rising.	6.00
1 do. Sun Setting.	6.00
1 do. Cupid's Pastime,	6.00
1 do. Cottage,	6.00
1 do. Herdsman,	6.00
Wash-Basin and Pitcher,	1.50

Andirons, Shovel, Tongs and Fender, . . $4.50

In the Small Room.

1 Dressing Table,	3.00
1 Wash Stand,	4.00
3 Windsor Chairs,	1.50
1 Bed and Bed-Stead,	40.00
1 Dressing Glass,	3.00
Glass and China in the China Closet, and that up Stairs, and also that in the Cellar,	850.00

In the Room which Mrs. Washington now keeps.

1 Bed-Stead and Mattress,	50.00
1 Oval Looking Glass,	10.00
1 Fender,	2.00
Andirons, Shovel and Tongs,	2.00
3 Chairs,	3.00
1 Table,	3.00
1 Carpet,	3.00

In Mrs. Washington's Old Room.

1 Bed, Bedstead, and Curtains,	70.00
1 Glass,	2.00
1 Dressing Table,	6.00
1 Writing Table,	25.00
1 Writing Chair,	2.00
1 Easy Chair,	10.00
2 Mahogany Chairs,	4.00
A Timepiece,	100.00
1 Chest of Drawers,	30.00
6 Paintings of Mrs. Washington's Family,	60.00
5 Small Drawings,	2.50
1 Picture, Countess of Huntington,	.75
1 do. General Knox,	1.00
1 do. A Parson,	1.00
5 Small Pictures,	2.00

In the Study.

7 Swords and Blades,	$120.00
4 Canes,	40.00
7 Guns,	35.00
11 Spy-Glasses,	110.00
1 Tin Canister of Drawing Paper,	.50
Trumbull's Prints,	36.00
1 Case Surveying Instruments,	10.00
1 Traveling Ink Case,	3.00
1 Globe,	5.00
1 Chest of Tools,	15.00
1 Box Containing two Paper Moulds,	25.00
1 Picture,	3.00
1 Bureau,	7.00
1 Dressing Table,	40.00
1 Tambour Secretary,	80.00
1 Walnut Table,	5.00
1 Copying Press,	30.00
1 Compass, Staff, and two Chains,	30.00
1 Case of Dentist's Instruments,	10.00
1 Old Copying Press,	11.00
2 Setts Money Weights,	20.00
1 Telescope,	50.00
1 Box of Paints, &c,	16.00
1 Bust of General Washington in Plaster, from the Life,	100 00
1 do. Marble,	50.00
1 Profile in Plaster,	25.00
2 Seals with Ivory Handles,	8.00
1 Pocket Compass,	.50
1 Brass Level	10.00
1 Japan Box containing a Mason's Apron,	40.00
1 Small Case containing three Straw Rings, one Farmer's Luncheon box	1.71
1 Silk Sash (Military,)	20.00
1 Velvet Housing for a Saddle and Holsters, trimmed with Silver Lace,	5.00

1 Piece of oil cloth, containing Orders of Masonry,	$50.00
Some Indian Presents,	5.00
1 Bust in Plaster, of Paul Jones,	20.00
2 Pine Writing Tables,	4.00
1 Circular Chair,	20.00
1 Box Military Figures	2.00
1 Brass Model Cannon,	15.00
2 Brass Candlesticks,	2.00
2 Horse Whips,	4.00
1 Pair of Steel Pistols,	50.00
1 Copper Wash Basin,	.75
1 Chest and its Contents, &c.	100.00
1 Arm Chair,	2.00
1 Writing Desk and Apparatus,	5.00
1 (Green) Field Book,	.25
Balloon Flag.	1.00
Tongs, Shovel and Fender,	1.00
A Painted Likeness, Lawrence Washington,	10.00
1 Oval Looking Glass,	2.00
3 Pair of Pistols,	50.00

In the Iron Chest.

Stock of the U. S. { 6 per cent., 3746; Dr. Deferred, 1873; 3 per cent., 2946 } 3746 2500	6,246.00
25 Shares Stock of the Bank of Alexandria,	5,000.00
24 do. do. Potomac Company, (at £100 st'g.)	10,666.00
Cash,	254.70
1 Sett of Shoe and Knee Buckles, Paste, in Gold,	250.00
1 Pair of Shoe and Knee Buckles, Silver,	5.00
2 Gold Cincinnati Eagles,	30.00
1 Diamond do.	387.00
1 Gold Watch, Chain, two Seals, and a Key,	175.00
1 Compass in Brass Case,	.50
1 Gold Box, Presented by the Corporation of New New York.	100.00
5 Shares of James River Stock at $100,	500.00

170 Shares of Columbia Stock at $40,	$6,800.00
1 Large Gold Medal of General Washington,	150.00
1 Gold Medal of St. Patrick's Society,	8.00
1 Ancient Medal (another Metal,)	2.00
11 Medals in a Case,	50.00
1 Large Medal of Paul Jones,	4.00
3 Other Metal Medals,	1.00
1 Brass Engraving of the Arms of the United States,	10.00
1 Pocket Compass,	5.00
1 Case of Instruments, Parallel Rule, &c.	17.50
1 Pocket Book,	5.00

Plate belonging to Mount Vernon.

44 Lbs. 15 oz.,	900.00

Plated Ware.

2 Bottle Stands,	2.00
1 Large Waiter,	8.00
2 Waiters, 2d Size,	6.00
4 Waiters,	8.00
1 Bread Basket,	8.00
1 Fish Knife,	2.00
6 Salt Stands,	12.00
4 Bottle Sliders,	4.00
1 Coffee Urn,	8.00
1 Tea Urn,	20.00
4 Pair of High Candlesticks,	40.00
3 Pair of Chamber Candlesticks,	9.00
1 Sett of Castors,	20.00
2 Cream Dishes,	6.00
2 Sugar Dishes,	8.00
2 Mustard Pots,	4.00
7 Salts,	17.00
1 Wine Strainer,	1.50
1 Cream Pot,	3.00

1 Snuffer Stand,	$1.00
1 Muffin Dish,	3.00
1 Tea Urn,	50.00
2 Pair of High Candlesticks,	30.00
1 Pair of Small Candlesticks,	3.00
1 Lamp,	10.00
1 Bread Basket,	10.00
1 Ladle,	.50
1 Pair of Large Coolers	60.00
2 Pair of Small Coolers,	60.00
1 Waiter,	10.00

WASHINGTON'S GREAT BARN.

On page 288 is printed part of a letter from Washington to Henry Lee, written in Philadelphia in October, 1793, concerning a new threshing machine, in which he complained of the difficulties he had experienced in trying to teach overseers and servants new ways of farm management and labor. "As a proof in point," he said, "of the almost impossibility of putting the overseers of this country out of the track they have been accustomed to walk in, I have one of the most convenient barns in this, or perhaps any other country, where thirty hands may with great ease be employed in thrashing. Half of the wheat of the farm was actually stowed in this barn, in the straw, by my order, for thrashing; notwithstanding, when I came home about the middle of September, I found a treading-yard not thirty feet from the barn door, the wheat again brought out of the barn, and horses treading it out in a open exposure, liable to the vicissitudes of weather."

The great barn here mentioned was circular in form, and the lower half of the wall was built of bricks. It was three or four miles from the Mount Vernon Mansion. It was yet

WASHINGTON'S CIRCULAR BARN.

standing in the sadly dilapidated state seen in the engraving when the writer visited Mount Vernon just before the late Civil War. It was taken down and rebuilt a few years ago.

POSTHUMOUS HONORS.

On page 346, we have noticed the funeral services in honor of Washington, held in Philadelphia by direction of Congress which was in session at the time of his death. It is mentioned that General Lee's oration, prepared at the request of Congress, was pronounced in the Lutheran Church in that city. It is yet used as a place of worship by the same denomination of Christians. I here give a correct picture of the edifice, copied from one in Lossings' *Pictorial Field Book of the War of* 1812, in which also appears the accompanying delineation of a silver medal in my possession, struck in commemoration of Washington, immediately after his death. It

LUTHERAN CHURCH IN PHILADELPHIA.

was designed by Dudley A. Tyng, then collector of customs at Newburyport, Massachusetts, and the die was cut and the medal published by Jacob Perkins, the eminent Mechanican and Engraver.

The medal is a little larger and thicker than a Spanish quarter of a dollar. On one side is a profile of Washington, inclosed in a wreath of laurel, and surrounded by the words, "HE IS IN GLORY, THE WORLD IN TEARS." On the reverse is a Memorial Urn, and

WASHINGTON MEDAL.

around it, forming two circles, are abbreviations seen in the engraving, signifying, "Born, February 11, 1732; General of the American Army 1775; resigned, 1783; President of the United States of America, 1789; retired in 1796; General of the Armies of the United States, 1798; died December, 14, 1799."

It is mentioned on page 349 that Bonaparte ordered crape to be suspended from all the flags and standards in the French service, for ten days. He did more. He directed a funeral oration to be pronounced before him and the civil and military authorities. This was done by Louis Fontaine in the Temple of Mars, at Paris, on the 8th of February, in the year 1800.

WASHINGTON'S WILL.

Washington wrote his Will at Mount Vernon, and signed it on the ninth of July, 1799, a few months before his death. The document, without the schedule of property mentioned in it, and attached to it, occupied several pages of manuscript, at the bottom of each of which he wrote his name. I will give here only such portions of his Will as may have an interest for the general reader.

After the usual form, and bequeathing to his wife the use, for the term of her natural life, almost his whole estate, he wrote, as the first object of his solicitude—

"*Item.*—Upon the decease of my wife, it is my will and desire that all the slaves whom I hold *in my own right* shall receive their freedom. To emancipate them during her life would, though eminently wished by me, be attended with such insuperable difficulties, on account of their intermixture by marriage with the dower negroes, as to excite the most painful sensations, if not disagreeable consequences to the latter, while both descriptions are in the occupancy of the same proprietor, it not being in my power, under the tenure by which the dower negroes are held, to manumit them. And whereas, among those who will receive freedom according to this devise, there may be some, who, from old age or bodily infirmities, and others, who, on account of their infancy, will be unable to support themselves, it is my will and desire, that all, who come under the first and second description, shall be comfortably clothed and fed by my heirs while they live; and that such of the latter description as have no parents living, or, if living, are unable or unwilling to provide for them, shall be bound by the court until they shall arrive at the age of twenty-five years; and in cases where no record can be produced, whereby their ages can be ascertained, the judgment of the court, upon its own view of the subject, shall be adequate and final. The negroes thus bound, are (by their masters or mistresses,) to be taught to read and write, and to be brought up to some useful occupation, agreeably to the laws of the Commonwealth of Virginia providing for the support of orphan and other poor children. And I do hereby expressly forbid the sale or transportation out of the Commonwealth, of any slave I may die possessed of, under any pretense whatsoever. And I do moreover, most pointedly and most solemnly enjoin it upon my executors hereafter named, or the survivors of them, to see that this clause respecting slaves, and every part thereof, be religiously fulfilled at the epoch at which it is directed to take place, without evasion, neglect or delay, after the crops, which may then be on the ground, are harvested, particularly as it respects the aged and infirm: seeing that a regular and permanent fund be established for their support, as long as there are subjects requiring it; not trusting to the uncertain provisions to be made by individuals. And as to my mulatto man, *William*, calling himself *William Lee*, I give immediate freedom, or, if he should prefer it, (on account of the accidents which have befallen him, and which have rendered him incapable of walking, or of any active employment,) to remain in the situation he now is, it shall be optional in him to do so; in either case, however, I allow him an annuity of thirty dollars during his natural life, which shall be independent of the victuals and clothes he has been accustomed to receive, if he chooses the last alternative; but in full, with his freedom, if he prefers the first; and this I give him, as a testimony of his attachment to me, and for his faithful services during the Revolutionary War."

The whole number of negroes left by Washington, in his own right was as follows: Men, 40; Women, 37; working boys, 4; working girls, 3; children, 40. total, 124. For the public good, he proceeded to write:

"*Item.*—To the Trustees, (Governors, or by whatsoever other name they may be designated,) of the Academy in the town of Alexandria, I give and bequeath, in trust, four thousand dollars, or in other words, twenty of the shares which I hold in the Bank of Alexandria, towards the support of a free School, established at or annexed to, the said Academy, for the purpose of educating such orphan children, or the children of such other poor and indigent persons, as are unable to accomplish it with their own means, and who, in the judgment of the trustees of the said seminary, are best entitled to the benefits of this donation. The aforesaid twenty shares I give and bequeath in perpetuity; the dividends only of which are to be drawn for, and applied, by the said trustees for the time being, for the uses above mentioned; the stock to remain entire and untouched, unless indications of the failure of the said bank should be so apparent, or a discontinuance thereof should render a removal of this fund necessary. In either of these cases, the amount of the stock here devised is to be vested in some other bank or public institution, whereby the interest may with regularity and certainty be drawn and applied as above. And to prevent misconception, my meaning is, and is hereby declared to be, that these twenty shares are in lieu of, and not in addition to, the thousand pounds given by a missive letter some years ago, in consequence whereof an annuity of fifty pounds has since been paid toward the support of this institution.

"*Item.*—Whereas by a law of the Commonwealth of Virginia enacted in the year 1785, the legislature thereof was pleased as an evidence of the approbation of the services I had rendered the public during the Revolution, and partly, I believe, in consideration of my having suggested the vast advantages which the community would derive by an extension of its inland navigation under legislative patronage, to present me with one hundred shares, of one hundred dollars each, in the incorporated Company, established for the purpose of extending the navigation of the James River from the tide water to the mountains; and also with fifty shares of £100 sterling each, in the corporation of another Company, likewise established for the similar purpose of opening the navigation of the river Potomac from the tide water to Fort Cumberland; the acceptance of which, although the offer was highly honorable, and grateful to my feelings was refused, as inconsistent with a principle which I had adopted, and I had never departed from, viz., not to receive pecuniary compensation for any services I could render my country in its arduous struggle with Great Britain for its rights, and because I had evaded similar propositions from other States in the Union; adding to the refusal, however, an intimation, that, if it should be the pleasure of the legislature to permit me to appropriate the said shares to *public uses*, I would receive them on those terms, with due sensibility; and this it having consented to, in flattering terms, as will appear by a subsequent law, and sundry resolutions, in the most ample and honorable manner;—I proceed after this recital, for the more correct understanding of the case, to declare that, as it has always been a source of serious regret with me, to see the youth of these United States sent to foreign countries for the purpose of education, often before their minds were formed, or they had imbibed any adequate ideas of the happiness of their own; contracting too frequently, not only habits of dissipation and extravagance, but principles unfriendly to Republican Government, and to the true and genuine liberties of mankind, which thereafter are rarely overcome; for these reasons it has been my ardent wish to see a plan devised on a liberal scale, which would have a tendency to spread systematic ideas through all parts of this rising empire, thereby to do away local attachments and State prejudices, as far as the nature of things would, or indeed ought to admit, from our national councils. Looking anxiously forward to the accomplishment of so desirable an object as this is (in my estimation,) my mind has not been able to contemplate any plan more likely to effect the measures, than the establishment of a UNIVERSITY in a central part of the United States, to which the youths of fortune and talents from all parts thereof may be sent for the completion of their education, in all the branches of polite literature, and in arts and sciences, in acquiring knowledge in the principles of politics and good government, and, as a matter of infinite importance, in my judgment, by associating with each other, and forming friendships in juvenile years, be enabled to free themselves in a proper degree from those local prejudices and habitual jealousies which have just been mentioned and which, when carried to excess, are never-failing sources of disquietude to the public mind, and pregnant of mischievous consequences, to this country.

"*Item.*—I give and bequeath, in perpetuity, the fifty shares which I hold in the Potomac Company, (under the aforesaid acts of the Legislature of Virginia,) towards the endowment of a University, to be established within the limits of the District of Columbia, under the auspices of the general government, if that government should incline to extend a fostering hand towards it; and, until such Seminary is established, and funds arising for these shares shall be required for its support, my further will and desire is, that the profit accruing therefrom shall, whenever the dividends are made, be laid out in purchasing stock in the Bank of Columbia, or some other bank, at the discretion of my executors, or by the Treasurer of the United States for the time being, under the direction of Congress, provided that honorable body should patronize the measure; and the dividends proceeding from the purchase of such stock, are to be vested in more stock, and so on, until a sum adequate to the accomplishment of the object is attained;

of which I have not the smallest doubt before many years pass away, even if no aid or encouragement is given by the legislative authority, or from any other source.

"*Item.*—The hundred shares which I hold in the James River Company, I have given and now confirm in perpetuity, to and for the use and benefit of Liberty Hall Academy, in the county of Rockbridge, in the Commonwealth of Virginia."

The Liberty Hall Academy thus so liberally endowed by Washington, is now a flourishing Seminary of learning in Lexington, Virginia, with the corporate title of Washington and Lee College.

Martha Washington, the wife of the testator, was appointed by this will, executrix, and his nephews, William Augustine Washington, Richard Washington, George Stephen Washington, and Lawrence Lewis, and his ward, George Washington Park Custis, ("when he shall have arrived at the age of twenty years,") were appointed executors of the Will, "in the construction of which," he said, "it will be perceived, that no professional character has been consulted, or has had any agency in the draft;" and he expressed a hope that no disputes would arise concerning it. If there should, he continued, "my will and direction expressly is, that all disputes shall be decided by three impartial and intelligent men, known for their probity and good understanding; two to be chosen by the disputants, each having the choice of one, and the third by those two; which three men, thus chosen, shall, unfettered by law or legal construction, declare their sense of the testator's intention; and such decision is, to all intents and purposes, to be as binding on the parties as if it had been given in the Supreme Court of the United States."

MRS. WASHINGTON'S WILL.

"'Tis well," said Mrs. Washington when told that her husband was dead. "All is now over; I shall soon follow him; I have no more trials to pass through." She survived her husband only two years and a half. So impressed was she that her death would soon follow his, that nine months afterwards, she had her last Will and Testament drawn up, as follows:

In the name of God, *Amen.*

"I MARTHA WASHINGTON, of Mount Vernon, in the county of Fairfax, being of sound mind and capable of disposing of my worldly estate, do make, ordain, and declare this to be my last Will and Testament, hereby revoking all other Wills and Testaments by me heretofore made.

Imprimis.—It is my desire that all my just debts may be punctually paid, and that as speedily as the same can be done.

Item.—I give and devise to my nephew, Bartholomew Dandridge, and his heirs, my lot in the town of Alexandria, situate on Pitt and Cameron streets devised to me by my late husband, George Washington, deceased.

Item.—I give and bequeath to my four nieces, Martha W. Dandridge, Mary Dandridge, Frances Lucy Dandridge, and Frances Henley, the debt of two thousand pounds due from Lawrence Lewis and secured by his bond, to be equally divided between them or such of them as shall be alive at my death, and to be paid to them respectively on the days of their respective marriage or arrival at the age of twenty-one years, whichsoever shall first happen, together with all the interest on said debt remaining unpaid at the time of my death; and in case the whole, or any part of said principal sum of two thousand pounds shall be paid to me during my life, then it is my will that so much money be raised out of my estate as shall be equal to what I shall have received of the said principal debt, and distributed among my four nieces aforesaid as herein has been bequeathed; and it is my meaning that the interest accruing after my death, on the said sum of two thousand pounds shall belong to my said nieces, and be equally divided between them, or such of them as shall be alive at the time of my death, and be paid annually for their respective uses, until they receive their shares of the principal.

"*Item.*—I give and bequeath to my grandson, George Washington Parke Custis, all the silver plate of every kind of which I shall die possessed, together with the two large plated coolers, the four small plated coolers, with bottle castors, and a pipe of wine, if there be one in the house at the time of my death also the sett of Cincinnati tea and table China, the bowl that has a —— in it, the fine old China jars which usually stand on the chimney-piece in the new room; also, all the family pictures of every sort and the pictures painted by his sister, and two small screens, worked one by his sister, and the other a present from Kitty Brown; also his choice of prints; also, the two girandoles and lustres that stand on them; also, the new bedstead which I caused to be made in Philadelphia, together with the bed, mattresses, bolsters, and pillows, and the white dimity curtains belonging thereto; also, two other beds with bolsters and pillows, and the white dimity window curtains in the new room; also, the iron chest and the desk in my closet which belonged to my first husband; also, all my books of every kind except the large Bible and Prayer-book; also, the set of tea china that was given me by Mr. Van Braam, every piece having M. W. on it.

Item.—I give and bequeath to my grand-daughter, Martha Peter, my writing table and the seat to it standing in my chamber; also, the print of General Washington hanging in the passage.

"*Item.*—I give and bequeath to my grand-daughter, Elizabeth Parke Law, the dressing table and glass that stands in the chamber called the yellow room, and General Washington's picture painted by Trumbull.

Item.—I give and bequeath to my grand-daughter, Eleanor Parke Lewis, the large looking-glass in the front parlor, and any other looking glass which she may choose; also, one of the new side-board tables in the new room; also twelve chairs with green bottoms, to be selected by herself; also, the marble table in the garret; also, the two prints of the Dead Soldier, a print of the Washington Family in a box in the garret, and the great chair standing in my chamber; also, all the plated ware not heretofore otherwise bequeathed; also, all the sheets, table linen, napkins, towels, pillow-cases remaining in the house at my death; also, three beds and bedsteads, curtains, bolsters, and pillows for each bed, such as she shall choose, and not herein particularly otherwise bequeathed, together with counterpanes and a pair of blankets for each bed; also, all the wine-glasses and decanters of every kind; and all the blue and white china in common use.

"*Item.*—It is my will and desire that all the wine in bottles in the vaults be equally divided between my grand daughters and grand-son, to each of whom I bequeath ten guineas to buy a ring for each.

Item.—It is my will and desire that Anna Maria Washington, the daughter of my niece, be put into handsome mourning at my death, at the expense of my estate: and I bequeath to her ten guineas to buy a ring.

" *Item.*—I give and bequeath to my neighbor, Mrs. Elizabeth Washington, five guineas to get something in remembrance of me.

Item.—I give and bequeath to Mrs. David Stuart, five guineas to buy her a ring.

Item.—I give and bequeath to Benjamin Lincoln Lear, one hundred pound specie, to be vested in funded stock of the United States, immediately after my decease, and to stand in his name as his property, which investment my executors are to cause to be made.

Item.—When the vestry of Truro Parish shall buy a glebe, I devise, will and bequeath that my executors shall pay one hundred pounds to them in aid of the purchase, provided the said purchase be made in my life-time, or within three years after my decease.

Item.—It is my will and desire that all the rest and residue of my estate, of whatever kind and description, not herein specifically devised or bequeathed, shall be sold by the executors of this, my last will, for ready money, as soon after my decease as the same can be done, and that the proceeds thereof together with all the money in the house and the debts due to me (the debts due from me and the legacies herein bequeathed being first satisfied,) shall be invested by my executors in eight per cent stock of the funds of the United States, and shall stand on the Book in the name of my executors in their character of executors of my will; and it is my desire that the interest thereof shall be applied to the education of Bartholomew Henley and Samuel Henley, the two youngest sons of my sister Henley, and also to the education of John Dandridge son of my deceased nephew, John Dandridge, so that they may be severally fitted and accomplished in some useful trade; and to each of them, who shall have lived to finish his education, or to reach the age of twenty-one years, I give and bequeath one hundred pounds, to set him up in his trade.

Item.—My debts and legacies being paid, and the education of Bartholomew Henley, Samuel Henley and John Dandridge, aforesaid, being completed, or they being all dead before the completion thereof, it is my will and desire that all my estates and interest in whatever form existing, whether in money, funded stock, or any other species of property, shall be equally divided among all the persons hereinafter named, who shall be living at the time that the interest of the funded stock shall cease to be applicable, in pursuance of my will hereinbefore expressed, to the education of my nephews, Bartholomew Henley, Samuel Henley and John Dandridge, namely: among Anna Maria Washington, daughter of my niece, and John Dandridge, son of my nephew, and all my great grandchildren living at the time that the interest of the said funded stock shall cease to be applicable to the education of the said B. Henley, S. Henley, and John Dandridge, and the interest shall cease to be so applied when all of them shall die before arriving at the age of twenty-one years, or those living shall have finished their education or have arrived at the age of twenty-one years, and so long as any one of the three lives who has not finished his education or arrived to the age of twenty-one years, the division of the said residue is to be deferred, and no longer.

Lastly.—I nominate and appoint my grandson, George Washington Parke Custis, my nephews, Julius B. Dandridge and Bartholomew Dandridge, and my son-in-law, Thomas Peter, executors of this, my last will and testament.

In Witness whereof I have hereunto set my hand and seal this twenty-second day of September, in the year eighteen hundred.

MARTHA WASHINGTON. [SEAL.]

Sealed, signed, acknowledged and delivered as her last will and testament, in the presence of the subscribing witnesses, who have been requested to subscribe the same, as such, in her presence.

ROGER FARRELL,
WILLIAM SPENCER,
LAWRENCE LEWIS,
MARTHA PETER.

MARCH 4, 1802.

I give to my grand-son, George Washington Parke Custis, my mulatto man Elish, that I bought of Mr. Butler Washington, to him and his heirs forever.

M. Washington

PRESENT CONDITION OF THE HOME OF WASHINGTON.

We have an account on page 369 and 370, of the purchase of the Mount Vernon estate—the Home of Washington—which was accomplished just before the beginning of the late Civil War. The possessors—the women of the land who contributed the purchase money, and who constitute *The Mount*

Vernon Ladies Association—are vested with the legal rights of owners of the property, by an act of incorporation passed by the Legislature of Virginia, (in which State the property lies,) on the 17th of March, 1856. This Act was afterward amended and re-enacted by the unanimous vote of both Houses of the Assembly of Virginia, in the following words:

"The Mount Vernon Ladies' Association of the Union, as heretofore organized, shall be, and they are hereby constituted a body politic and corporate, under the name and style of 'The Mount Vernon Ladies' Association of the Union,' and by this name and style shall be subject to all the provisions, and entitled to all the rights, powers, privileges and immunities, prescribed by existing laws, in so far as the same are applicable to like corporations, and not inconsistent with this Act.

"2. It shall be lawful for the said Mount Vernon Ladies' Association of the Union to purchase, hold and improve two hundred acres of Mount Vernon, including the late mansion, as well as the tomb of George Washington, together with the garden-grounds and wharf, and landing now constructed on the Potomac river; and to this end they may receive from the owner and proprietor of the said land, a deed in fee simple, and shall have and exercise full power over the use and management of the same, as they may by by-laws and rules declare; provided, however, that the said Mount Vernon Ladies' Association of the Union shall not have power to alienate the said land, or any part thereof, or to create a charge thereon, or to lease the same without the consent of the General Assembly of Virginia first had and obtained.

"3. The capital stock of the said Mount Vernon Ladies' Association of the Union shall not, including the two hundred acres of land aforesaid, exceed the sum of five hundred thousand dollars. The said Association, in contracting with the proprietor of Mount Vernon for the purchase of the same, may covenant with him, so as to reserve to him the right to inter the remains of such persons whose remains are in the vault at Mount Vernon, as are not now interred, and to place the said vault in such a secure and permanent condition as he shall see fit, and to inclose the same so as not to include more than a half acre of land; and the said vault, the remains in and around it, and the enclosure, shall never be removed nor disturbed; nor shall any other person hereafter ever be interred or entombed within the said vault or enclosure.

"4. The said property herein authorized to be purchased by the said Mount Vernon Ladies' Association of the Union shall be forever held by it, sacred to the Father of his Country; and if from any cause the said Association shall cease to exist, the property owned by the said Association shall revert to the Commonwealth of Virginia, sacred to the purposes for which it was originally purchased.

"5. This act shall be in force from its passage.

Under this act of incorporation *The Mount Vernon Ladies' Association* was organized by the appointment of Miss Ann Pamela Cunningham, (the daughter of the "Southern Matron, mentioned on page 370,) to be "Regent" or President, for life, having for her associates in the management, a number of Vice-regents, composed of one person in each state, nominated by the Regent. These constitute an Executive Committee to whom is intrusted the entire control and management of the affairs of the *Association*. The Committee and

Regent hold the relation towards each other like that of the National Senate and the President of the Republic. Her nominations may be confirmed or rejected by the Vice-regents.

When the late civil war broke out, the Managers were preparing to make a final appeal to their country-women for a sum of money, the interest on which should be ample to keep the Mount Vernon Mansion and Estate in the best order. The purchase money was all paid, and nothing was wanted to crown the efforts of the *Association* with complete success, but such liberal endowment. Already much had been done toward the renovation of the property. So early as July, 1859, a year before all the purchase money was paid and a deed given, the late proprietor allowed the work of repairing to commence. A Superintendent and fourteen men of various trades were at once occupied in the labor. Attention was first given to the renovation and restoration of the exterior of buildings, garden walls, et cetera. A new wharf was built, and a good road and paths were constructed between it and the Tomb and Mansion. But little had been done to the interior, when the war broke out in 1861, and the income derived from visitors, ceased.

During the war, the Home of Washington was in charge of an accomplished woman whom *The Mount Vernon Ladies' Association* had placed there, assisted by a Superintendant of the buildings and farm. And it is a pleasure to record, in honor of the American character, that while the war raged, at times, with intense and destructive energy in the vicinity of Mount Vernon, and the soldiery of both parties engaged in the contest were there, the most profound and reverential respect for the Home of Washington was observed by all.

The sentiment of love for the Great Patriot was too deeply rooted in the American heart to be eradicated by the intense hatred which such a war engenders. It was shown at Mount Vernon in the most delicate manner. No notable injury was inflicted upon building, tree or shrub during all the time of the internecine strife.

After the close of the war the Regent of *The Mount Vernon Ladies' Association*, resided at the Mansion and, with the assistance of a Secretary, had a general supervision of affairs there. The work of interior renovation has gone on slowly, until now, (1882,) a greater portion of the wood-work has been painted, and the roof of the Mansion has been newly shingled. The whole building is now in a state of fair preservation. An appropriation by Congress, has been spent in the work of renovation, mostly in the rebuilding of the Conservatory for plants, on a larger scale, which was destroyed by fire in 1863, and with it, the ancient Lemon Tree, Century Plant and Sago Palm—all there in Washington's time—delineated on pages 158 and 159 of this work. From the sale of plants and flowers reared in the Conservatory, a considerable income each year has been derived (among them descendants of the Sago Palm). Much of the old Vegetable garden, yet surrounded by the brick wall built by Washington, is devoted to the raising of strawberries, the sale of which, to early summer visitors is a source of considerable profit. These fountains of revenue, the sale of hickory canes cut from the forest of the estate, the price of admission to the grounds and Mansion, and per centage of the receipts of the steamboat from passengers to and from Mount Vernon, constitute the entire income of the Association. These are insufficient to put and keep the grounds and buildings in good order and to make the restoration complete. There should be an endowment, either by Congress or by the free gift of the American people large enough for the interest on the sum to be ample for making Mount Vernon, aside from its associations, one of the most attractive spots in our country. Now it is quite otherwise. Nature has done much, but art and labor has done so little, that from the Wharf to the Tomb and up to the Mansion, the visitor sees, at every step, evidences of poverty. The Tomb and its neighborhood have a most forbidding appearance; while the Mansion itself, bereft of nearly every thing mentioned in this work, is less attractive than it might be, if its surroundings could be beautified by Art and skilled Labor, and its rooms present an exhibition of objects of every kind, yet in existence, that were associated with Washington's life. Already, some contributions of that kind have been made by patriotic citizens. These may and should be increased until the Mansion of Mount Vernon shall become a rich Museum of relics of that classic period in our history, the old War for independence and the establishment of our National Government.

Considered in its relations, historic and patriotic, Mount Vernon should be one of the most precious objects of the care of the American people. The means to make it creditable to our patriotism, gratitude and generosity, should be given with a quick and lavish hand; and it is to be hoped that the *Association* may yet be able to proclaim, as a part of its own experience, that the great Republic of the West is not ungrateful toward its Founders.

INDEX.

A.

	PAGE
Adams, John, description of the inauguration of	294
Adams, Mr. and Mrs., visit Mrs. Washington after the death of her husband	349
Adams, President, nominates Washington to the Senate, as commander-in-chief	322
Adams, Robert, watch that belonged to Washington willed to	220
Adams, Vice-President, at Washington's table	323
Address card of Washington	362
Alexandria, Washington invited to partake of a public dinner at	209
Alison, remarks of, respecting Washington's Farewell Address	281
Amelung, J. P., glass manufacturer, visits Mount Vernon in 1789	204
" presents some specimens of his art to Washington	204
Ancient entrance to Mount Vernon, picture of	210
" present condition of	210
Appearance, personal, of Washington, when on horseback	77
Arch, triumphal, at Trenton, in honor of Washington	113
Arlington Spring, kitchen and dancing hall erected at, by Mr. Custis	267
" Washington's tent at	140
Arms of the Washington family, picture of	27
Armstrong, John, letter of, to General Gates respecting Washington's reception in New York, in 1789	214
Army, American, disbanded	131
" officers of part with Washington	131
Army, British, evacuates New York	134
Army, Continental, adopted by Congress	113
" Washington made commander-in-chief of	114
" popular one formed	106
" its character	106
Asses presented to Washington by the King of Spain	189
" Mr. Custis's account of	190
Atkins, Rev. A. B., wife of, has Washington's telescope	49
" Washington's butter-bowl in possession of	255
Aurora, letter hostile to Washington published in, soon after his retirement from office	293
Autographs of Jane and Mary Washington	32

INDEX.

B.

	PAGE
Bachelor, London orders of Washington when a	68
Baldwin, John Y., owner of Washington's pistols	246
Ball at Annapolis, attended by Washington	132
" Fredericksburg, attended by Washington	129
Ball, Colonel William, ancestor of Washington's mother	33
" arms of his family	33
Ball, Joseph, letter of, to Washington's mother	45
Baptism of Washington	33
Barge, Washington's, returned to the giver	230
Bartram, John, garden of, near Philadelphia	157
Bartram, William, explorations of	157
Bassett, Colonel, J. P. Custis dies at the house of	127
Bastile, key of, presented to Washington	231
" sketch of	231
" destruction of	234
" site of	234
" picture of destruction of	235
" picture of key of	237
Battle-sword of Washington preserved	134
" where manufactured	134
" with Franklin's staff	134
Bed and bedstead on which Washington died kept as sacred mementos at Arlington House	337
" description of	337
" picture of	337
Belvoir, the seat of the Fairfaxes	43
" mansion of the Fairfaxes consumed by fire	106
" owner of never returned from England	106
Bianca, Florica, the Spanish premier, letter of, to Washington	190
Bible on which Washington took the oath of office in 1789	216
" inscription on	216
" picture of	216
" in possession of St. John's Lodge, in New York	217
Bier upon which the body of Washington was conveyed to the tomb	343
Billy, one of Washington's favorite servants, known to Westford	352
" death of, hastened by intemperate habits	353
Birth of Washington	33
Birth-place of Washington	34
" present desolation of	35
" picture of the inscribed stone that marks it	36
Bishop, Washington's body-servant	77, 120
Bishop White, at the farewell dinner given by Washington in Philadelphia, in 1797	294
Blues, McPherson's, picture of uniform of	348
" six survivors of, in 1859	347
Bonaparte, respect paid to the memory of Washington by	350
Book-plate, Washington's, picture of	27
Boot-jack, Washington's travelling, picture of	109
Boundary disputes between the French and English	52
Box made of the wood of the oak tree that sheltered Wallace after the battle at Falkirk, sent to Washington by the Earl of Buchan	272
Box sent to Washington by the Earl of Buchan recommitted to his care by the will of the General	275

INDEX.   433

	PAGE
Braddock, General	55
" calls a council at Alexandria	56
" invites Colonel Washington to his quarters	56
" invites Washington to become his aide	57
Bradford, Mr., impromptu effusion of, on learning the misfortunes of Lafayette	301
Brevoort, J. Carson, owner of Pine's portrait of Washington	182
Bridport, Lord, respect paid to the memory of Washington by	349
Brienne, Marchioness de, sister of Count de Moustier, at Mount Vernon	198
" painted a miniature of Washington	198
" her picture of Washington and Lafayette	199
Brown, Dr., called to attend Washington in his last illness	333
Burgesses, Virginia, Washington a member of, the House of	85
Bushrod Washington, nephew of the General, comes into possession of Mount Vernon, on the death of Mrs. Washington	350
" appointed by President Adams to be Judge of the Supreme Court of the United States	357
" portrait of	351
Butter-bowl, china, that belonged to Washington	356
Button, military, belonging to Washington's coat	95
Buttons stolen from military coat of Washington	95

C.

Calvert, Benedict, miniature of daughter of, painted by Peale	98
" daughter of, wife of John Parke Custis	98
Camp-chest, leathern, used by Washington in 1753, picture of	53
Candelabra, mural, used in Washington's dining-room at Philadelphia, described	315
" picture of	315
Candlesticks, Washington's, massive silver	317
" picture of	317
Capitol, singular historical fact respecting the site of the	260
" corner-stone of the north Wing of, laid in September, 1793	261
" plan for the, submitted by Dr. Thornton, approved by Washington	261
Carey's House, at Alexandria, place where Braddock had his quarters	56
" picture of	56
Carpenter's Hall, place of meeting of the first Congress	104
Carrington, Mrs., her description of Mrs. Washington at home	218
Carroll, Charles, of Carrollton	140
" son of, a suitor of the hand of Nelly Custis	325
" letter of G. W. P. Custis to Washington, respecting son of, as a suitor for the hand of Nelly Custis	325
Carthagena, British soldiers perish at	41
Casseday, Alexander, drawing by, of Washington's secretary	228
Cave Castle, the seat of Washington's ancestors in England	29
" picture of	29
Century plant at Mount Vernon	158
Chairs at Mount Vernon, pictures of	69
" described by Washington	69
Chamberlayne, Mr., the host of Washington where he first saw Mrs. Custis	62
" Colonel Washington lingers at the house of	62
Chastellux, Marquis de, at Mount Vernon in 1781	120
" Sketch of	122
" portrait of	123
" Washington's letter to	23
Chatham, Earl of, his opinion of the Continental Congress	105

INDEX

	PAGE
Children, great fondness of Washington for	280
Chimney-piece presented to Washington by Samuel Vaughan, of London	185
" picture of	186
China, Sèvres, belonging to Washington	253
China, Cincinnati, presented to Washington	253
" picture of	254
" Mrs. Washington's	254
" picture of Mrs. Washington's	255
Christ Church, Alexandria, Washington a vestryman of	90
" Washington's pew in	90
" picture of	91
Christmas at Mount Vernon in 1783	146
Cincinnati china, picture of	254
Cincinnati, Society of the, account of the formation of	141
" object of	142
" constitution	142
" order of	143
" splendid order of, presented to Washington by French soldiers	144
" member's certificate of	145
" Washington president-general of the Society of the	146
" Knox secretary of the Society of the	146
City Tavern, Philadelphia, Washington entertained at a sumptuous banquet at	212
Clarke, maker of Washington's coach	249
Clinton, George, Washington's letter to, on Peace	131
" at Washington's inauguration in 1789	216
" at the President's table	223
Clothes, military, Washington lays aside his	133
Coach, Washington's English	245
" picture and description of	246
" emblazoning upon	247
" picture on panel of	248
" Washington's letters about	249
" fate of	249
" used by him on his journey from Philadelphia to Mount Vernon in 1791	267
Coasters, wine, invented by Washington	263
" their popularity	264
" picture of	265
Cochran, Dr. John, Washington's letter to	136
Coffee-pot, Washington's silver	265
Coffins, marble, remains of Washington and his wife re-entombed in, in 1837	354
Coffin of Washington	340
" inscription on plates on	340
Coffin, marble, of Washington, picture of	356
" sculptured lid of Washington's, picture of	356
Column of July in the *Place de Bastile*	234
Commission as commander-in-chief resigned by Washington in 1783	132
Commissioners of Maryland and Virginia, consult Washington in 1785	193
Confederation Articles of, inefficiency of	192
" movement toward the amendment of	192
Congress, general, proposed by Dr. Franklin, meets at Philadelphia	100
" assembling of delegates to	102
" opening of the session of	103
" officers of	104
" resolution adopted by	104

INDEX. 435

	PAGE
Congress, adjourned to meet in May, 1775, if necessary	106
Congress, Continental, action of	113
" adopt an army	113
" choose Washington commander-in-chief	113
Congress, Federal, vote a bronze equestrian statue to Washington in 1783	171
Congress, meeting of, at Philadelphia	256
" action of concerning seat of Government	259
" verses, respecting the removal of	260
" effects of removal of	261
" joint resolutions adopted by, on the occasion of the death of Washington	345
Conogocheague	257, 258
Conservatory at Mount Vernon destroyed by fire	160
" ruins of	160
Continental Congress Washington a member of the	101
Convention, federal, adopt a constitution for the United States	194
" Washington a member of	194
Correspondence of Washington, extensive, in 1792	271
Cornwallis, Earl, joy caused by surrender of	127
Costume and manners of Washington while president	225
Craik, Dr. James, attends John Parke Custis	127
" at Mount Vernon	107
" mentioned in Washington's will	228
" called to attend Washington in his last illness	333
" portrait of	342
" short biographical sketch of	339
Craik, Rev. James, owns the secretary that belonged to Washington	228
Crayon profile of Washington	210
" of Mrs. Washington	211
Crest of Washington engraved upon his family plate	265
Cunningham, Miss Anna Pamela, regent of Mount Vernon	372
Cushing, wife of Judge, extract from a letter of, describing her visit at Mount Vernon in February, 1799	323
Custis, Daniel Parke, Mrs. Washington's first husband	63
" portrait of	64
Custis, Eleanor Parke, marriage of, with Lawrence Lewis	128
" portrait of	128
Custis, Elizabeth Parke, description of the portrait of	181
" portrait of	182
Custis, G. W. P., places an inscribed stone on Washington's birth-place	36
" his *Recollections of Washington*	61
" description by, of Washington on his farm	82
" portrait of, when a child	183
" portrait of, at the age of seventeen years	308
" and G. W. Lafayette, personal friendship between, in youth	309
" letter of, to Washington, respecting the son of Charles Carroll, of Carrollton, as a suitor for the hand of Nelly Custis	325
" massive gold ring presented to Lafayette by, at the tomb of Washington	354
Custis, John Parke, articles ordered from London for	73
" arms of family of	74
" portrait of, painted by Peale	98
" portrait of wife of, painted by Peale	98
" at Mount Vernon	118
" Washington's letter to, during his stay at Mount Vernon	118
" children of, at Mount Vernon	125

INDEX

	PAGE
Custis, John Parke, aide-de-camp of Washington	126
" death of	127
" two children of, adopted by Washington	127
Custis, Mrs. Martha, affianced to Colonel Washington	63
" her fortune	63
" her iron chest	64
" articles for, ordered from London by Washington	70
Custis, Martha, daughter of Mrs. Washington, her sickness and death	99
" grief of Washington at the death of	99
Custis, Master and Miss, London orders of Washington for	74
" accompany Mrs. Washington to New York	222
Custis, Nelly, a son of Charles Carroll, of Carrollton, a suitor of the hand of	325
" Lawrence Lewis a suitor for the hand of	325
" interesting anecdote of, told by Mr. Irving	326
" and Lawrence Lewis married on Washington's birthday, 1799	327

D.

Daggett, Dr., president of Yale College	195
Dandrige, Mr., private secretary of Washington in 1793	288
Davis, Rev. Thomas, books presented to him by Washington on the occasion of his officiating at the marriage of Nelly Custis	328
Death-bed of Washington, resignation of Mrs. Washington exhibited at	336
" why no clergyman was present at	336
Death-Chamber of Washington, thoughts suggested to the author by a visit to	339
Death of George A. Washington, nephew of the General	278
" of Washington, system of management, written by the General, completed only four days before	329
" health and vigor of Washington only a few days before	329
" detailed account of the illness preceding	330, 335
" announced to Congress by Hon. John Marshall of Virginia	345
Delaunay, Governor of the Bastile	333
D'Estaing presents a bust of M. Necker to Washington	241
" fate of	242
" letters of	243
"Destiny of Washington," an allegorical painting	199
" picture of	200
" description of	200
" history of	201
Diary, Washington's, kept in the blank leaves of the *Virginia Almanac*	80
" headings of pages in	80
" fac-simile of entry in	81
" extract from, concerning furniture	227, 228
" note made in it on the 11th of December, 1799	330
Dick, Dr., consulted by Dr. Craik on the occasion of Washington's last illness	333
Dinner, at the table of Washington, the artist Robertson's description of	273
Dinner, farewell, of Washington, at Philadelphia in 1797	294
Dinner, Washington sits down to, without changing his damp clothes, December 12, 1799	330
Dinwiddie, Governor, sends Washington to Ohio	53
Dress of Washington at his second inauguration minutely described	285
Dress-sword of Washington, picture of	245
Dry-well at Mount Vernon	161
Duer, President, on the anxiety of citizens to see Washington on his retirement from office	295

INDEX. 437

PAGE

Dunlap, William, paints Washington's portrait 172
Dunmore, unsuccessful attempt of, to desolate Mount Vernon 119
Dunn, Washington's coachman 248
Dutch tile in Washington's birth-place, picture of 34

E.

Earl of Buchan, letter of, accompanying the oaken box sent by him to Washington 272
Elizabethtown Point, Washington met at, by a committee of Congress 216
Elkanah Watson, anecdote of his, respecting his visit at Mount Vernon 318
Ellenborough, Lord, nephew of, marries the granddaughter of Mrs. Washington .. 124
Emblazoning on Washington's coach 247
English traders driven away from the Ohio by the French 53
Etiquette, doubts of Washington in relation to 219
Eulogy of Washington, written on the back of the *Pitcher Portrait* 364
Eulogy of Washington, written on the back of the Sharpless profile 366, 368
Evans, Mrs. Eliza, daughter of General Anthony Walton White 80
Evening—a landscape, by Winstanley 319
Everett, Edward, large sums paid by, into the treasury of the *Ladies' Mount Vernon Association* 371

F.

Fairfax Anné, wife of Lawrence Washington 42
Fairfax, Bryan, at Mount Vernon with Major Gates 112
Fairfax, General, leader of the Parliamentary Forces 28
Fairfax, Lord 43
    " large domain of, in Virginia 44
    " death of, at Greenway Court, in 1782 44
Fairfax, Sir William 43
    " a soldier in the Indies 45
    " narratives of, influence young Washington 45
Fairfax, Washington a vestryman of the parish of 86
Family dinner at Washington's house in New York 223
Family plate of Washington made over again in New York, and additions made to, in 1789 265
    " several pieces of, now in use at Arlington House 265
Farewell Address of Washington, prepared by Washington at Mount Vernon 290
    " profound sensation caused by its publication 291
    " said by Allison to be unequaled as an uninspired composition 291
Farewell dinner of Washington at Philadelphia, in 1797 294
Federal city, Major L'Enfant employed to make a plan and survey of 270
    " named by the Commissioners without Washington's knowledge 270
    " point of land selected by Washington for the 270
    " singular historical fact respecting the site of the 270
    " Washington meets commissioners to lay out 270
Federal Convention, Washington president of 191
Fencing, Washington takes lessons in, from Van Braam 50
Field, an English painter, takes a button from Washington's coat 95
    " anecdote of 96
    " becomes a bishop in Canada 97
First President of the United States, Washington elected 203
Flag, British, captured at Yorktown, presented to Washington, picture of 118
Flag, Hessian, presented to Washington 116
    " picture and description of 117

INDEX.

	PAGE
Flower-garden at Mount Vernon, plants in	157
Fort du Quesne taken possession of by Colonel Washington	60
France, hostile attitude of, in 1795	320
" preparations made for war with, in 1798	321
" pacific relations with, on the overthrow of the Directory by Napoleon Bonaparte	324
" unanimity of military leaders in looking to Washington in the impending war with	321
Franklin, Dr., to superintend making a statue of Washington	172
Franklin's staff willed to Washington	134
Frances' Tavern, at New York, Washington parted with his officers at	131
Frederick the Great, his praise of Washington	116
Fredericksburg, Washington visits his mother at, in 1781	129
Freemasons at the funeral of Washington	341, 343
French Directory, insolent attitude of, toward the United States	321
French Dominion ceases south of Lake Erie, on Washington's taking Fort du Quesne	61
French Minister, furniture of, purchased by Washington	228
French officers' admiration of Washington's mother	129
Frestel, M., tutor of young Lafayette, favorable mention of, by Washington	307
Funeral of Washington, detailed account of	340, 343
" minute guns fired from schooner of Mr. Robert Hamilton, during	341
Funeral procession of Washington, gentlemen who made the arrangements for	341
" composition and order of	342

G.

	PAGE
Galveston, Spanish ship-of-war, salutes Washington	214
Garden-house at Mount Vernon, picture of	157
Gardens at Mount Vernon	156
Gardoqui, Don Diego, at Washington's table	222
Gates, Major Horatio, at Mount Vernon	107
" sketch of portrait of	110
" with Bryan Fairfax, at Mount Vernon	112
Germantown, Washington proposes to call Congress together at, in consequence of the presence of yellow fever in Philadelphia	297
" family of Washington, at, in the summer of 1794	288
Giles, Tommy, notice of	260, 261
Gist, agent of English Ohio Company, questioned by an Indian	52
Glass-ware, first manufactured in the United States	204
" Washington's letter to Jefferson respecting	255
Gloucester, Duke of, speaks of the Americans in presence of Lafayette	163
Goblets, silver, belonging to Washington	137
" picture of one	138
Gold medal decreed to Washington by Congress for the recovery of Boston	115
" picture of	116
Gorget, silver, worn by Washington while in the colonial service, history of, by Mr. Quincy	359
Graham, Mrs. Macaulay, modest allusion of Washington to the visit of, in 1785	328
Gray's Ferry, Washington's reception at	212
Greene, General, Washington dines widow of, in 1791	260
Greene, Rev. Ashbel, particular description by, of Washington's habits at table	267
Greenway Court	41
Greenwood, Isaac L., owner of Washington's pistols	240
Gunston Hall, the seat of George Mason	85

INDEX. 439

PAGE

H.

Hale, Sir Matthew, his "Contemplations Moral and Divine," read by Washington's mother.. 34
Hallam, Lewis, at the head of a company of players.. 78
Hamilton, Alexander, letter of, to Washington, on peace... 130
" proposes a convention of states to mend the *Articles of Confederation*..... 192
" urges Washington to accept office a second term................................. 283
" appointed first major-general of the Provisional Army........................... 323
Hamilton, Mr. Robert, fires minute guns from his schooner during the funeral of Washington... 341
Harpsichord presented to Nelly Custis by Washington.. 281
" now at Mount Vernon.. 282
Harrison, Benjamin, goes with Washington to the Congress in 1775.......................... 113
" governor of Virginia, letter of, respecting the statue of Washington......... 175
Hay, Colonel Samuel, pistols presented to, by Washington.. 240
Henry Lee, General, portrait of... 246
Henry, Patrick, speech of, in Virginia Assembly.. 85
" at Mount Vernon, on his way to the first Congress............................. 102
" portrait of.. 103
" business of Congress opened by.. 104
Head-quarters, Washington's first... 54
" picture of.. 55
Home of Washington, as it was in 1759... 67
Home and tomb of Washington to be ever cherished as memorial treasures............ 373
Hopkinson, Francis, portrait of, painted by Pine... 184
" letter of Washington to, in relation to his sitting to Pine for his portrait... 180
Hospitalities, Washington's, reasons for declining on his Southern tour in 1791..... 268
Houdon, the sculptor, engaged to make a statue of Washington.............................. 175
" his bust of Washington.. 176
" letter of Washington to.. 176
Houdon's bust of Washington, picture of 163—the Original mask............................ 374
Hounds, French, presented to Washington by Lafayette.. 182
" anecdote of one of them.. 181
Humphreys, Colonel, accompanies Washington to Mount Vernon in 1781................. 120
" resident guest at Mount Vernon.. 195
" portrait of.. 195
" brings the picture of King Lewis to Washington............................... 196
" writes his Life of Putnam at Mount Vernon...................................... 196
Hunting establishment at Mount Vernon broken up.. 184

I.

Ice house at Mount Vernon, picture of... 161
Inauguration of John Adams.. 290
Inauguration of Washington, as first president of the United States........................ 215
" less parade at the second than at the first....................................... 284
" pleasant picture of the second.. 284
Inkstand of Washington, description of... 313
" picture of.. 314

J.

Jackson, Major, accompanies Washington to Mount Vernon and on his Southern tour, in 1791... 267
Jane and Mary Washington, autographs of.. 32

	PAGE
Jay, John, letter of Washington to, in 1786	193
" anxiety of Washington respecting the treaty made by	289
Jay, Rev. William, impromptu lines of, on seeing a picture of Mount Vernon	373
Jefferson, Thomas, letter of, respecting Houdon	175
" letter of, respecting bust of Lafayette	243

K.

Key of the Bastile, letter of Washington to Lafayette respecting the	237
Kitchen and dancing-hall erected by Mr. Custis at Arlington Spring	267
Knox, General, Washington's letter to, respecting his going into office	205
" at Washington's inauguration	216
" letter of Washington to, two days before his retirement to private life	292, 297
" appointed third major-general of the Provisional Army	323

L.

Ladies' Mount Vernon Association the present owners of Mount Vernon	371
Lafayette, Marquis de, visit of, at Mount Vernon in 1784	163
" arrival at New York, in 1784	164
" Washington's intuitive perception of his character on his arrival	164
" letter of, Washington at New York	165
" portrait of	166
" commander of National Guard in France	233
" sends key of Bastile to Thomas Payne, to be sent by him to Washington	234
" letter of, to Washington, presenting key of the Bastile	236
" bust of, at Mount Vernon	243
" picture of bust of	244
" ceremony at the presentation of the bust of, to the city of Paris	245
" anxiety of Washington respecting the misfortunes of	299
" a prisoner in a dungeon at Olmutz for three years	303
" wife and daughters of, share his prison at Olmutz	303
" letter of Washington to, respecting his son	206
" massive gold ring presented to, by Mr. Custis, at the tomb of Washington	355
Lafayette, George Washington, accompanies Washington to Mount Vernon, on his retirement from office in 1797	299
" portrait of	300
" arrives at Boston from France in 1795	303
" parental feelings of Washington toward	303
" reasons of state govern Washington's manner receiving, on his arrival from France	303
" letter of Edward Livingston to	305
" resolution of Congress respecting	305
" return of, to France, in 1797	306
" letter to G. W. P. Custis, in 1825	309
Lafayette, Madame, letter of Washington to	148
" her admiration of Washington	166
" sends Masonic apron to Washington	167
" picture of Masonic apron sent by, to Washington	167
"Lament of Washington," poem from the pen of Attorney-General Bradford, respecting the misfortunes of Lafayette	301
Langdon, John, president of the United States Senate *pro tempore*	206
" informs Washington by letter of his elevation to the presidency	206
Lantern, ancient iron, eighty years at Mount Vernon, then at Arlington House	316
" picture of	315

INDEX. 441

	PAGE
La Salle, commander-in-chief of the militia of Paris	232
Last illness of Washington, detailed account of	330, 335
Last words of Washington	335
Lawrence Washington goes to Barbadoes for his health	51
Lawrence Washington accompanied to Barbadoes by his brother George	51
" his return home from Barbadoes, and death	51
Lear, Tobias, becomes a resident at Mount Vernon	191
" his stay there remembered in Washington's will	191
" letters of Washington to, relating to his coach	249
" letters of Washington to, relating to his house and furniture in Philadelphia	250, 253
" residing in the family of Washington at the time of his last illness	330
Lee, General Charles, at Mount Vernon	107
" portrait of	108
Lee, Richard Henry, letter of, to Washington, when a child	37
" the first to congratulate Washington after his taking the oath of office	216
" his opinion of *The Rights of Man*, by Thomas Paine	276
" letter of Washington to, respecting a newly-invented threshing machine	286
" invited to pronounce an oration on the occasion of Washington's funeral	346
" anecdotes of, showing his familiarity with Washington	347
Lee, Mrs. Robert E., the great-granddaughter of Mrs. Washington	99
Lemon-tree at Mount Vernon	158
L'Enfant, Major, employed to furnish a plan and survey of the national city	270
" his plan of the national city approved by Congress	271
Lepine, watches made by, purchased by Washington	220
Levees, Washington's	225
Lewis, George, inherits a sword from Washington	226
Lewis, Lawrence, a suitor for the hand of Nelly Custis	325
" invited to take up his residence at Mount Vernon in 1798	324
" and Nelly Custis married on Washington's birthday, 1799	337
Lewis, Major, re-entombs remains of Washington and his wife in marble sarcophagi, in 1837	354
Lewis, Robert, instructed by Washington in the management of his estate	371
Lexington, effects of the news of the battle of, at Mount Vernon	112
Liquor-chest that belonged to Washington, remaining at Mount Vernon in 1857	360
" picture of	361
Livermore, Mr. George, his account of a silver gorget, a relic of Washington's earlier life	358
Livingston, Chancellor, administers the oath of office to Washington in 1789	215
Livingston, Edward, letter of, to George Washington Lafayette	305
Livingston, Governor, entertains Mrs. Washington	323
Livingston, Robert R., secretary for foreign affairs	130
" letter of, to Washington, communicating the news of the conclusion of peace, in 1783	130
London Chronicle, sketch of Washington in	225
Louis XVI sends an engraving of himself to Washington	196
Lunt, his lines on the burial-place of Washington	348

M.

McCoombs, house of, occupied by Washington	228
Macubbin, Mrs., opens a ball at Annapolis with Washington	132
McHenry, Mr., letter of Washington to, from Mount Vernon, after his retirement	312
" letter of Washington to, respecting the anticipated troubles with France	322
" anxiety of Washington expressed to, that his affairs might be found in order after his death	329

INDEX.

	PAGE
McKean, Sally, becomes the wife of the Marquis d'Yrugo	390
McPherson's Blues, six survivors of, in 1859	347
" picture of uniform of	348
Madison, James, writes an inscription for the statue of Washington	174
" at Mount Vernon with Houdon, the French sculptor	177
Mansion near the Potomac, the home of the Washington family	32
Mansion, the presidential, at Philadelphia, picture of	267
Manuscript memorandum of Washington	163
Marble coffin of Washington, picture of	356
Marquée and Tent of Washington	138, 139
" picture of portmanteaux containing	140
Marriages of foreign envoys with American women, numerous	190
Marshall, Hon. John, announces the death of Washington to Congress	345
Mason, George, Washington's neighbor and friend	85
Masonic apron presented to Washington by Madame Lafayette	167
" picture of	167
Massey, Rev. Lee, minister of Pohick Church	89
Maurepas, Count, remark of, in relation to Lafayette	164
Meade, Bishop, notice of Mason L. Weems, by	89
" letter of, in relation to Washington's English coach	249
Mercer, Dr. Hugh, at Mount Vernon	107
Mifflin, Governor, meets Washington on the frontiers of Pennsylvania	211
Military clothes of Washington, picture of	133
Miniature of Washington, by Mrs. Sharpless	310
Miniature portrait of Mrs Washington, painted by Robertson in 1792	274
Mirror of Washington still at Mt. Vernon	362
" picture of	361
Monuments of several members of the Washington family on the east side of the tomb of the General	358
"Morning" and "Evening"—landscapes painted for Washington, by Winstanley, now at Arlington House	320
Morris, George P, his ode on Washington's sword and Franklin's staff	135
Morris, Governor, stands to Houdon for the figure of Washington	179
" sends wine-coolers to Washington	262
Morris, Mrs. accompanies Mrs. Washington to New York	223
Morris, Robert, builds a studio for Pine the portrait painter	180
" house of, in Philadelphia, rented for Washington's residence	250
Morris, Roger, marries Mary Phillipse	59
" picture of his residence	60
" proscribed as an "enemy to his country"	60
Mortar, bronze, that belonged to Cimon Washington in 1664, picture of	30
Mossom, Rev. David, unites Washington and Mrs. Custis in Marriage	65
Mother of Washington, visited by him for the last time	208
Motier, a family name of Lafayette, assumed by his son in 1795	304
Motto of the Washington family	30
Mount Vernon, the mansion at, built by Lawrence Washington	42
" style of living at, before the Revolution	75
" picture of present landing at	83
" changes in and around	106
" little children at	124
" sorrow at, in 1781	126
" mansion at, and its surroundings described	150
" mansion and other buildings at, found by the General much in want of repair, after his eight years' absence	313

INDEX. 443

	PAGE

Mount Vernon, hospitalities at, continued after the death of the General............ 350
" passes into the possession of Bushrod Washington, nephew of the General, on the death of Mrs. Washington.. 358
" becomes the property of John Augustine Washington in 1829,............... 354
" Mrs. Jane Washington mistress of, in 1832.. 354
" few articles of the personal property of Washington remaining at.......... 358
" articles that belonged to Washington, remaining at, in 1857..................... 360
" engravings that belonged to Washington still remaining at................... 363
" successive owners of, for one hundred and sixteen years........................ 369
" inconsiderate conduct of visitors at.. 369
" for many years falling into decay.. 369
" proposition to make it a national possession... 370
" high price offered by speculators for, rejected.. 370
" the property of the *Mount Vernon Ladies' Association*............................... 371
" the work of renovation and restoration commenced at............................. 371
" moral associations connected with the name of.. 372
Moustier, Count de, French Minister, at Mount Vernon,..................................... 198
Mural candelabra, used in Washington's dining-room at Philadelphia, picture of, 315
Necker, M., dismissed from his post as minister of finance, in France............... 243
" bust of, presented to Washington.. 241
" inscription on bust of, presented to Washington.. 242
" picture of bust of, presented to Washington.. 243
Newport, Rhode Island, Washington makes a voyage to, for the benefit of his health... 228
North, Lord, emotions of, on hearing of the defeat of Cornwallis....................... 130

O.

Oath of office administered to Washington in 1793, by Judge Cushing............. 283
Occoquan Falls, mills at, destroyed by Lord Dunmore.. 119
Ode to Washington, sung at Trenton.. 213
Ogden, Charles S., original study of Peale's first portrait of Washington, in possession of.. 97
Olmutz, dungeon at, the prison of Lafayette for three years............................... 303
Oration pronounced by General Henry Lee, on the occasion of the funeral of Washington 346
Otis, Mr., holds the Bible at Washington's inauguration...................................... 215

P.

Packsaddle used by Washington on his expedition to the Ohio country in 1753, picture of... 53
Paine, Thomas, letter of, to Washington, respecting the key of the Bastile........ 236
" letter of, to Washington, respecting the success of "*Rights of Man*"........ 276
" Washington shamefully abused by, in a published letter........................... 277
Patrick Henry's opinion of Washington.. 105
Patrick Henry, Washington heard the burning words of, in the Virginia Assembly 111
Peace, desire for, in England.. 130
" Washington's letter to Clinton on the subject of... 130
Peale, Angelica, crowns Washington at Grey's Ferry in 1789.............................. 212
Peale, Charles Willson, beginning of artist life of... 94
" paints Washington in Mount Vernon in 1772... 94
" portrait of... 95
" fac-simile of his receipt for ten ginueas for painting miniature of Mrs. Washington.. 97
" ordered by Gov. Harrison to paint a portrait of Washington to make a statue from.. 175

444 INDEX.

PAGE

Peale, Charles Willson, emblematic paintings by, on the occasion of Washington's retirement from office 206
Peale, Rembrandt, his history of the *Pitcher Portrait* and the eulogy on the back of it 263
Pendleton, Edmund, at Mount Vernon on his way to the first Congress........... 102
Peters, Judge, meets Washington on the frontiers of Pennsylvania.................. 211
Philadelphia the federal city for ten years.. 238
Phillipse, Mary, Washington in love with... 59
" marries Roger Morris... 59
" portrait of... 59
Pinckney, Gov. Charles Cotesworth, receives Washington at the wharf in Charleston, in 1791 269
" reply of, to the insulting proposition of the French Directory........ 321
" appointed second major-general of the Provisional Army 333
Pine, Robert Edge, an English painter, at Mount Vernon............................. 179
" his portrait of Washington in Montreal.................................... 182
Pistols, Washington's, description and picture of....................................... 240
Pitcher Portrait, and eulogy of Washington on the back of it 363, 368
Plan of the grounds at Mount Vernon... 155, 156
Plaster cask taken of the face of Washington... 172
Plate, Washington's, picture of pieces of, at Arlington House...................... 256
Pohick Church, Washington attends.. 87
" rebuilding of.. 87
" Washington's drawing of.. 87
" author's visit to... 91
" picture of.. 92
" present condition of 93
" picture of pulpit.. 93
Precedents established for the President of the United States...................... 219
Presence of Washington, remarkable scene of awe caused by....................... 285
Presidential mansion at Philadelphia, picture of.. 267
Profile portrait of Washington.. 310
Profile portrait of Mrs. Washington... 311
Protestant Episcopal Church, burial service of Washington according to the ritual of 314
Provisional Army, Washington appointed commander-in-chief of, in view of the impending war with France.. 322
" major-generals and other officers appointed by Washington.......... 323
Punch-bowl, tea-table and sideboard, picture of....................................... 317
Putnam, Life of, written at Mount Vernon by Humphreys............................ 196

R.

Randolph, Peyton, chosen president of first Congress................................ 104
Ranney, letter of Washington to, in relation to his sending flag-stones, &c., from England.. 153
Rawlins, Mr., one of Washington's overseers, sent for to bleed Washington in his last illness.. 332
Reading of Washington at his second inauguration.................................... 286
Reception of Mrs. Washington... 224
Reception of Washington at New York and Philadelphia..................... 225, 226
Recollections and Private Memoirs of Washington, interesting correspondence of Washington to be found in... 326
Remains of Washington, account of the re-entombment of, in 1837........ 354, 357
Resolution, important, passed by the first Congress.................................. 104

INDEX. 445

	PAGE
Retirement from office of Washington, extract from a newspaper of the day, describing a public entertainment on the occasion of	296
Revolution, flames of, kindling, in 1773	100
Revolution, involuntary tribute by ladies to the memory of	267
Revolution, French, breaking out of	282
Ripon, Earl of, present owner of the English seat of the Washington family	30
Rochambeau, Count de, at Mount Vernon in 1781	120
" portrait of	121
Room in which Washington died, picture of	338
Roosevelt, Mr., funeral of the wife of	219
Rush, Dr., remarks of, in relation to the seat of government	257
Rush, the late venerable Richard, incident related by, illustrating the feelings of Washington toward Lafayette in misfortune	301

S.

Sago palm at Mount Vernon	159
St. John's Lodge, in New York, in possession of the Bible used at Washington's inauguration	217
Sarcophagi of Washington and his wife, description of	356
Seal, impression of Washington's, attached to a death-warrant	31
Seal, impression of Washington's last watch, picture of	221
Seal-ring, picture of Washington's	31
Seals, Washington's watch, lost on Braddock's field and in Virginia, and afterward found	31
" pictures of	31
Secretary, Washington's, willed to Dr. Craik	228
" picture of	229
Sharpless, James, his profile portraits of Washington and Mrs. Washington, said to be the best likeness extant	300
Sharpless, Mrs , beautiful miniature of Washington by	310
Shield, silver, on Washington's coffin, picture of	341
Sideboard, black walnut, that belonged to Lawrence Washington, now at Arlington House	316
Silver candlestick, Washington's picture of	317
Silver inkstand of Washington, description of	319
Sotomayer, Duke of, a native of Philadelphia	290
Southern States, tour of Washington through, in 1791	278
Spaniards, depredations of, on British commerce in the West Indies	49
Spy-glass, Washington's anecdote in connection with	238
" picture of	238
Statuary, orders of Washington for, from London	72
Statue, bronze, of Washington, ordered by Congress	171
" to be made by the best sculptor in Europe	172
Statue of Washington, ordered by the legislature of Virginia	173
Steuben, Baron, at Washington's inauguration	216
Stockton, Annis, assistance of, in honoring Washington at Trenton	313
Strickland, Mr., his description of the personal appearance of Major Lewis in 1837	255
Struthers, Mr. John, marble sarcophagi presented by, for the re-entombing of the remains of Washington and his wife, in 1837	354
Stuart, David, Washington wills his telescope and shaving apparatus to	49, 79
" marries the widow of John Parke Custis	49
Stuart, Gilbert, painter of Eleanor Parke Custis	129
Style, old and new, how it originated	34
Summer-house at Mount Vernon, picture of	162

INDEX.

PAGE

Sword and Staff, Washington's and Franklin's, picture of, and ode by George P. Morris, ... 135
Sword, Washington's, picture of 232
" will concerning 226

T.

Table, particular description by Rev. Ashbel Greene of Washington's habits at . 297
Tea-table, Washington's, at Arlington House, description of 316
Telescope, Washington's, in the possession of the wife of Rev. A. B. Atkinson.... 49
" picture of 50
Telescope, Washington's pocket, presented to General Jackson............................ 239
The Entry, a satire, published in 1789... 215
Thompson, Charles, secretary of Congress, carries to Washington, at Mount Vernon, a notice of his election to the presidency 206
" portrait of 207
Thornton, Dr., his plan for the capitol approved of by Washington...................... 271
Threshing-machine, letter of Washington to General Henry Lee respecting one... 287
Tomb of Washington broken into thirty years after his death 344
" description of 356, 558
" picture of 357
Traveling writing-case, Washington's picture of 139
Tray, Washington's silver, anecdote respecting 206
Trenton, triumphal arch at, in honor of Washington 213
Trunk, Washington's traveling, described... 135
" picture of 136
Truro Parish, Washington a vestryman of... 86

V.

Van Braam, teaches Washington the art of fencing... 50
Vases, porcelain, that belonged to Washington, picture of.................................. 188
Vaughan, Samuel, presents a marble chimney-piece to Washington, ... 185
Vault, the Washington family, site of a proposed new one indicated to Major Lewis by Washington, a few days before his death 329
Vault, the Washington family, directions left in the General's will concerning..... 343
Vault, old, of the Washington family, picture of... 344
Vernon, Admiral, commander-in-chief of the English Navy in the West Indies... 39
" portrait of 40
" medal in commemoration of his capture of Porto Bello, preserved at Mount Vernon 41
Virginia, address of legislature of, to Washington... 174
" legislature of, vote a statue of Washington... 173
Von Berckel, copy of an allegorical picture painted by the wife of..................... 200
Vulcan, a French hound, anecdote of... 185

W.

Walker, Colonel, aide to Baron Steuben, takes a letter to Gov. Clinton from Mount Vernon 132
Wallace, words of, brought to memory of the author, while occupied in sketching the death chamber of Washington... 339
Warville, Brissot de, at Mount Vernon,... 201
Washington and the Fairfaxes in Virginia in political opposition........................ 30
Washington, a page of Charles I., dies at Madrid... 28
Washington, Augustine, father of George, death of.. 38
" bequeaths Hunting Creek estate to Lawrence.. 38
Washington Benevolent Society, recipient of Washington's masonic apron......... 168
Washington, Bushrod, wills his watch to Mr. Adams.. 220

INDEX.   447

	PAGE
Washington, Bushrod, receives a sword from General Washington	226
" becomes master of Mount Vernon on the death of Mrs. Washington	250
Washington, Colonel William, hospitalities of, proffered to Washington on his Southern tour	268
Washington family emigrate to America nine years after the death of Charles I,	29
Washington, George, a boy at Mount Vernon	43
" about to enter the navy	45
" a letter from his uncle to his mother decides her against his going to sea,	46
" returns to school and loves a "lowland beauty"	46
" goes to live with his brother at Mount Vernon	47
" the friend of George William Fairfax	47
" admires Fairfax's wife's sister	47
" hunts with old Lord Fairfax	47
" goes beyond the Blue Ridge as a surveyor	48
" appointed public surveyor	48
" record of his commission	49
" commissioned adjutant of his military district	49
" heir to the Mount Vernon estate	51
" his property on the Rappahannock	51
" sent by Dinwiddie to the Ohio	53
" again in the field in 1754	54
" made Colonel in 1754	55
" leaves the service and retires to Mount Vernon	55
" his mother endeavors to dissuade him from going to the field again	57
" enters Braddock's family	57
" preserved on the field of blood	57
" most of the time in camp for four years afterward, except when sick	58
" his journey to Boston in 1756	58
" sick at Mount Vernon	61
" a member of the house of Burgesses of Virginia	61
" story of his love and courtship	61
" takes his bride to Mount Vernon	65
" personal appearance of, at the time of his marriage	66
" present from Frederick the Great to	73
" with his wife at the Virginia capital	78
" attends the theatre at Williamsburg	78
" end of his dancing days	78
" appearance of, on his farms	82
" chief crops of his farms	82
" views calmly the approaching political storm	85
" activity of, in public affairs	86
" a vestryman of Truro and Fairfax parishes	86
" first portrait of, by Peale, at the age of forty	96
" journey of, to Philadelphia as delegate in the first Congress	103
" in conference with Bryan Fairfax and Major Gates	112
" appointed commander-in-chief of the Continental army	114
" gold medal decreed by Congress in his honor	115
" letters of, alluding to his retirement after the war, to Knox and Lafayette,	147
Washington, George A., ill health of, in 1792	271, 277
" distress of Washington on account of the moral sickness of	277
Washington, George Steptoe, receives a sword from the General	226
Washington, Harriet, a resident of Mount Vernon	279
Washington, Henry, defender of the English city of Worcester, against Fairfax,	28
Washington, John A., sends a watch to Mr. Adams	221

INDEX.

PAGE

Washington, John A., Mount Vernon bequeathed to, by Judge Washington.... 354
Washington, Lawrence, portrait of.. 39
    "   his military spirit.. 39
    "   present at the attack of Admiral Vernon and General Wentworth on Cartagena.. 40
    "   friendship of Wentworth and Vernon for................................... 41
    "   his marriage.. 42
    "   takes possession of the estate after the death of his father, and names it Mount Vernon... 42
    "   adjutant-general of his district.. 45
    "   portrait of, at Mount Vernon... 363
Washington Lodge, Alexandria, Washington's masonic apron in................ 170
Washington, Lund, the General's overseer... 118
    "   reproved by the General for saving Mount Vernon from destruction by giving aid to the enemies of his country................................... 119
Washington, Mrs., portraits of children of.. 66
    "   portraits of.. 67, 275, 311
    "   in camp and at head-quarters.. 114
    "   letters to, from her husband, destroyed by her......................... 114
    "   grandchildren of, painted by Pine.. 181
    "   letter of, asking Fanny for an apron..................................... 221
    "   honors paid to, on her way to New York................................. 222
    "   first drawing-room of, at New York...................................... 224
    "   first public reception of, in Philadelphia............................. 261
    "   company at public receptions of... 262
    "   excessive fondness of, for her grandchildren........................... 280
    "   resignation of, exhibited at the death bed of her husband.............. 336
    "   reply of, to Congress, respecting the disposition of the remains of her husband... 348
    "   letters and visits of condolence to, after the death of her husband... 349
    "   death of, in 1802... 350
Washington, Mrs. Jane, mistress of Mount Vernon in 1832.......................... 354
Washington, Samuel, receives a sword from the General............................ 226
Washingtons an ancient English family.. 28
Watch, owned by Washington, picture of... 221
Water-mark, on paper made for Washington, picture of.............................. 357
Watson and Cossoul, correspondence of, with Washington respecting his masonic apron... 169
Watson, Elkanah, anecdote of his, respecting his visit at Mount Vernon...... 318
    "   remarks of, in relation to Washington's masonic apron................. 170
Watson, John F., owns Washington's military button................................. 95
Weems, Rev. Mason L., officiates at Pohick Church................................... 89
    "   portrait of.. 89
Westford, sole survivor of Judge Washington's slaves, portrait of............. 352
White, General Anthony Walton, picture of gold pen presented to, by Washington, 80
"Widow of Malabar," translated by Humphreys at Mt. Vernon, performed at Philadelphia.. 197
Will of Washington, executed in July, 1799, written out entirely by himself.. 329
Wine-coolers, disposition of, that belonged to Washington........................ 264
    "   picture of.. 265
Winstanley, William, landscapes "Morning" and "Evening," painted for Washington, by.. 320
Wolcott, Oliver, of Connecticut, prudence of.. 259
    "   letter of, respecting the president's habits of economy................ 257
Worcester, English city of, defended by Henry Washington against Fairfax.. 28
Wright, Joseph, paints portraits of Washington and his wife...................... 182
    "   attempts to take a plaster mould from Washington's face.............. 173
    "   makes a medal die of Washington.. 173
Wright, Mrs. Patience, wax figures of.. 172

Y.

Yellow fever in Philadelphia in 1794, Washington retires to Mount Vernon to avoid... 286
Yrujo, Marquis d', the Spanish minister, the guest of Washington in 1796, at Mount Vernon... 289
    "   becomes the husband of Sally McKean.................................... 290

www.ingramcontent.com/pod-product-compliance
Lightning Source LLC
Chambersburg PA
CBHW022134300426
44115CB00006B/182